At Home with the Bella Coola Indians

Edited by John Barker
and Douglas Cole

At Home with the Bella Coola Indians

T.F. MCILWRAITH'S
FIELD LETTERS, 1922-4

UBC Press · Vancouver · Toronto

09 08 07 06 05 04 03 5 4 3 2 1

Printed in Canada on acid-free paper ∞

National Library of Canada Cataloguing in Publication Data

McIlwraith, T. F. (Thomas Forsyth), 1899-1964
At home with the Bella Coola Indians: T.F. McIlwraith's field letters, 1922-4 / edited by John Barker and Douglas Cole.

Includes bibliographical references and index.
ISBN 0-7748-0979-5 (bound); ISBN 0-7748-0980-9 (pbk.)

1. McIlwraith, T. F. (Thomas Forsyth), 1899-1964 - Correspondence. 2. Bella Coola Indians. 3. Bella Coola (B.C.) 4. Bella Coola (B.C.) - Biography. 5. Anthropologists - Canada - Correspondence. I. Barker, John, 1953- II. Cole, Douglas, 1938-1998. III. Title.
E99.B39M49 2003 971.1′1004979 C2002-911312-1

Canadä

UBC Press gratefully acknowledges the financial support for our publishing program of the Government of Canada through the Book Publishing Industry Development Program (BPIDP), and of the Canada Council for the Arts, and the British Columbia Arts Council.

This book has been published with the help of a grant from the Canadian Federation for the Humanities and Social Sciences, using funds provided by the Social Sciences and Humanities Research Council of Canada, and with the help of the K.D. Srivastava Fund.

UBC Press
The University of British Columbia
2029 West Mall
Vancouver, BC V6T 1Z2
604-822-5959 / Fax: 604-822-6083
www.ubcpress.ca

To Anne and Jake

Contents

Illustrations

Foreword

As with *The Bella Coola Indians*, we are most grateful for the publication of T.F. McIlwraith's edited letters and manuscripts. McIlwraith's personal and factual recordings, made while he lived with our ancestors, have had a positive and significant impact on our lives today.

Alongside the oral histories passed to us by our ancestors, the works of McIlwraith in book form will aid us in the revival of cultural, spiritual, and historical aspects of our lives today.

At Home with the Bella Coola Indians will also aid us in educating our people, the direct descendants of the families and individuals appearing in the letters, about the historical and human events that occurred to their ancestors.

Most important, this book reinforces the need for us, as Nuxalkmc today, to remember who we are and where we come from. The strength and dignity of our ancestors, as portrayed within these works, will assist us in accomplishing that.

We extend our greatest appreciation to Dr. John Barker and the McIlwraith family for the publication of these important works.

Stutwinii,

Hereditary Chief Nuximlayc (Lawrence Pootlass)
Nuxalk Nation

Preface

This book was conceived around 1980 after the two editors independently read parts of a rich trove of letters written by the anthropologist T.F. McIlwraith from Bella Coola in 1922 and 1923-4. In 1976-7, I had decided to write a senior undergraduate research paper on McIlwraith for a course I was taking at the University of Western Ontario on the history of anthropology. I had the opportunity to travel to Ottawa, where I came across McIlwraith's letters to Edward Sapir in the files of the Canadian Ethnology Service, part of the (then) National Museum of Man. I was both intrigued and inspired by McIlwraith's experience as a pioneering Canadian anthropologist and decided, after completing my BA in 1977, to inquire further. I contacted Beulah Knox McIlwraith in Toronto, McIlwraith's widow. She graciously welcomed me into the family home and, fulfilling the fantasy of any budding historian, invited me to explore the contents of several cartons in the basement containing her husband's papers. Around the same time, Douglas Cole had come across some of McIlwraith's letters to A.C. Haddon while carrying out research on the history of Canadian anthropology at Cambridge University. Following Beulah McIlwraith's death in 1978, the family invited Cole to examine McIlwraith's private papers and prepare them for donation to the University of Toronto Archives, where most of them now reside. Doug Cole and I were immediately impressed by the letters. They were important for the light they shed on life in a small BC community, split between the Nuxalk and White settlers, in the early decades of the century; and they revealed a great deal about the methods and challenges faced by anthropological research during its formative years in Canada. But beyond this the letters were wonderfully written – vivid, perceptive, and often funny. With the family's blessing, we decided to collate the letters in our possession and prepare them for publication.

With his characteristic generosity, Doug insisted on sharing equal billing as editor with me, although I was at this point just beginning my

PhD and unable to give much attention to the project. In 1982, while I was conducting fieldwork in Papua New Guinea, Cole completed a sixty-six-page manuscript of the letters with extensive annotations and a short introduction. For reasons that were never made entirely clear to me, he decided to withdraw from the project soon after completing the manuscript. I received a copy and placed it in my files, where it resided for several years.

I returned periodically to my earlier research on McIlwraith, publishing an article on his career at the University of Toronto and republishing, with annotations, an article he had written about his fieldwork for the popular press in 1924 (Barker 1987a; Barker 1987b). I soon after initiated a move to have University of Toronto Press reissue McIlwraith's major work, *The Bella Coola Indians*, which had become quite rare and expensive since its initial publication in 1948. This project encouraged me to renew my connections with the McIlwraith family and to finally visit Bella Coola myself, which I did in 1990. University of Toronto Press reissued an excellent facsimile version of the original two-volume work with a new introduction in 1992.

Nuxalk elders used the occasion of a memorial potlatch held in October 1991 to celebrate the reissuing of *The Bella Coola Indians* and to honour the memory of T.F. McIlwraith and the ancestors with whom he had worked. The potlatch was attended by all three of McIlwraith's children and many of his grandchildren. The McIlwraith family presented copies of the field letters to the Nuxalk. They had found several new letters, including several covering the period during which McIlwraith had been involved in the winter ceremonials. I had by this time also turned up additional letters in Ottawa and, in the course of researching my Introduction to *The Bella Coola Indians*, a great deal of contextual material as well. The time was right to resurrect the field letters project.

Over the next few years, as time permitted, I had Doug's original manuscript entered into the computer, added the additional letters (about one-quarter of the total), and revised and added to the annotations. I was greatly aided in this work by two of McIlwraith's grandsons – Tad McIlwraith, then a master's student in anthropology at the University of British Columbia, and Hugh Matheson, who carefully proofread the text. While he did not involve himself in the renewed project, Douglas Cole was very encouraging. Sadly, this great historian died in 1997, long before his time.

It is a pleasure to acknowledge Carole Farber, who first suggested I look into McIlwraith's work and career; Andrea Laforet, who introduced me to the wonders of the Canadian Ethnology Service Archives; and, especially, the late Beulah Knox McIlwraith, who took a tremendous personal interest in this project. Douglas Cole and I have both greatly appreciated the professionalism and dedication of the staffs of several archives and libraries, notably the Cambridge University Library and Museum of Anthropology and Archaeology, the Canadian Museum of Civilization, the University of Toronto Archives and Thomas Fisher Rare Book Library, and the Provincial Archives of the University of British Columbia. Dorothy Kennedy made several helpful suggestions in the early stages of this project. Meeting the late Wilf Christensen, who appears in McIlwraith's letters as a twelve-year-old boy, was a thrill, as was an evening spent with the late Clayton Mack, a marvellous raconteur whose mother greatly assisted McIlwraith in 1923. I also appreciated hearing from Geraldine Ward and Joan Janis, who shared some of their childhood memories of Bella Coola in the Christensen, Robson, and Clayton families. I thank my colleagues at the University of British Columbia for many stimulating discussions about McIlwraith and his Bella Coola research, particularly Julie Cruikshank, Bruce Miller, Bill McKellin, and Cole Harris. I am also grateful to Wendy Wickwire of the University of Victoria for her enthusiastic support for this project and for her helpful suggestions for the Introduction. My greatest debts are to T.F. McIlwraith's two families. Besides contributing the main letters, Mary Brian, Tom McIlwraith, and Peggy Matheson clarified many details, offered consistent support, and displayed remarkable patience as this project slowly moved towards completion. I am also mindful of my debt to the Nuxalk Nation that adopted McIlwraith. My thanks, in particular, go to Chief Lawrence Pootlas, Melina Mack, Wilma Mack, and Karen Anderson. Jean Wilson and Darcy Cullen of UBC Press and copy editor Joanne Richardson all helped enormously in bringing the manuscript to its final form.

Last, but far from least, I am grateful for the keen interest my wife Anne Marie Tietjen has taken in this project. While she bears no responsibility for the weaknesses that remain, her clear-sighted reading of an early draft of the Introduction led me to better appreciate the value of McIlwraith's letters to an audience beyond academic specialists.

John Barker

At Home with the Bella Coola Indians

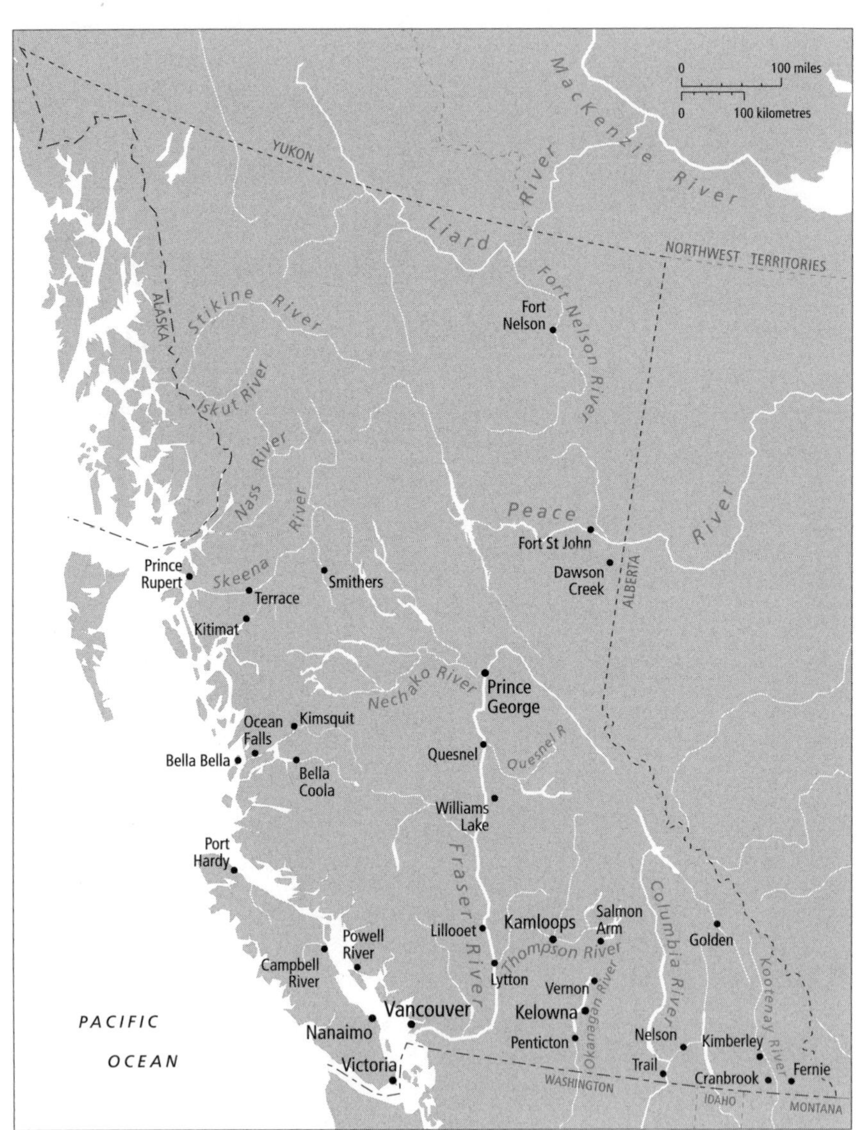

British Columbia, showing location of Bella Coola

Introduction

Ethnographic fieldwork is anthropology's crucible. During fieldwork, as Jean E. Jackson (1990, 29) observes, "one must work out one's relationship to the field, to the natives, and to one's mind and emotions (as data-gathering instruments and as bias-producing impediments)." Fieldwork is at once a scientific pursuit that draws upon shared techniques and technologies and an intensively personal experience that is always unique. Anthropologists have written and taught about fieldwork from anthropology's earliest days as an academic discipline. Most students now must take training courses in ethnographic methods and read a wide variety of case studies before undertaking their own fieldwork. Historians have done much to reveal the connections (and disconnections) between fieldwork – with all of its ambiguities and compromises – and authoritative ethnographic monographs penned after the return from the field. All of the studies, courses, and critiques have done little to demystify the fieldwork experience itself, however. It remains for most anthropologists at the defining centre of the discipline – a rite of passage that at once engenders personal transformation and provides insight into alien cultural ways. Fieldwork moulds both the anthropologist and the products of his/her intellectual labours.

T.F. McIlwraith, who, along with Marius Barbeau, was one of the pioneers of Canadian anthropology, certainly understood fieldwork in this way. In 1948 he published *The Bella Coola Indians,* regarded as one of the finest ethnographies ever written about a Northwest Coast people.

As with most ethnographers of that time and since, he restricted his discussion of the fieldwork upon which it was based to a few notes in the Preface. But he took great delight in telling about his experiences among the Nuxalk people of Bella Coola in other venues – in a magazine article (reproduced in this volume), in academic conferences, before students, and in addresses to popular audiences. As befits a splendidly comprehensive and thematically coherent study, McIlwraith's fieldwork experiences were remarkable. He had arrived in Bella Coola in the twilight years of the old culture, when a handful of elders still lived in the richly adorned longhouses of their ancestors. He gained their trust, becoming a sort of repository into which they poured ancestral mythologies, histories, songs, and details about ceremonials, religion, and social organization. Capping it all, he had the extraordinary good fortune not only to witness but also to participate in the winter ceremonies of a Northwest Coast secret society.

Over the course of two stints of fieldwork in Bella Coola, totalling almost eleven months between 1922 and 1924, McIlwraith wrote about the progress of his work and his experience in weekly letters to his family, less regularly to his professors at Cambridge University and his employer in Ottawa. Written with a keen eye for telling detail, a clear prose style, and an engaging wit, the letters provide a vivid record of his experiences and open a precious window onto the character of anthropological fieldwork on the Northwest Coast during this period. The letters enhance the value of *The Bella Coola Indians* by allowing us to better understand the underlying research upon which it was based. But the importance of the letters goes well beyond their connection to anthropology. They are invaluable historical records for Bella Coola in general and for the Nuxalk Nation in particular. McIlwraith's correspondence gives readers a unique glimpse into life in a frontier community, then divided equally between First Nations peoples and White settlers. Even more important, they contain priceless information about the grandparents and great-grandparents of today's Nuxalk, a generation that took crucial steps towards saving the memory of their past culture when all appeared to be lost.

Although written eight decades ago, the letters remain fresh and engaging. They require no introduction to be enjoyed and appreciated. My aim here is to provide readers interested in exploring the greater significance of McIlwraith's correspondence with some background information and discussion about the letters' implications for our understandings of the evolution of anthropological fieldwork and our perspectives on the fate of indigenous peoples. I begin below with a brief biography and description of the setting within which McIlwraith carried out his fieldwork. I then turn to a more extended discussion of what the letters reveal about Aboriginal-White relations in Bella Coola in the early 1920s, about the working assumptions underlying McIlwraith's field methods, and about the critical role certain Nuxalk elders played in shaping the anthropologist's understanding of their cultural traditions. As a work of "salvage anthropology" that aimed to describe Nuxalk traditions as they may have existed before the arrival of Whites, *The Bella Coola Indians* neglects the contemporary conditions under which the people actually lived and denies them a role as active agents who shaped their own destinies within the confines of colonialism. The letters open a door to a historical critique of *The Bella Coola Indians* – not to denounce the work as flawed but to reclaim it as an essential part of a living and continuously evolving Nuxalk culture.

T.F. McIlwraith's Life and Work[1]

Thomas Forsyth McIlwraith was born on 9 April 1899 in Hamilton, Ontario, to Mary and Thomas McIlwraith, a local coal importer. He attended the private Highfield School for Boys in Hamilton and then studied for a year at McGill University. Upon turning eighteen he applied to join the officer corps as part of the First World War effort. He undertook the requisite training in Toronto and Cambridge, was commissioned as a second lieutenant with the King's Own Scottish Borderers, and was sent to France in October 1918, shortly before the Armistice was signed and before (to his disappointment) seeing any action. McIlwraith then moved with his battalion into Germany and stayed on as an assistant education officer until demobilization in 1919.

Reluctant to return immediately to Canada, McIlwraith inquired about joining the British Colonial Service. While on leave in Cambridge, he had met Alfred Cort Haddon and W.H.R. Rivers, the two most prominent British anthropologists of the day, who encouraged him to include anthropology in his training for the service. Aided with an Imperial Settlement Scholarship and a year's credit from McGill, McIlwraith arrived at Cambridge University in September 1919 to begin two intensive years of anthropological study. He quickly developed a passion for museum work, spending many hours sorting through the extensive ethnological collection in the Cambridge Museum. By the time he completed the new Anthropology Tripos, with a first class standing, McIlwraith had set his sights on an academic career. He was awarded a scholarship, which enabled him to teach during the fall of 1921 and promised the prestigious Anthony

Wilken Scholarship for the following year. McIlwraith began making tentative plans for field research in New Guinea, where both Haddon and Rivers had previously conducted their fieldwork.

The American anthropologist Paul Radin now intervened. A superb fieldworker, Radin had worked under contract to the Anthropology Division at the Victoria Memorial Museum in Ottawa for several seasons. He met McIlwraith while a visiting professor at Cambridge and, much taken by the young man's enthusiasm and ability, urged him to write to the division chief, Edward Sapir (like Radin, a student of Franz Boas and a close friend), to see if a position might be available. None was; however, impressed by Radin's endorsement, Sapir offered McIlwraith a contractual appointment to carry out a few months' fieldwork: "You would do well to tackle the Bella Coola Indians of British Columbia: Mr. H.I. Smith, our archaeologist, has spent two seasons among them on technological research. I would suggest, subject to his eventual agreement, that you take up the non-material aspects of Bella Coola culture with special reference to social organization."[2] With Haddon's blessing, McIlwraith accepted.

Sapir was not able to fund the position until the end of January. McIlwraith lingered on at Cambridge through the Michaelmas term, giving lectures on African ethnology and installing a Uganda collection in the museum. After a holiday in Italy, he departed from England on 8 February 1922 and spent much of the next month on trains. He visited New York, where he had a brief and rather unencouraging encounter with Franz Boas (who had briefly worked in Bella Coola in 1897) before returning home to Hamilton. While in Toronto, he had lunch with the president of the University of Toronto, Sir Robert Falconer, and was interviewed by Playfair McMurrich (a professor of anatomy) and Charles Trick Currelly (the director of the Royal Ontario Museum of Archaeology) for a possible position as an anthropologist. From there, he visited Ottawa, where he had a helpful talk with Harlan I. Smith, the museum's archaeologist. Almost an habitué of the Pacific coast, Smith gave him some suggestions about living arrangements and informants in Bella Coola, where Smith himself intended to return later that summer. On the evening of 9 March, McIlwraith descended the gangplank of the SS *Camosun* as it lay aside the steamer wharf at Bella Coola, some 500 kilometres north of Vancouver. He was a month shy of his twenty-third birthday.

McIlwraith stayed in Bella Coola until early August, amassing a huge quantity of fieldnotes on the Bella Coola Indians (now known as the Nuxalk). Had the University of Toronto job come through, his research in Bella Coola would likely have concluded at this point, but it did not. Fortunately, Sapir scraped up some money to allow him to organize and transcribe his notes and offered him a contract for a second season of fieldwork, which was to commence in the spring of 1923. McIlwraith was set to go when his mother was diagnosed with cancer. He delayed his departure until a month after his mother died (which was in August). Already in mourning, upon his return to Bella Coola he was shocked to learn that his favourite informant, Captain Schooner, with whom he had become very close, had died only a few weeks earlier. He thus found himself back in the community during the winter ceremonial season and, as one of Captain Schooner's heirs, obliged to participate in the proceedings. At first his participation was limited to some dancing and speech making. Soon after, however, the Nuxalk arranged for him to write down songs composed for the dances and to act as a prompter for the choir accompanying the dancers. All in all, his involvement in the ceremonials was a demanding honour, often requiring his presence in the community hall from early evening until the small hours of the morning throughout the six-week ceremonies. McIlwraith brought his fieldwork to a conclusion in February by recording a large collection of Nuxalk songs on wax cylinders. He left in March, never to return.

Upon returning to Hamilton, McIlwraith spent the next few months writing up his notes, supported by another small grant from Ottawa, while looking for a job. He had just taken up a limited-term research position at the new Institute of Psychology at Yale University when the Toronto position finally received funding. McIlwraith had time to complete a report on shamanism and a rough draft of his Bella Coola manuscript before returning to Ontario to marry Beulah Gillet Knox, a long-time family acquaintance, and begin his new career as lecturer in anthropology and keeper of the ethnological collections of the Royal Ontario Museum of Archaeology.

It was for many years a demanding and lonely post. McIlwraith immediately plunged into a schedule split between managing the extensive ethnological collection at the museum and giving lectures in a wide range of anthropological courses. In 1933 the University of Toronto financed a second position in anthropology and, at long last, officially created a Department of Anthropology in 1936, to which McIlwraith was appointed professor and head. Although the entire staff hovered between two and three men before the war, the new department managed to initiate a popular archaeological program along with courses in social anthropology and material culture. McIlwraith's major achievement during these years was to organize, with C.T. Loram of Yale, the first international conference in Indian welfare, hosted at the University of Toronto for two weeks in 1943 (Loram and McIlwraith 1943).

Meanwhile, McIlwraith encountered numerous obstacles in his attempts to publish his Bella Coola monograph. The manuscript was huge – over 1,800 typed pages – and, given the specialized typographical characters required for the Nuxalk language, technically difficult to produce. Sapir left the museum in 1925 but fortunately his successor, Diamond Jenness, was willing to work through the manuscript with McIlwraith. In those days the Anthropology Division and the museum itself were part of the Geological Survey of Canada. In the past, the division had provoked the ire of senior geologists and some politicians by publishing monographs containing explicit descriptions of sexual activities. Warned by Sapir and Jenness, McIlwraith had taken the precaution of having the more explicit passages of Nuxalk narratives translated into Latin. This proved inadequate. The supervisor of government publications came across the first chapters of *The Bella Coola Indians* as they were being set for printing. Scandalized, he sent them back to Jenness, declaring "that Latin was no better than English, and [he] would admit neither."[3] Jenness and McIlwraith went over the entire manuscript, eliminating the most offensive passages and rendering still more into Latin. The exercise seems to have done little more than confirm to the director of the museum and to the deputy minister responsible that the Anthropology Division harboured pornographers and perhaps should be eliminated. After a lengthy conference, the parties agreed to publish part of the manuscript. The first volume was actually set to be printed in 1930 but was cancelled when the museum had its budget slashed at the start of the Depression. This is where matters and the manuscript stood until the early 1940s, when the Canadian Social Science Research Council, of which McIlwraith was a founding member, offered a subvention to University of Toronto Press to publish the monograph. *The Bella Coola Indians* eventually appeared as a two-volume work in 1948, the censored and translated passages all fully restored, more than twenty years after it had first been written (Barker 1992).

McIlwraith never again carried out ethnographic research; instead, he threw himself into administrative and public work in Toronto. In 1950 the Royal Ontario Museum and the Department of Anthropology were formally separated, and the dormant anthropology program began to grow rapidly. As head, McIlwraith oversaw the founding of both honours and graduate programs in anthropology. In addition, he filled key roles in several government commissions and private organizations, addressing historical, archaeological, and conservation issues. In the early

1960s he toured parts of the Canadian Arctic as a technical advisor to the Department of Indian Affairs. Soon afterwards he fell ill. McIlwraith died in Toronto in 1964, shortly before his mandatory retirement from the department he had founded. During all these years, he did not revisit Bella Coola; however, it is clear from the reminiscences of his students and friends that his experiences as a young man living with the Nuxalk formed a key part of his identity as an anthropologist and as a teacher. *The Bella Coola Indians* is the work of an energetic and gifted ethnographer. Despite the central role McIlwraith took with regard to the institutionalization of academic anthropology in Canada, he will likely be mostly remembered for this remarkable study.

The Setting

The landscape of the traditional territory of the Nuxalk Nation is dense with sacred meaning. At the beginning of time, *Äłquntäm*,[4] the creator, created Carpenters who, in turn, carved and painted all things in their original home in the heavens, *Nusmät·a*, "The Place of Myths." The first

Bella Coola township on North Bentinck Arm facing south, 24 June 1921. The Indian reserve lies to the north of the Bella Coola River, on the left side of the photograph.

human beings selected a cloak of an animal or bird from the walls of *Nusmät·a* before descending to the earth. From their landings on the mountaintops, they sent the cloaks back and then climbed down to settle in the valley. Nuxalk hold that the ancestors' names, their associated cloaked forms, and their places of landing and settlement form an eternal and inalienable unity. Throughout their lives people inherit ancestral names and associated prerogatives, place names, and histories. These names must be validated before witnesses at potlatches and then released to succeeding generations upon the deaths of their temporal custodians (Kirk 1986, 41; McIlwraith 1948 I, chap. 2).

The Bella Coola Indians attempts to reconstruct Nuxalk religion and social organization as they may have existed prior to the great nineteenth-century epidemics that decimated the population and the arrival of White settlers who displaced the Nuxalk from most of their lands. It describes an intensely spiritual terrain inhabited solely by the Nuxalk and their deities. The terrain in which McIlwraith worked and from which he wrote his letters was very different. He lived in a boarding house in the White township, walking a total of six kilometres or so a day to visit Nuxalk informants living either in new frame houses on a reserve or in the decayed remains of a traditional village at the mouth of the Bella Coola River. A rough wagon road led deep into the valley, past small White homesteads, up to a village settled by a colony of hardy Norwegians. Whites and Aboriginal people alike now exploited the great marine and forest resources of the region, working for new canneries and lumber mills. Almost all of these changes had occurred within living memory.

The people McIlwraith knew as the Bella Coola Indians[5] were among the first of the coastal Aboriginal cultures to be described in any detail by European visitors. In July 1793, about a month after Captain George Vancouver's crew made a brief landing in the west, Alexander Mackenzie entered the Bella Coola valley from the east at the end of his epic overland journey to the Pacific Ocean. At that time, the Nuxalk – to use their modern name – occupied as many as twenty villages along the lower Bella Coola River, North and South Bentinck Arms, Dean Channel, and Kwatna Inlet (Kennedy and Bouchard 1990, 323). Lacking any overall political order, the villages shared a common language, social organization, and ceremonial system. Nuxalk is a Salishan language; but the Nuxalk society and culture more closely resembled neighbouring Heiltsuk (Bella Bella) and Kwakwa̱ka̱'wakw (Southern Kwakiutl) societies than the distant Coast Salish societies far to the south. Like all Aboriginal peoples in what is now British Columbia, during the nineteenth century the Nuxalk suffered a horrendous loss of life to introduced diseases. Boyd (1990, 136) estimates that a pre-contact population of 2,910 had dropped to 402 by 1868. By the time McIlwraith arrived, the population had reached its lowest point – around 300 people – and had begun a slow increase.

Following first contact, Nuxalk gradually abandoned their traditional villages to concentrate along the lower Bella Coola River. This came, in part, as a response to the collapse of the population. But the survivors also wished to live closer to the Hudson's Bay Company trading post (which operated from 1867 to 1882) and the new Methodist mission (which was begun in 1883). The government's reduction of Indian lands to tiny reserves during the 1880s accelerated the process. As the White population in the area grew, the Nuxalk found seasonal work at small canneries and logging operations. Most Nuxalk settled on a reserve on the north side of the Bella Coola River across from the old trading post and the decaying village of Q̓omqo·ts. In 1922 Kimsquit, the last of the outlying villages, was abandoned. Before this time there was no general name for the people. Following consolidation, they began to refer to themselves collectively as Nuxalkmx, the traditional name for the people of the Bella Coola valley. Around 1980 this was modernized to the present "Nuxalk" (Kennedy and Bouchard 1990, 338).

White traders began visiting Bella Coola regularly in the mid-nineteenth century, after the establishment of a Hudson's Bay Company trading post at Bella Bella in 1843. Permanent settlement came in 1867, when a Hudson's Bay Company post was opened in Bella Coola itself on the south side of the river's mouth. In 1878 an adventurous young Englishman, John Clayton, travelled overland from the Cariboo gold fields to work at the trading post. By 1885 he had bought out the company's interests in both Bella Bella and Bella Coola. By 1894 the White population had grown to about sixteen (Kopas 1974, 238). That year they were joined by the first eighty-four members of a new colony of Norwegian immigrants, who had decided to leave their new homes in the depressed agricultural economy of Minnesota for the promise of free lands in a fjord-like setting in Bella Coola. With some aid from the provincial government, the settlers constructed a wagon road into the interior. Most settled about thirty-two kilometres inland from the sea at a place they christened Hagensborg; however, a few established homesteads closer to Clayton's residence in the old Hudson's Bay Company post. Clayton remained by far the largest landowner, having acquired much of the flat land at the southern end of the river when the Bella Coola reserve was laid out several years earlier. He became the foremost entrepreneur of the area, running the largest general store and setting up the first cannery as well as a local shipping service.

In 1904 the provincial government built a new wharf on the south shore of the inlet. However, in order to cut off competition to his store from Norwegian entrepreneurs (especially from the Brynildsen family, who had built a general store on the edge of his land), John Clayton refused to grant a right of way through his property. The province decided to relocate the wharf and lay a new townsite on the north shore of North Bentinck Inlet just beyond the Necleetsconnay River, about three kilometres west of the reserve. The Christensen and Brynildsen families relocated their general stores from up the valley to the new settlement. Boosted by the arrival of new settlers lured by the government's offer of free land and intense speculation that Bella Coola would soon be developed as a railway terminus and port,[6] by the time of the outbreak of the First World War the town boasted two canneries, a sawmill, several stores (including a bakery), a hotel, a local telephone system, a police outpost, and a lively newspaper (the *Courier*). The new prosperity allowed the town fathers to sponsor a small hospital and a community hall (although not the one where McIlwraith would later attend dances). But the boom soon turned to bust with the opening of the Prince Rupert terminus of the Grand Trunk Pacific Railway in 1914. After a series of floods in the early 1920s, it became clear that the town would need to be moved. During the boom years, speculators had bought up most of the Clayton estate, which was now acquired by the provincial government and developed as a new townsite. By 1929 the White community had shifted buildings to the new site. In 1936, following a flood that washed away the bridge across the Bella Coola River, the Nuxalk village moved to the old village site adjacent to the White community.

The Letters

> Letters can be a way of occasionally righting the balance as, for an hour or so, one relates oneself to people who are part of one's other world and tries to make a little more real for them this world which absorbs one, waking and sleeping.
>
> — Margaret Mead, *Letters from the Field, 1925-1975*

Anthropologists generate several types of documents during the course of fieldwork. Most contain the "data" from which later ethnographic works will be constructed: transcriptions of texts related by "informants" (e.g., oral traditions and interviews); scratch notes jotting down observations and ideas as they occur; fieldnotes proper, in which the ethnographer simultaneously records and orders information while taking the first steps towards a more comprehensive understanding of her/his material (these useful categories are suggested by Sanjek 1990b). Fieldworkers may also create additional non-discursive forms of documentation, such as photographs, audio recordings, films, and so forth. Finally, most people write letters from the field to family, friends, professors, and colleagues; and many also keep journals and diaries. Letters and diaries, far more than more direct forms of documentation, tend to reveal the experiential and personal aspects of fieldwork. Diaries are private places, written for oneself in the immediacy of the moment. In some cases – Bronislaw Malinowski's diaries and Boas's journals come to mind – diaries reveal a great deal about the personality of the fieldworker and the nature of the fieldwork situation; but they are often very cryptic to those who come across them in archives. Letters are another matter. As Margaret Mead observed in the epigraph opening this section, it is in letters that anthropologists start the task of explaining the cultures they are studying. Letters may be personal and immediate, but they are not as personal and immediate as diaries. They are reports from the field that provide a crucial historical link between historical experience and the research process itself.

McIlwraith wrote most of his research notes as transcriptions of interviews and narratives, taken down as they were dictated and later annotated, sometimes quite heavily. He rarely dates the notes or indicates his informant, reducing their usefulness for reconstructing his fieldwork experience. If he kept a diary, it has long been lost. His letters thus give the most detailed and informative chronicle of his time in Bella Coola – one that both expands upon his published comments and contributes much additional information.

Sunday provided the best opportunity for writing letters as the Nuxalk refused to antagonize the missionary by working on the Sabbath. McIlwraith also took advantage of breaks in interviews and evenings during the week, often racing to complete his letters to meet the weekly coastal steamer that provided the main link to the outside world. Most of his letters to his family have survived, and it is they that make up the bulk of this collection. He also wrote periodic reports to Sapir concerning the progress of his research as well as detailed and frank summaries to Haddon. The latter were written after he returned to his family home in Hamilton at the conclusion of the first and second seasons of fieldwork. The collection is rounded out with shorter letters written while in the field to Haddon, Rivers, and other figures at Cambridge as well as to Harlan Smith. This leads to some repetition of subject matter; for example, in his correspondence of 1923-4 McIlwraith returns repeatedly to his involvement in the winter ceremonials. But he was very attuned to the interests of his different readers, never simply copying sections of one letter into another. The correspondence as a whole thus provides a variety of perspectives, enriching our understanding of their author's experiences and observations.

McIlwraith relied almost entirely upon informant testimonies for the materials making up *The Bella Coola Indians*. The subtle and insightful analysis provided in that book, particularly in the chapters dealing with religion and social organization, demonstrate that he was more than a mere scribe. But it is only with the letters that we come to appreciate the full scope of his talent, particularly his ability to earn the respect and cooperation of the Nuxalk elders and his keen eye for observation. The letters provide information on the contemporary lives of the Nuxalk, material that McIlwraith largely omits from his study. Furthermore, the letters greatly deepen our understanding of the fieldwork that generated the material and the insights that later became *The Bella Coola Indians*, and they help us to better appreciate the strengths as well as the limitations of that ethnography. Last, but certainly not least, they provide intriguing clues that support a Nuxalk-based understanding of that First Nation's history in the early twentieth century – an understanding that is at odds with McIlwraith's own pessimistic assessment.

CONTEMPORARY CONDITIONS

Like other anthropologists of his day, McIlwraith came to Bella Coola to salvage what information he could on Nuxalk culture as it existed prior to extensive European influence. *The Bella Coola Indians* is largely silent about contemporary conditions, but the letters are more forthcoming, permitting a partial and fragmentary glimpse of Bella Coola at a critical moment of transition for the Nuxalk people. The physical links with the pre-European past were then rapidly disappearing, and the local White population had steadily increased to a point where they outnumbered the Nuxalk. A handful of old people, several stubbornly resisting baptism, continued to live in the ruins of the old village, but most of the Nuxalk now dwelled in single-frame family houses on the reserve across the river. McIlwraith suggests that they enjoyed a modestly comfortable lifestyle by combining several months of paid work in the late spring and summer – as fishers, loggers, and cannery workers – with more traditional subsistence and leisure activities, especially during the winter. They had, in his opinion, an extraordinarily high tolerance for dirt and germs; however, he does not seem to have considered the population to be abnormally unhealthy. Even the instances he describes of drunkenness, mostly from imbibing a potent homemade wine, pale in comparison with the self-destructive alcoholism evinced by several Whites. The church and a popular brass band provided a focus for many community functions, along with traditional ceremonials and potlatching, which were now performed in a recently constructed community hall on the reserve. In his early letters, and even more so in the concluding chapter of *The Bella Coola Indians,* McIlwraith insists that younger men had nothing but contempt for the traditions of their ancestors. However, until the early 1930s, no Nuxalk had to leave Bella Coola to attend residential school. Children retained their language, grew up with their parents, and were nurtured within a dense network of intermarried kin groups.

The letters also open an intriguing window onto the various groups of White settlers residing in the Bella Coola region. McIlwraith had little to do with the Norwegians (with the exception of Andy Christensen, the son of his landlord, with whom he became good friends). Most of the Norwegians at this time were eking out a living as farmers, loggers, or operators of small local businesses like the Christensen general store. McIlwraith felt more comfortable in the company of the few Anglo-Canadians in the area. He became particularly close to Bert Robson and the Clayton family, perhaps because they came closer in education and outlook to his own background than did others but also because, with their long involvement in trading on the coast, they spoke Chinook jargon (the simplified trade language of the coast) and were comfortable around the Nuxalk. At that time the Robson and Clayton families resided on John Clayton's old estate and probably shared McIlwraith's opinion of the Norwegians. John Clayton's widow Elizabeth, for instance, so opposed the marriage of her daughter to Andy Christensen that the two contemplated eloping (with McIlwraith's reluctant connivance). Life in this frontier settlement could be rough. McIlwraith describes a number of instances of serious alcohol and drug abuse, particularly on the part of the local doctor. But the community was not without law or a social life. The town supported its own tiny police force as well as a court, and it sponsored community dances at the town hall.

In the early 1920s the Nuxalk and White communities appeared to be more than physically separated. When the first European settlers entered the Bella Coola valley, they had depended upon the Nuxalk residents to supply them with transportation as well as with fur and fish for trade. Now the dependencies had begun to reverse, with Nuxalk working as employees in the new canneries and mills. Few Whites seemed to have much to do with them, including, according to McIlwraith, the two representatives of Canadian authority over Aboriginal peoples. He describes the missionary as an "amiable fool" who had not bothered to learn Chinook and thus could not communicate directly with his charges. And the Indian agent never went near the reserve unless there was trouble. The Nuxalk, apparently at the request of the missionary, occasionally invited their White neighbours to performances featuring masked dancers and the brass band, but this hospitality does not seem to have been reciprocated. McIlwraith mentions Whites attending a few of the ceremonials he himself witnessed, but he felt that in general the settlers were at best indifferent to, and often contemptuous of, the Nuxalk and their traditions. At times he took a malicious delight in transgressing boundaries. For example, in a letter to Harlan Smith he describes surprising the Whites in the audience at a Christmas show by performing a traditional dance with some Nuxalk and then delivering a song and speech. "Needless to say the whites thought I was a damn fool, but they do anyway, especially as I have quarreled with almost all the community" (TFM to Smith, 7 January 1924).

FIELDWORK

McIlwraith's main concern in the letters, of course, is his progress on the project of documenting Nuxalk religion and social organization. And this was impressive by any measure. His first letters from Bella Coola, written only five days after arriving, show him hard at work recording information from Joshua Moody, who remained his primary informant for the next month. Although it was at times difficult to find Nuxalk elders who were available and/or willing to talk, he managed to amass a huge quantity of data during the first season, often working for nine or more hours a day. He allowed himself to slow down somewhat during the second season, but even so he added considerably to his collection of texts and his deeper knowledge of traditional Nuxalk culture. McIlwraith clearly possessed a remarkable capacity for focused intellectual labour. He hit the ground running upon his arrival, which suggests that he came with a clear notion of the kind of information he needed and how to get it.

He received his main brief from the Anthropology Division at the Victoria Memorial Museum. The Canadian government had established the division in 1910 in order to undertake a survey of Canada's Aboriginal peoples. This was in response to a resolution of the British Association for the Advancement of Science (BAAS), which stated:

> that with the rapid development of the country, the native population is inevitably losing its separate existence and characteristics; that it is therefore of urgent importance to initiate, without delay, systematic observations and records of native

> physical types, languages, beliefs and customs, and to provide for the preservation of a complete collection of examples of native arts and industries in some central institution. (Quoted in Burke 1993, 92-3)

Prior to this, the BAAS had created the Committee on the Northwestern Tribes of Canada and had hired a young German geographer, Franz Boas, to work on the Northwest Coast for five periods of fieldwork between 1888 and 1894 (Cole 1973). Boas continued to focus upon the Northwest Coast after finding a permanent position at Columbia University. He did this by working with part-Aboriginal collaborators such as George Hunt in Alert Bay (who recorded and sent indigenous texts to him), by sending associates and students to conduct their own fieldwork in the region, and by visiting on numerous occasions (as late as 1931) (Rohner 1969). Edward Sapir, one of Boas's most gifted students, built the Anthropology Division according to his teacher's vision of the discipline; that is, as an intensively empirical endeavour. The division's anthropologists carried out extensive fieldwork across the country, but the Northwest Coast continued to be given special priority – as much for building the museum's collection as for documenting cultures. Most of the permanent staff, including Sapir himself, carried out research on the Northwest Coast.

The Nuxalk had been the object of intermittent anthropological attention throughout this period.[7] In 1885, under directions from the Museum für Völkerkunde in Berlin to recruit Northwest Coast Indians for a living exhibition, the Norwegian brothers J. Adrian and Fillip B. Jacobsen convinced nine Nuxalk, who were travelling via Victoria to work in the hopfields of Washington State, to go to Germany instead. Between their public performances across Germany, a number of scientists, including Franz Boas (fresh from his first fieldwork on Baffin Island), studied their language, stories, and music (Cole 1982; Cole 1985, 72). The following year Boas ran into two of the troop members in Victoria, who assisted him at the start of his survey of coastal societies.[8] This early work resulted in several short publications on mythology, masks, and ceremonialism. In 1897 Boas spent about two weeks in Bella Coola itself, during which time he recorded, from a single unnamed Nuxalk, most of the texts that make up *The Mythology of the Bella Coola Indians,* which was published the following year. The Jacobsens also lived in Bella Coola around 1890, during which time they observed and wrote short articles on Nuxalk mythology and ceremonies. As we have seen, beginning in 1920 Harlan I. Smith made four trips to Bella Coola and the Interior to study material culture and to collect for the museum. This resulted in a few short articles, but Smith's copious and mostly unreadable fieldnotes remain unpublished to this day. In 1897 Boas had been impressed by the unusual complexity of Nuxalk cosmology, and he recognized the need for more systematic research into the rich religious and ceremonial system of that culture. Sapir himself had played with the idea of working in Bella Coola and, in 1916, tried without success to hire Paul Radin. McIlwraith was thus brought on board to fill in a long-recognized gap in Northwest Coast ethnology.

By the time McIlwraith arrived in Bella Coola, the basic routines of anthropological fieldwork had been established for more than half a century. Fieldworkers rarely "lived with the Indians, participated in their daily routines, or learned their language" (Rohner 1969, xxviii). They usually stayed at a local hotel or boarding house within walking distance of Aboriginal communities. They observed and documented customary rituals if these happened to occur while they were in the field – sometimes they would sponsor them for this purpose – but they relied primarily upon employed informants who were paid a set rate to provide ethnological information and translations. Usually, fieldworkers worked in a place for no more than a few weeks before moving on. Fieldwork was principally a matter of collecting various types of things – objects for museum display, measurements of physical types, texts of stories and songs, customary routines for curing, and so forth. The task of making sense of the patterning of a culture, if it were taken up at all, tended to be taken up after the enthnologist returned from the field.

Main street of old Bella Coola (Q̓omqo·ts), 1897. Twenty-five years later only a handful of elderly people continued to live in and among the deteriorating long houses. Most Nuxalk had resettled in European-style single family dwellings on the Indian reserve across the river.

In general, McIlwraith's fieldwork conformed with the established procedures of what has since become known as "salvage ethnography" (Gruber 1970). His letters help us to see how such methods actually worked in the field as well as some of their consequences for the relationship between the anthropologist and his subjects. Probably before he even arrived in Bella Coola, or certainly not long thereafter, McIlwraith determined that the culture was largely moribund. He thus relied for his information almost exclusively upon a small number of elders whom he hired to talk to him at the rate of forty cents per hour. The job of informant required more than knowledge of traditional Nuxalk ways. The best informants needed to be available to work long hours, and they needed to have the ability and patience to dictate narratives, answer questions about a wide range of customs, and aid in clarifying key Nuxalk ideas. The letters suggest that McIlwraith worked mostly with five people: Joshua Moody, Jim Pollard, Captain Schooner, Mary Mack, and "Steamboat" Annie (Mrs. Tallio Charlie). Finding and keeping informants was a persistent preoccupation. He chafed when informants went off to fish, plant potatoes – indeed, sometimes even when they participated in ceremonials – as this tended to stop the steady flow of information. Keeping a good informant at times proved challenging. They became bored, annoyed by some of the questions, worried that neighbours would suspect that they were telling stories to which they had no rights. Once he started getting information, McIlwraith also had to be concerned about quality control. He attempted to sift "corrupting" elements (e.g., Moody's frequent references to the Bible) out of the testimonies he recorded, and he checked information with as wide a number of elders as he could. While necessary, this cross-checking sometimes had the unfortunate side effect of stirring up old animosities between Nuxalk who claimed the same ancestral names and associated ceremonial rights.

Nothing illustrates the underlying assumptions of salvage fieldwork better than McIlwraith's account of the various ceremonies he witnessed and in which he participated, particularly the six weeks of winter dances in 1923-4 when, as the late Schooner's adopted son, he became a full participating member and performer. It would be hard to imagine a more romantic invocation of the idea of anthropological fieldwork as a rite of passage. McIlwraith tells the story of his participation well, with a compelling mix of vivid detail concerning backstage business; descriptions of the masks and performances; and self-deprecating comments about his own wobbly attempts to make speeches in Nuxalk, to sing traditional songs, and to dance. Participating in the ceremonials was a personal triumph as it was a clear indication that he was trusted by the Nuxalk elders. And yet in many of the letters, especially those written to other anthropologists, McIlwraith often comes across as apologetic, even defensive, about his involvement in the ceremonies. In the spring of 1922, when he could not have anticipated seeing the winter ceremonials, he was already explaining to Sapir that they "are only generate survivals of the old dances" suitable mainly as "a jumping off-place for studying the old" (27 May 1922). He confirmed this opinion the following year, complaining to Sapir that his obligation to attend and participate in the ceremonials "interferes very seriously with my work" (26 December 1923). Clearly, he assumed that the senior anthropologist would agree. And, in fact, the detailed descriptions of the winter ceremonials that appear in *The Bella Coola Indians* were drawn almost exclusively from informant testimonies, mostly recorded during the first season. McIlwraith took great joy in recounting his participation in the ceremonials before general audiences and his students,[9] but he left the only detailed record of this involvement buried in private letters to his family and associates.

McIlwraith (1948) later insisted that, as a Cambridge-trained man, he pursued a markedly different style of fieldwork from that adopted in American anthropology. The correspondence clearly shows that, while he did indeed take his lead from Cambridge, this resulted in a modification of, rather than in a break with, the standard approach and underlying assumptions of salvage anthropology. Dissatisfied with the limitations of regional ethnographic surveys, they typical approach of the time, Haddon and Rivers had advocated a new approach, dubbed "the intensive study of limited areas," which required the anthropologist to live among his/her subjects for at least a year, learning their language, winning their trust, and thus working towards a comprehensive understanding of their culture (Stocking 1983). This model presumed that the anthropologist was studying a "living" culture, and it would find its most brilliant and compelling expression in Bronislaw Malinowski's statement about, and demonstration of, participant observation in *The Argonauts of the Western Pacific* (1922). This book is regarded by many as the first example of a modern anthropological study. Within a few weeks of arriving in Bella Coola, McIlwraith tried to employ Rivers's signature methodology by collecting genealogies. But few Nuxalk could recall or were willing to share such information, confirming for McIlwraith that the culture was largely dead. He seems to have then rethought the salvage model in terms of the Cambridge ideals. Through the intensive study of a single people, he sought, in conjunction with Smith's work on technology, to produce a comprehensive account of traditional Nuxalk culture. By modern standards, his notion of a comprehensive understanding, in which he would make the Nuxalk "his people," was very circumscribed. Learning the language, for instance, meant acquiring competence in Chinook jargon rather than in Nuxalk itself (by his own admission, McIlwraith had a poor ear for Nuxalk phonology). Gaining rapport with the people in effect meant gaining rapport with the elders, who were the custodians of the old culture, as, in McIlwraith's view, the younger people had turned their backs on the past. And learning Nuxalk culture meant largely ignoring the contemporary lives of the people in favour of exploring the esoteric knowledge contained in the "memory culture" he elicited from a handful of old people.

McIlwraith's Cambridge training had its greatest effect upon his attitude towards the data he was recording. This can best be illustrated by comparing his fieldwork to that of Franz Boas. Over the course of his many trips to the coast, Boas had developed an approach to salvage ethnography that focused upon the transcription of texts recited by Aboriginal informants, preferably in the vernacular. Most of his first generation of students pursued a similar strategy, with mixed success, depending upon their own linguistic abilities (Suttles and Joanaitis 1990, 80). Collecting texts was, for Boas, an end in itself, a means of presenting Aboriginal culture "as it appears to the Indian himself," free from "contaminating" interpretations on the part of the ethnographer (Codere 1966, xv).[10] McIlwraith also wrote down hundreds of myths, stories, anecdotes, and songs, but he did not accord them the same importance as did Boas and his students. In fact, he took a fairly casual approach to recording them. With the exception of song texts transcribed in the final weeks of his fieldwork, he wrote all of his fieldnotes in English interspersed with Chinook and Nuxalk words, even though his informants spoke to him solely in Chinook. His main object, the one he returned to repeatedly in his letters to Sapir and Haddon, was to discover the underlying logic of traditional Nuxalk religion and social organization. Cross-checking information between informants served not just to ensure accuracy but also to reveal general patterns. Some texts contributed directly to this larger analysis, but most were by-products of the basic method of salvage anthropology (texts are the easiest form of information to record from single informants) and, most significantly, the Nuxalk elders' insistence that he write them down.[11] Historians of anthropology on the Northwest Coast have sometimes lumped McIlwraith in with the Boasians, in part because Sapir employed him and in part because so much of *The Bella Coola Indians* is taken up with texts (Barker 2000; Darnell 1998). But McIlwraith was no Boasian. Boas never managed to produce a coherent ethnography of a Northwest Coast people. McIlwraith did.

To sum up, the letters reveal McIlwraith as an extraordinarily focused, hard-working, and resourceful fieldworker. He did not break new methodological ground, but he did manage to stretch the boundaries of salvage ethnography by exploring the interrelations of key cultural elements as far as these could be traced in informants' testimonies. This research provided the basis for an exceptionally well-rounded and thorough account of a Northwest Coast culture, one "notable for demonstrating the relationship of myth, ceremony, and social organization" (Suttles and Joanaitis 1990, 81).

RESISTANCE AND RESILIENCE: AN ALTERNATIVE READING

In his letters McIlwraith returns over and over again to themes of cultural abandonment and decay. He complains about how Christianity has contaminated Nuxalk religious thought and altered the rhythms of daily life; he finds that the gas lights of the community hall, built in White man's style, drain masked dances of much of their former splendour; he cringes at the contempt towards Nuxalk traditions coming from the lips of not only some of their White neighbours but also of young Nuxalk men; he is baffled by the Canadian government's uncompromising opposition to the potlatch, which has caused the Nuxalk to carry out in secret a much diminished form of the exchange. He is often moved to anger at the intolerance of "our so-called civilization" (TFM to family, 30 June

Eastern part of the village on the Bella Coola Indian reserve, 29 August 1920. The town hall on the right, next to the flag pole, provided the main venue for the winter ceremonials in 1923-4.

1922). At times he is even defiant, taking upon his own shoulders the burden of resisting the petty incursions of White authority that Nuxalk suffered every day. For example, he boasts to Haddon:

> I have named babies (not to mention nursing the dirty and howling brats on all occasions), helped hide wine from the police, prevented a murder (out of respect for the intending murderer, NOT for the victim), helped in a potlatch (forbidden by law), taken part in horse-play in the village, helped old men with their salmon nets, put drunk Indians to bed, taken their part against the missionary, agreed emphatically that much in the white man's bible was wrong and inferior to their own religion, given my valuable (?) assistance to settling disputes, and done many other things that would be considered undignified by the majority of American anthropologists. (29 August 1922)

"In this kind of way," he adds, "I have made myself popular with most of the Indians and they showed it."

That these feelings came from a deep and sincere respect for the Nuxalk and their traditions cannot be doubted. McIlwraith was an uncomfortable witness to the devastating consequences of European conquest and the daily indignities Nuxalk continued to suffer in its colonial aftermath. Still, one can detect in passages such as the one I have just quoted another familiar theme – the White man who does not just penetrate the cultural "Other" but who is elevated by the Natives to be their leader: Kipling's "the man who would be king" or Captain Cook apotheosized in a Hawaiian god.[12] In such fables, as they are related by Europeans to each other, the White hero arrives at the moment before the exotic world of the Aboriginals crumbles under the juggernaut of European civilization. McIlwraith hints at this fantasy in his letters on the winter ceremonials. He takes pride in his central role, asserting (incorrectly) that he was the first White man to perform in them and that his presence had made the 1922-3 ceremonies the best for many a year. In a letter to Harlan Smith, he goes further: "Thanks to these performances I feel that I am fairly well established with the community, so much so that I have had the pleasure of bawling out several Indians whom I dislike, a thing which last year I never dared to do." To be fair, such outbursts of boastfulness are rare and are more than balanced by self-deprecating jokes concerning his awkwardness as a performer. All the same, it is significant that McIlwraith was often tempted to imagine himself as something more than a student of Nuxalk culture, that he imagined himself as its representative.

Such passages suggest that, however critical McIlwraith may have been of Canadian attitudes and policies towards Aboriginal peoples, he was not able to escape the underlying assumptions of his own class and culture. Nuxalk culture was doomed, its people unable to resist the pressures and enticements of the colonizer. Figures like Captain Schooner, whom he described as "the original, uncontaminated Bella Coola type," stood alone, elderly and frail, impotent and bitter about the passing of the old ways (McIlwraith 1948 II, 525). Although "the individual may suffer," McIlwraith insisted, "civilization must press onward and the life of the Indian will soon disappear" (1948 I, xlvi). Such fatalism, of course, provided salvage anthropology with both its justification and its urgency.

But Nuxalk culture did not disappear. For a time, its decline continued and even accelerated. In the early 1930s, a Nuxalk chief convinced the people to abandon the winter ceremonials and potlatch. Nuxalk children began to attend distant residential schools. The painfully familiar spiral of language and culture loss, attended by increasing alcohol and drug abuse and other forms of social disintegration, took their toll. But the Nuxalk continued to perform traditional dances on such special occasions as the celebration of the ending of the Second World War. The 1960s and 1970s witnessed a strong revival of Nuxalk carving, painting, dancing, and songs, culminating in the reinstitution of ceremonial potlatching in 1979 (Kennedy and Bouchard 1990; Stott 1975; Walmsley 1987). A Nuxalk elementary school now draws upon the elders of the community to teach children the rudiments of their language and ceremonial heritage. The House of Smayusta, created by Nuxalk hereditary chiefs, holds a resource library containing publications, reports, archival documents, and taped oral histories that serve as a base of traditional knowledge – knowledge that is essential to the revitalization of Nuxalk culture and the struggle to regain control over traditional lands. In an irony he would have appreciated, McIlwraith's writings have played a central part in the Nuxalk revival. Indeed, some people refer to *The Bella Coola Indians* as the "Nuxalk Bible."

Viewed retrospectively, in terms of the Nuxalk present and future, it is possible – indeed, imperative – to read McIlwraith's correspondence differently from what he intended. The letters provide clues to the attitudes and to the way of life of the immediate ancestors of today's elders at a critical time of transition. From this perspective, the "informants" McIlwraith writes about appear less as passive victims than as active participants in the unfolding of their own history. Consider Joshua Moody. McIlwraith thought that Moody's interest in Christianity and White man's knowledge in general had corrupted his understanding of Nuxalk traditions and thus represented a decline in traditional knowledge. In retrospect, Moody's insistence on interpreting Christianity in terms of Nuxalk religious understanding is better understood as an endorsement of the latter and as a sign of its continuing relevance and vitality. In rising to the intellectual challenge of mission Christianity, Moody certainly altered his understanding of the spiritual beliefs he had been taught as a child. But this is surely a sign of a living culture, an indication of intellectual flexibility as well as of intellectual wonder.

And consider the controversies created by McIlwraith's requests to record traditions. The anthropologist recognized that the Nuxalk elders were very sensitive about ownership of stories, songs, and dances and, thus, about who had the right to allow them to be recorded. But he regarded the elders as "informants" whose disputes involved him only insofar as they created an impediment to his project – an impediment that had to be overcome. In retrospect, it is clear that the Nuxalk drew an unwitting McIlwraith into an ongoing politics of cultural ownership and reproduction. I think that the same is true of the dances. When I interviewed Nuxalk elders in 1990, I found that no one thought of McIlwraith as the successor to Captain Schooner, although they knew that he had participated in the winter ceremonials. This suggests that McIlwraith's adoption was a means of incorporating him into the dance rather than of creating a particular right for him. It would have been important for them to do this because, by this time, McIlwraith had come into possession of valuable cultural knowledge. By obliging him to support the ceremonials, the Nuxalk elders exercised a means of controlling him and assessing his intentions.

McIlwraith's own observations thus inadvertently lend supporting evidence that, even in the dark days of the early twentieth century, Nuxalk culture possessed an underlying vitality that continued to provide meaning to its people. Attuned to an imagined Nuxalk past, the anthropologist was unable to see clearly the present, let alone the future. He believed that the elders had given him their precious histories, mythologies, ceremonies, and other possessions because he had shown them respect and because they believed the younger generation was no longer interested in them. He was largely correct. The older Nuxalk who befriended him probably did believe that the old ways would soon disappear; they were probably no more able than was he to perceive the future. Still, from the perspective of the present, these elders appear not as "informants" but as teachers who wisely chose to incorporate a sympathetic young outsider into their circle despite the risks and the political tensions this move engendered. They, and previous generations of Nuxalk back to the time of creation, are the true authors of *The Bella Coola*

Indians. Rather than entombing the remains of a way of life soon to be forgotten, this book, like the anthropologist, is itself encompassed within and transformed by a vibrant, evolving culture. The Nuxalk have long claimed *The Bella Coola Indians* as their own. McIlwraith's letters lend further support to this act of reclamation.

Note on Texts and Annotations

The letters reproduced here are held by the McIlwraith family, by the Canadian Ethnology Service at the Canadian Museum of Civilization, by the Cambridge University Library, and by the Cambridge Museum of Archaeology and Anthropology. The 1922 letters were handwritten; most of those from 1923-4 were typed. McIlwraith's hand is quite clear, but some of the earlier letters are faint and hard to read. One letter is torn at the edge, rendering the text slightly incomplete. Such omissions and ambiguities have been noted in the text.

The editors have reproduced the letters as closely to their original holograph or type as possible. The following exceptions should be noted. First, in a very few cases, we have omitted material quite extraneous to the field experience. Summaries of the deleted passages are inserted in brackets when they concern academic matters. A few paragraphs of purely family concerns have been silently deleted. Second, "slips of the pen" – or of the typewriter key – have been silently corrected.

The annotations serve a number of purposes. They provide background information on people and places mentioned by McIlwraith as well as references to key historical developments that influenced the Nuxalk and, thus, his fieldwork (e.g., the campaign against the potlatch). We have also provided extensive cross-references to the text of *The Bella Coola Indians* (abbreviated as either "*BCI* I" or "*BCI* II," depending on the volume). Annotations are, of course, only useful to the extent that they enhance rather than detract from the main text. We hope we have been able to strike the right balance here.

The spelling of Nuxalk terms presents a special problem. As he began to learn Nuxalk words, McIlwraith experimented with different spellings, many of which are not consistent with the final versions in *The Bella Coola Indians*. To make matters more complicated, other anthropologists and linguists have recorded different variants of several of the key terms appearing in the letters and ethnography, and they have used quite distinct orthographies (see, for example, Nater 1984; Nater 1990). For the sake of simplicity, but likely at the cost of some accuracy, our annotations rely upon the spellings that appear in *The Bella Coola Indians*.

One delicate matter remains. McIlwraith's letters are still remarkably fresh and immediate after eighty years. But language usages shift over time, sometimes dramatically. Nowhere is this more obvious than with words such as "chink" and "nigger." While certainly not for polite society in the 1920s, such words are now among the most offensive racist slurs in the English language. There is nothing in the letters to suggest that, on the very few occasions he uses them (and never in reference to the Nuxalk, one might add), McIlwraith does so with conscious racist intent. After a great deal of consideration, the editors have decided to leave the words in to keep the letters as close to the originals as possible.

We have also included in this volume three short articles McIlwraith wrote about the Nuxalk shortly after the conclusion of his fieldwork. The first, "At Home with the Bella Coola Indians," is a popular journalistic piece, written for the *Toronto Sunday World* newspaper in August 1924. It describes McIlwraith's field experiences. Readers may want to start with it before plunging into the detail of the letters. The other two articles have not been previously published. McIlwraith read the first, "Certain Aspects of the Potlatch among the Bella Coola," before the British Association for the Advancement of Science in Toronto in August 1924. The last article reproduced here, "Observations on the Medical Lore of the Bella Coola Indians, British Columbia," was apparently written in the late 1920s. Besides the magisterial *The Bella Coola Indians,* McIlwraith published only two short papers on the Nuxalk (McIlwraith 1925; McIlwraith 1964).

PART I

The Bella Coola Field Letters of T.F. McIlwraith 1922–4

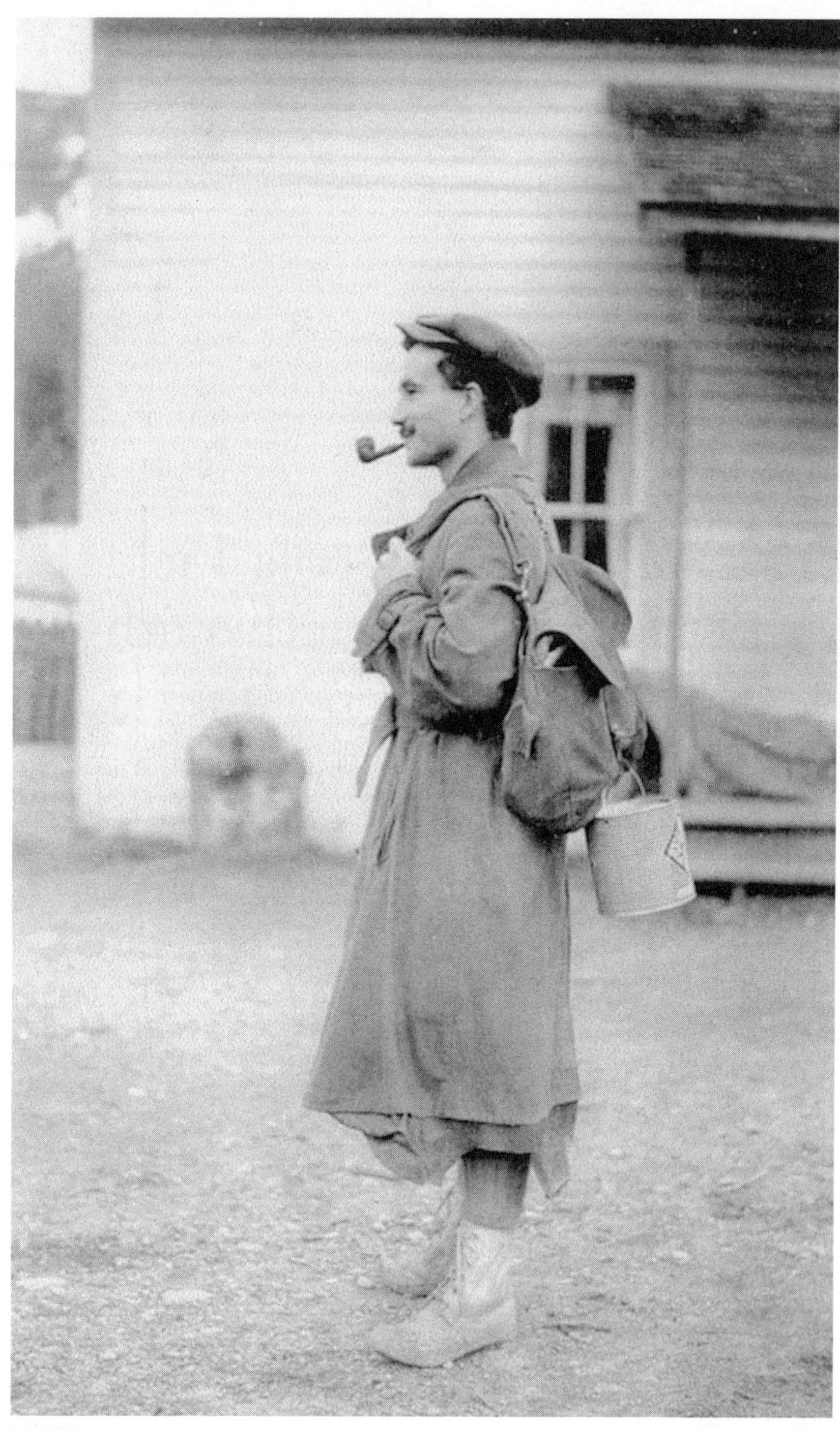

McIlwraith in his winter kit, complete with haversack and lunch pail, February 1924.

The First Season, March to July 1922

For convenience the following identifactory symbols are used, printed at the heading of each letter, to identify their location: [C] Canadian Ethnology Service, Canadian Museum of Civilization; [F] Family; [H] Haddon Collection, Cambridge University Library; and [M] Cambridge Museum.

[F] *(Postcard)*
Vancouver
7:00 P.M. 7/3/22

Dear Family,[1]

I have struck luck with regards to catching a boat for Bella Coola. The weekly "Camosun"[2] leaves at 11.00 tonight – with me on board. As far as I know this is the only way of getting to the place, so I am in luck. I get to Bella Coola sometime on Thursday, don't know when. Have had a fairly busy day poking around Vancouver, which seems to be a decent city. It feels like spring here, and the ice has all gone from the streets. If mail only leaves Bella Coola once a week, there will be a gap after this P.C., but it cannot be helped.

Heaps of love,

Tom

[H] 14/3/22

[To A.C. Haddon.[3] The first two pages are missing. Page 3 bears a note, in another's hand, "First part a 'raven' string fig."[4]]

I have been here five days, which have really been four, as the Indians refuse to talk on Sunday. This is my chief difficulty, there are only 3 pagans in the village. I have been working with one old man[5] who has been a "Christian" for 32 years, but who remembers a lot and is willing to talk, although he tells me about once an hour that he knows a great deal more about the bible than about ancient times. I have been unable to get an interpreter; I tried one young man who spoke good English but who scorned all Indian things. He is now in jail so even his doubtful aid is lacking. My old man speaks broken English, but helps it out with a wealth of gesture. I think all native handicrafts have disappeared; the people live in a row of ugly frame houses set on posts over a sea of mud. They seem to spend much of their time sitting inside and playing gramophones. I tried to collect pedigrees and failed, thanks to the multiplicity of names that each man owns. They depend on ceremonies of various kinds. I have more or less sorted out the names, and am now in a position to go ahead on pedigrees again. I have got into the problem of potlatches, really ƚɔm[6] (in my best Bella Coola), and am doing my best to get at the local positions of various animal and bird groups. Even my unsuccessful pursuits of pedigrees show that these are not exogamous. Cats' Cradles are common, I have obtained several and more are to be had for the collecting. The language is horrible, nothing but grunts and gasps, the difficulty of recognizing these when heard again adds considerably to the difficulties of the genealogical method.[7] I hope that in time things will become less complicated.

Kindest regards to Mrs. Haddon and all my Cambridge friends.

Yours sincerely,
T.F. McIlwraith

[C] *Bella Coola, BC*
14/3/22

Dear Dr. Sapir,[8]

With this mail I am returning the copy of "Language"[9] which you were kind enough to lend me. I read it on the train and boat, and found it both interesting and helpful. It is certainly a remarkably good book.

I reached here on the evening of the 9th, and have been hard at work since. I tried one of the younger Indians as an interpreter, the only one here who speaks good English, but found that his scorn of old customs made him of little use. Since then I have worked entirely with Joshua, whose English is broken but fairly intelligible, and who knows a great deal about early times. Owing to multiple names I have found difficulty in recording pedigrees, but have now got enough information about names to clear this trouble. The language is certainly a brute.

It is unfortunate that I cannot use an interpreter when there is plenty of money, but I think I will be able to use Joshua in this capacity later on when I have exhausted his own stock of knowledge. Information is coming in, which is the important thing.

Please excuse this scrawl, which is written in bed, the only warm place at night for writing. Yours very sincerely,

T.F. McIlwraith

[H] *Bella Coola, BC*
March 21st(?) 1922 [sic]

Dear Dr. Rivers,[10]

I am enclosing herewith the manuscript of the paper I gave at the B.A. last year,[11] with various additions and alterations – my own feeling is that it is only fit for waste paper. If, however, you think it worth publishing, I would be very grateful if you would send it in for me. Perhaps it would be improved by cutting out certain parts; in this case please do so, I turn the thing over to you unreservedly. At one time you spoke of sending it to the "Journal of Egyptian Archaeology," I do not know whether such a course is still open. However, as I said, please do with it what you think fit.

I have now been here for nearly two weeks, and have got my bearings, though results have not been as good as I could have wished. Conditions are, I imagine, very different from Melanesia.[12] The Bella Coola live in a long row of crude wooden houses (European style) set in an ocean of mud. When needing money they work for a few weeks at logging or in the canneries, then each family retires to its own house where the members spend their time sleeping, moping, playing gramophones, singing hymns, and getting consumption. The white man's movements are of no interest, and I am convinced that I could loaf around the village for a year without attracting a single spectator, much less a crowd interested in my questions. With three exceptions all are nominal Christians, eager to exhibit their knowledge of bible stories. Most speak a few words of broken English, but the younger men, who speak tolerable West Coast slang,[13] have such a supreme contempt for the old customs that they are almost useless as interpreters. No information is gratis, one must pay an informant by the hour.

I have been working for a week with a white man as interpreter,[14] and have found it quite successful. Lord knows the Chinook lingua franca well, and can eke out its deficiencies with a little Bella Coola. His chief objection is that he tries to turn my informant's statements into too clear English instead of bringing out the contradictions. Also, as with many other good Scotsmen, he had studied a certain amount of theology, and at times plunges into an animated argument in Chinook with my informant, leaving me out in the cold.

So far I have worked entirely with one man, Joshua. He is an old man, willing to talk, in fact eager to have the white man know "Indian law," with a good memory for the things that happened when he was a boy. He is hard to keep to the point, and has an unpleasant habit of comparing Indian theology with parts of the Old Testament, about which he knows much more than I. Yesterday he assured me that the angels at Mons[15] were due to siut power, which is the power that a man attains in dreams and fasting when he wishes to gain rank. Details of this kind rather interrupt the flow of information.

I have taken advantage of Joshua's willingness to talk and Lord's interpreting to plunge into religion, reserving pedigrees etc. for a time when a good interpreter is not available. I have got enough information from the few pedigrees I have taken to convince myself that kinship is the important feature, the "clan" concept being very vague. The collection of genealogies is complicated by the multiplicity and transference of names, while the names themselves are so difficult that the later recognition of them is not easy. Slaves[16] merge easily into the common people, while the nobles, tahi,[17] are not strictly endogamous.

Religious matters are so complicated that I am at present bewildered. Every living creature has a himanoas,[18] one part of which urges him to good, another to evil. At death this splits into four, one part staying with the body, one going up above, one passing into a wolf, and one into an owl.[19] The himanoas resides in the base of the skull, and exerts a guiding influence over the individual; if it leaves, the man becomes sick and, if not brought back, he dies. Men who have obtained siut power band together, I think, to perform dances etc., in which the common people are deceived. One man, e.g., has power to eat a corpse. The "corpse" is a wooden frame over which bear's meat is smeared, and which is buried in a coffin – this is dug up and eaten in the dance, during which the performer revolves sunwise.[20] Siut power is at the command of the successful giver of a potlatch (klim),[21] but the exact relation of klim men, tahi men, and men with siut remains to be worked out. Plenty of work is available here, and I hope that in a few months I will be less confused about these things than at present. I have already got copious notes, and hope to be able to straighten things out.

This is the most wonderful country – snowcapped mountains, forests and sea in close proximity. I am living in the home of a Norwegian family,[22] about two miles from the Indian Village. After breakfast I set out for the latter, taking lunch with me, and put in about seven hours of solid talk. By that time my interpreter's head is reeling, Joshua complains that a head-ache keeps him awake at night, while I have been known to talk in my sleep. The day's work is shorter than I like, but under the circumstances I cannot see how to lengthen it.

Please give my regards to all my Cambridge friends. I hope you will show this letter to Dr. Haddon and any others who may be interested, I have no time to write to each individually.

Yours very sincerely,
T.F. McIlwraith

[F] *Bella Coola, BC*
26/3/22

Dear Family,

The way time slips away here is amazing, it seems impossible that another week has gone, – at this rate the last of July will be here before I know it. Things are going here as well as could be expected, in fact rather better than I hoped, while the place itself improves all the time.

This last week there has been brilliant sunshine all the time, with heavy frosts at night. The snow has almost gone from the valley and even the road through the woods to the Indian village is dry in a few isolated spots. In the open it is drying fast and there is a glorious feel of spring in the air. This is at least my third spring this year, Italy, England and now B.C., with a few warm days in New York and Hamilton thrown in. Birds are beginning to arrive, in the last few days I have seen song sparrows and hermit thrushes. A few birds were around before that, the woods were full of chickadees and winter wrens, with crows around the open space in front of the Indian village. By the way I have seen several non-Ontario birds, I do not know whether there is any *small* (pocket) guide to birds west of the Rockies. If so I would like one very much.

This afternoon I walked up the valley for about four miles with the Indian agent, an old Norwegian who came into the valley 29 years ago.[23]

We went up to where the road crosses the Bella Coola River by a big bridge, and where, looking up the valley we could see Mt. Nusatsum shining in the distance. This is the highest peak in the valley, a huge pinnacle of a mountain with bare snow-covered top. The view was certainly one that would be hard to beat. Looking down into the river we could see the first straggling salmon, the run will not be for another five weeks. Speaking of salmon I have had samples of several for supper, and very fine they seem too.

Friday night I had supper with the missionary and his wife,[24] a young English couple who have been in B.C. for about 4 years. I liked them very much, but cannot help thinking they are out of place. I admire their pluck immensely, coming to live in a place like Bella Coola. Mrs. Peat is rather a frail looking lady who must have her hands full with three small children, not to mention keeping a biggish ramshackle house in order, and lending a hand to the woes of any of the Indians. Mr. Peat pointed out to me with much glee two plum trees growing within a few yards of his pantry-window; last fall they were stripped by a black bear. The Peats watched it from their window for over half an hour, within touching distance with a walking-stick.[25]

Things are continuing with fluctuations as regards information and Joshua. One morning the old man was not on the scenc, and when he did turn up, it was with a long face. Several of the important Indians had been to him complaining about his telling tribal legends to me – or rather about his combining them with biblical allusions. Joshua was very worried, he believes his fathers and uncles were killed off by black magic and half dreaded the same fate, though realizing that jealousy on the part of the other men was the cause of their outbreak. For two hours I slung taffy to him about his honesty and virtue, and then suggested that I had better go and talk to other chiefs. Herewith greed and jealousy got the upper hand of his many sided nature, he became smiling at once, and stories have continued as of yore.

My interpreter, Lord, goes to work in the cannery on Monday week. He has been very useful, but I do not think would do for a permanency, even if available. He is interested in a general way in the pursuit of information, but would not have the patience to spend months trying to get at facts which seem so obvious to the Indian that he cannot understand our stupidity in failing to appreciate them. Lord put me on to another man,[26] also white, whom I am going to try. I certainly like the looks of him, he appears to be all that could be wanted. He is quite well educated, a returned man, the son of a Hudson's Bay factor who has lived all his life among the Indians. He has plenty of money, so that I think his acceptance of the job of interpreter is more in the way of helping the work. If he proves satisfactory things should go well.

I have had my full week's ration of Joshua's idiosyncrasies. One of them is to learn what the white man would call any custom or fact related by Joshua. In his mind this means that the white man has the same belief, and therefore he is willing to discuss it with him. There are difficulties. At some point in his life Joshua told some white man of a mythical beast, and was told that it was like a gorilla. J. promptly informed me that his grandfather, with story complete, had met a "jolilya." With all the good-will in the world I looked blank, and J. decided that either I or the earlier white man had lied; otherwise why should I not recognize what the white man had said? Luckily the Indian is like a child in his willingness to swallow taffy and be pacified. I have been partly guilty for his learning a new word. We had been struggling for hours to get at the meaning of the word OM.K̓ŁV.NST'MANAM, apparently divine power when visible to human beings during its use by a powerful man, e.g. the rod in the bible. Joshua promptly asked for the English equivalent. At this instant in came Mr. Peat, to whom the question was carried. He suggested "theophany." At intervals for hours afterwards Joshua kept muttering this word; when last I heard it had become chèobany. Any future inquires from J. will be in trouble unless he can recognize cheobany.

The old man has an amazing memory. Something came up about killing a man, according to J—, "all same litley." I said, "yes, you sabby good" – without any idea what he was talking about. Unluckily I could not choke him off and in a minute I was caught. The pained expression came to his face, but he murmured, "litley and lattimer." A stroke of luck to me in that I remembered about the burning of Ridley and Lattimer,[27] so promptly gave him the story, which agreed with what he knew, and tickled him with the unpronounceables of "Reformation" and "Martin Luther."[28] In this case he had been told 29 years ago and had treasured up this instance of the white man killing other white men.

Both last mail and this I had two very excellent letters from New York, nine to fifteen days seems to be their time. By the way I *think* my next week's letter will be later; in summer the boat comes on Sundays instead of Thursdays, and I think the change comes after this week. I like awfully to hear of your doings in N.Y., but do not think I have anything to answer in the letters. Am glad Aunt Jean[29] has got a house, that is, always provided it suits.

I forget when Dorf's[30] P-puzzle had to be sent in. I saw the enclosed answers to another puzzle in one of the Vancouver papers, and am sending it along in hopes that it will be on time; it might contain some p's not in the dictionary.

Heaps and heaps of love,
Tom

[C] *Bellakula [sic], BC*
2/4/22

Dear Dr. Sapir,

Acting on instruction from Mr. McInnes, I posted yesterday to Mr. Marshall a statement of my expenditure to date, and also a letter to Mr. McInnes[31] asking for an advance of $300. I hope they will find that the accounts have been made out in a manner suitable to them, and that the vouchers contain the requisite information. My expenditure has been considerably less than the amount authorized, largely through the non-utilization of the $150.00 for museum specimens. I am sorry about this, but any attempt to go around trying to buy things would have interfered with the collection of ethnological information, so I concentrated on the latter.

Joshua Moody in Q̓omqo·ts, c. 1920. Moody had worked as the chief Nuxalk informant for archaeologist Harlan I. Smith, who in turn recommended Moody to McIlwraith.

I started with Joshua, and my opinion of him as an informant has increased steadily. I think I have flattered my way into his good graces, at any rate he has shown me his secret dance whistles[32] and so on. Joshua realizes that the old order is changing rapidly, and is willing, therefore, to describe customs which were secret in olden times, and which he does not want to have the other Indians know about his communicating to me. Unluckily he is very jealous, and any attempt on my part to go to other people, even to purchase specimens, would check the flow of information from him. I propose to spend several more weeks, or even longer, with Joshua, getting all the information I can from him, and then make my peace with one of the other old men. I do not think this will be at all difficult, the lure of money and a few compliments should make the way easy. So far I have had no trouble with Joshua about working for 40 cents an hour, but find that I can only use him profitably for six or seven hours a day, after that he becomes tired. I spend several hours a day poking around the village taking photographs, learning cat's cradles, and other small items of information, so that the time spent with Joshua does not constitute my working day. I have found it unprofitable to work on Sunday; the Indians are careful observers of the ritual of Christianity, I doubt if it goes much deeper, and I do not want to offend them.

Naturally I have taken all possible steps to test Joshua's accuracy. My interpreter, an intelligent white man, has verified a number of his statements when talking with other Indians. Several times Joshua has mentioned practices which, he says, are not Bella Coola ones, but those of the Kwakuitl, or the Kitkatlas.[33] I have found that such statements agree with published accounts. Taking a large number of small points into consideration, I have come to the conclusion that he is telling the truth, and accordingly have no hesitation in getting all possible information from him. He has a good memory and, as a member of one of the leading families of chiefs, took part in much of the secret ceremonial in his younger days.

I have gathered a good deal of information on many subjects, and am trying to fill in details. The Bella Coola formerly lived in small villages without the important chiefs of the northern tribes. Marriage depends entirely on kinship, but many of the villages were virtually endogamous through the desire of the people to prevent their "story" from going to strangers. The "story," which comprises the history of the "crest" is inherited from both father and mother, the family name in the patrilineal line alone. Family privileges pass in the patrilineal line, including the right to take part in ku'siut dances.[34] The right to give a sɪsaok[35] dance, mentioned by Boas,[36] also passes in the patrilineal line, but depends on the giving of a ɫɪm.[37] The distinction between chiefs and commoners is clear, though the offspring of a marriage between a chief's daughter and a commoner can be raised to chiefly rank. The transference of names is causing me a great deal of trouble and I do not feel certain that I have got to the root of the matter. At every turn I have come upon siut, the animating power of living objects. I think I have got fairly clear ideas on this subject, including the way in which an added supply of it is obtained by revelation and fasting. The possession of siut gives power to both healers and workers of "black magic," about whose methods I have obtained a good deal of information.

This will show you the kind of information I have been getting, and I hope you will think I am on the right track. In spite of Joshua's willingness to talk, I have found plenty of difficulties in trying to work out the complicated social life of the people, in which religion is closely bound up. At present I am much confused on many points, but hope to be able to clear them up in time. My greatest trouble is the phonetic system. It is nothing less than a brute. I can record names with sufficient accuracy to read them in a recognizable form when something turns up on the same subject a week or so later. This seems to suffice for the collection of information in the field, but I am afraid my records will be of little use from the linguistic viewpoint. I am doing my best, but am in endless trouble over words which seem to consist of consonants by glottal stops.

Please remember me kindly to Smith, Barbeau, and Jenness.[38]

Yours very sincerely
T.F. McIlwraith

[F] *Bella Coola, BC*
28/4/22

Dear Family,

All kinds of thanks for the Easter eggs and ever-sharp.[39] The former disappeared swiftly, while I am using the pencil all the time. I find that I have to take my notes in pencil and the ever-sharp seems to do the trick. I lost the one Dorothy once gave me, over a year ago, and am glad to get it replaced.

Thanks also for mother's letter of the 15th. I am awfully glad that father's knee has got into shape again and that he can get around again. A knee is a tricky business and he is lucky to get it in shape. I wrenched mine a few days ago and began to get worried when I was reduced to a stick and a limp, but luckily it seems all right again. I do hope that mother can manage to work in a visit to the Townships on her way home;[40] that would be fine.

This last week has been by far my slackest since I got here. There has been a tremendous run of oulachons,[41] the biggest for fifteen years, and all the Indians are hard at work. For about four days I hardly got in a decent hour's work and, if I had only known, would certainly have gone up the valley. As it was I took life easy and went through my notes, I have about 700 pages more or less filled. The oulachons are now over, and I am hard at it again.

Much to my amazement old Joshua gave me a mask to-day. The old sinner has sworn repeatedly that he had none, but I am far less surprised at his having one, as at his giving it away. The Indians are business people from the word go, and Robson, who knows them probably better than any other white man, was as stumped as I. It is not a very good one but any is hard to get. I was glad to tell the old boy that I had written away for a "strong picture" for his wall, in other words the monstrosity that I asked you to get for me last week.

A few days ago Robson and I were shown four dandy masks, big fellows with original trimmings of eagle down. The owner wanted $200.00 for the four, and was inclined to be rude when I offered $50.00. It should have been worth something to sit in his house discussing the matter, you could have got [sic] the air with a knife. The old man was blind and the smell in the house was wonderful. I am supposed to buy some of these things for the government, but not knowing much about the business am disposed to let it slide. There are still a few masks around, in fact I missed a good haul by only two or three days, but they are deucedly hard to get. Pretty soon I hope to know enough Chinook to be able to get along without an interpreter, which would help a lot in buying these secret objects. Robson is an absolute gem, but occasionally two white men double the difficulty of getting information, and it is hard enough to get things straight anyway.

With spare time this last week I have turned my hand to a couple of new jobs. One was shoe-repairing, thanks to my worthy army boots suddenly needing new soles. There is no shoe-repairer here, however, a decent individual with a last and nails volunteered to help, and I bought the half-soles in the store. The job has been a success. The actual job finished with the other man doing most of the work, with me lending very doubtful help.

Another job is gardening. Bella Coola owns a government financed doctor and hospital, the latter a frame building with about four beds. The old doctor died soon after my arrival, much to everyone's relief as he was a drunken old German.[42] The new doctor seems a very decent young fellow, a Toronto graduate, and, as the hospital is near the Christensens,

I have seen a good deal of him. I usually walk down and fool around in the garden a couple of nights a week till driven in by the mosquitoes which are now here in swarms. People swear they are not bad in summer, but I doubt it.

I enclose a few snaps,[43] they fail to give much idea of the mountains which dominate everything. The grandeur of the scenery is not in any particular view, it depends on the mass impression of rugged power, and the camera fails to get it. Still they show a bit of it anyway.

Heaps and heaps of love,
Tom

[C] *Bella Coola*
British Columbia
1/5/22

Dear Smith,[44]

I certainly agree with all you said about Bella Coola; it is a fine place inhabited by decent people. I am enjoying myself, though I often think that material is not coming in as fast as it should. I have been working pretty steadily with Joshua, though work this last week has been badly upset by a record catch of oulachons. Everybody has been busy and I have been driven back to talking to Myers,[45] Hump-back Tommy and others who are almost in their dotage. I hope you will be out soon; a wish in which everyone in Bella Coola seems to wish to join.

I was talking to Schooner to-day,[46] he seems to have a bit of a grievance with you. He says you took a "stone face" (? plaster cast) of him, and promised him a copy. In order to placate the old fellow, I promised to write you, and if you are coming here soon and could bring him one, it would put him in a good temper if you want any information from him. Naturally I know nothing about the thing, but thought it might be as well to write in case you wished to get on his right side for future information.

Yours very sincerely,
T.F. McIlwraith

[F] *Bella Coola, BC*
4/5/22

Dear Family,

Before plunging into an account of my week's doings, or lack thereof, I had better answer some queries in last mail's batch of letters from you. I like the look of the type of my (to be) typewriter, as shown in father's letter of the 19th. My return ticket is via Canadian National, T&NO,[47] and Grand Trunk to Toronto from Vancouver. These composite tickets can be bought at any G.T.R., or Canadian National office. They give alternate routings, mine is Vancouver-Winnipeg-Cochrane-North Bay-Toronto. If Dorothy likes she can take the alternate route going, via Port Arthur I think, or we can both take it coming back which might be better. My ticket can be changed without trouble.

Now for Dorf's[48] two letters. First of all Dorf, don't bank too strongly on Bella Coola, for I don't think it can be worked. You see the only boarding house where I stay, is also the place where lumbermen, canners and so forth put up. It suits me O.K., the people are decent enough, but it is decidedly not the place for you. It is the established rule of the place that the women eat scraps in the kitchen, which does *not* appeal to me for you. Smith, an archaeologist from Ottawa is coming out with his daughter (I think) in about a month. Last year he took a house, and will probably do the same this year, and it is just possible that he might feel disposed to put us up. Also, I may have to follow the Indians to a cannery[49] a few miles away, only returning to Bella Coola on Sundays. Even as it is I am away all day, sitting and working among more or less filth, and without some base it would be impossible for you. Robson would, I know put you up, but his house has only three rooms, so that is a wash-out. All told I think the chances are most slim of us foregathering in Bella Coola. The wretched part of it is that this is a bon place, but I can't see any way of working it.

Now what I would like to do is meet you either on the boat or somewhere near Vancouver about Aug. 1st, and then play around for a couple of weeks – all being well. I don't think the Ottawa people would object to my playing around and then coming back on their ticket, in fact I know there would be no trouble. All this sounds most complicated, but it simply means that I cannot see how to wangle us to stay around in Bella Coola, and that I am all in favour of us playing round either down below or in the Rockies. Gee it will be great. It seems to be that Miss Trapp[50] is the likely person to pump for a place for us to stay somewhere further south.

Also in last mail came the bird-book, for which much thanks. Also, alas, came word from Toronto that they have no money to start anything new in Anthropology. Prof. McMurrich[51] says, no, I will send his letter. It is a bit of a blow but may be best after all. I wrote him asking whether this also washed out any chance for a museum job under Currelly.[52] Until I hear I won't think of any plans for the future. It may be that I will finish up in the Colonial Service in Africa after all.

This last week can best be summed up as rotten fish ad infinitum. Every Indian family has one or more big lined holes on the bank filled with oulachons, tens of thousands of them. As they begin to rot they're shovelled into huge cauldrons and boiled, the grease skimmed off, the fish mashed to a pulp in the process, and the pulp run off. The smell absolutely hits one in the face. Every person in the community is working at it, so I have had to follow them to the bank and for several hours a day Robson and I get fumigated in fumes of rotten fish, to the mingled scorn, disgust and admiration of the Norwegians who would not go near the place without a gas-mask.

Last Saturday we took the afternoon off and went up to investigate the site of an ancient Indian village,[53] discovered by an Indian when clearing a potato field in an apparently casual spot in the midst of the forest. We took spades and dug holes in a vile tangle of roots and thorns, finding cooking stones under a foot and a half of earth. The most interesting find was a layer of mussel shells under 18 inches of soil, certain proof of human habitation. We found nothing worth taking away, but proved the site of the village and had a hot and pleasant afternoon.

To-day we went on another expedition, to investigate an ancient tree-burial.[54] I spotted the box in a tree fork, about 18 ft. from the ground, so we went for it. The tree was a huge cedar, absolutely unclimbable, however we threw a rope over a branch and I swarmed up, not perhaps à la squirrel, but anyway, up. It seemed about a million feet before I got there. The box was empty, practically fallen to pieces, and grown into the bark, but what I was interested in was that it was one of the very old boxes. Formerly these were made of cedar, bent into a square with the fourth corner and bottom laced with fibre. When the white man came with metal nails these were used instead, and all which I had seen were of this sort. However the one in the tree was the old original laced variety.

Other than this my news is nil. The weather has been rather bad the last week, plenty of rain. There is a pleasant plan afoot for me to take two days off next week and go hunting grizzlies, it sounds O.K., but I doubt if it gets any further.

Heaps and heaps of love,
Tom

[F] *Bella Coola, BC*
12/5/22

Dear Family,

Another very, very slack week. The cooking of oulachons and the planting of potatoes has interfered a lot with my work, one cannot object to the Indians doing their own jobs, though it interferes a lot with mine. In a few weeks they will be leaving for the canneries, and I may be in trouble for anyone to talk to; in fact I may have to follow them to a cannery, if I can get put up at one. That will be the end of this very comfortable and lazy life, instead of which I will be reduced to talking to old women as they clean fish.

Just at present I am working with the cleverest Indian on the reserve, a little too clever to suit my tastes.[55] The worthy man has been seen to read a newspaper, but swears he cannot speak English. Part of this English he learnt when in jail on trial for murder, he got off all right, but the general opinion is that it was more through his skill in lies than on the score of innocence.[56] When I go into his house he always hauls out a scrupulously clean table in front of the window, brings a chair for me, and starts to tell stories. He is perfectly willing to use English words when there is no Chinook equivalent, and I have found it child's play to collect fables from him. The difficulty is that he is too clever to be taffied and worked around the way one could with Joshua, and I know perfectly well that he will lie if he feels like it. The annoying part of it is that he knows a tremendous lot about the old customs and is, therefore, a useful man to work with.

The other man I have been working with this week has been an old hunch-back who swears he is 100 years old, and looks it. He is a stupid old man, very hard to understand owing to poor Chinook, and the owner of a house that smells from here to the next world. He is also a perpetual beggar, chiefly of tobacco, and swears he will be your friend forever when he gets it, which gratitude may last for as much as two minutes. I have got on far enough in Chinook now that I can get along without an interpreter, which simplifies matters a lot, especially as Robson will be fishing in a few days.

Nothing much to answer in last week's letters, though I was sorry to hear of the death of the Cruikshank grandchild.[57] Was glad to hear of father's safe arrival home, and also to get his letters forwarded from New York. Aunt Jean seems to have struck oil, for which I am glad.

This is a very short scrappy letter, but there is really no news here. The weather has stayed cold and dull, a very late spring. I had a most excellent trip into the woods the other day to try and locate an old cemetery, but I failed to come across it, though I filled in the afternoon comfortably.

Heaps and heaps of love.
Tom

[F] *Bella Coola, BC*
12/5/22

Dear Father,

Many happy returns of the day! As far as I can tell this letter will reach you on your birthday, I hope it will be a happy one. Whatever else may or may not be found in Bella Coola, there are certainly no birthday presents to be had here. I have just returned from investigating the store pretty thoroughly, and find the only possible thing to be a box of candy, which I hereby send with all the love. They are probably stale as blazes, but that can't be helped.

At present it is about 11.00 p.m., but the store is busier than I have ever seen it. Two interior Indians, Chilcotins, have just come down with their winter's catch of furs which they have traded for supplies, sugar, flour, rice and the rest of it. They are now engaged in smoking the Christensens' cigars, and will no doubt stay most of the night while he tries to talk and look pleasant. They are staying the night and as I left the question was raised as to where they were to sleep. They quite freely agreed that they were "plenty lousy," but said, "all right, you no see our lice." The last I heard was that they were to be put in the hay mow with some horse blankets.

I have had a brute of a day, to-day, in some respects the worst since I got here. At present I am working with a very disreputable member of the community, but by far the smartest. He is supposed to have murdered a couple of women a few years ago, but managed to lie his way out of it. He is one of the leading chiefs here, a fact which he keeps drumming into me, and with which I pretend to be duly impressed, although several other Indians have pointed out to me that some ancestor of his married a slave woman, and that, therefore, he is really no chief. Well the Indian agent summoned this worthy individual to him yesterday, and told him that some white man had told him (the agent), that this Indian was no chief and that he was stirring up trouble against the government. There has been endless discussion about it to-day, and Pollard, my chief, is in a regular blaze of excitement against the unknown white man. The Indian agent refused to tell his name, which complicated matters. Some of them suspected me as the one who had been prying into ancient history, and I have been busy vindicating myself and trying to turn their suspicions elsewhere. As a matter of fact I am guiltless, and most of them seem to believe me. Thank goodness I know enough Chinook to talk to them direct, and the worthy Pollard himself is disposed to be friendly, and even cheerfully asked me to listen to the Norwegians' gossip to try to find out who was causing the trouble. It is a – nuisance, but to-day has passed safely, and if I can hang off for a few more days more it will pacify things over. A few more days of this kind will turn my hair gray. I wish to blazes they would keep their troubles till I was away, naturally everything gets foisted at me.

Heaps and heaps of love; kindest regards to the Capt. & Mrs. H.[58]

Tom

[C] *Bella Coola, BC*
May 27th 1922

Dear Dr. Sapir,

Thanks for your letter of May 4th, received last mail. I am sorry to hear that your wife is still sick,[59] but I trust that she has received benefit from her stay and treatment in New York. It was good of you to write me in the midst of your numerous duties.

Things here have not been going as well as I should have liked. The chief trouble is that the people are busy. About the 1st of May came a huge run of oulachons, and every person who could move was working at them. For about two weeks I was reduced to talking to senile old men, or to sitting on the river-bank among the oulachons and gossiping with the people. Neither practice brought very good results. Since then there has been potato planting. They would be willing to work for me if I would agree to hire them for, perhaps, a month, but I do not feel justified in doing this – in most cases it would be a waste of money, their information would not last that long. Several of the Indians have begun to fish spring salmon now, but the general exodus will not take place till June 20th when the sockeye come. I expect a lot of trouble then, and may be forced to follow the Indians to one of the canneries, if I can arrange to do so. I am convinced that the best time to work in Bella Coola would be October, November and December, when most of the Indians are at home and when the dances take place. These are only degenerate survivals of the old dances, but they would form a jumping off-place for studying the old.

In spite of these inevitable difficulties information has been coming in steadily. I have been pleased to find that Joshua's testimony has been borne out on almost every point. The hardest thing to work out is the social organization. Small-pox killed off the Bella Coola in thousands (?) some seventy years ago, and dislocated the whole social life of the people.[60] Villages were abandoned, people fled away, and many of the old beliefs and practices were lost; then, before things had been firmly re-established, the white man's influence upset them again. That at least is the way it appears to me. Pedigrees are not carefully remembered, though the people know with what families they are connected. Kinship terms have been largely forgotten, and I had a great deal of trouble before I could get a complete set. I believe that individual relatives never played an important part in the people's lives, dances, and names, and duties passed at the will of an old man to whomever he wished. Chieftainship was hereditary, but was influenced by the ability of the person concerned to give ɬım ("potlatch"). I forget whether I told you about these points in my last letter – if so, please forgive the repetition, I have recently been getting confirmatory evidence about these points from several men and it is hard to remember when I first learnt the facts.

Among other matters I have recently gathered a good deal of folklore. I hope you will not think this is too far from my original aims. A large part of it is the basis for dances and masks, and the stories have a definite sociological importance in this connection. Others again seem valuable in connection with religion, particularly with regard to the house of the dead etc. Unluckily there is much over-lapping, not only with stories collected by Boas,[61] but also with those I get myself. One informant gives me a story which he claims is his own, and then frequently I get the same story from someone else. If I confessed that I had heard it before there would be trouble on the ground that I did not keep secret what was told to me, and nearly everyone in the village would refuse to talk.[62] I see no way of avoiding this over-lapping though it is most unfortunate.

I have now over 1000 pages of notes, and I certainly wish it would be possible to write them up after completing my field-work here. I had hoped to get a job in Toronto for the winter when I might have had time to work up the material, but this has fallen through. If by any chance the department should be disposed to give me a chance of doing this work, I hope you will let me know. You told me, I think, to write you an official letter to this effect at the conclusion of my field-work; I will certainly do so on the chance that funds might be available. Of course I understand that this is most unlikely, but if there should be any chance, I would like to have a shot at it.

Yours very sincerely,
T.F. McIlwraith

[H] June 7th 1922

Dear Dr. Haddon,

Thanks very much for your letter of May 12th. I know how busy you are, and accordingly appreciated all the more your kindness in writing. I am glad for your sake that you are giving up the curatorship of the museum, though it will be a bad thing for the museum. Before leaving Cambridge I knew of WHRR'S proposed leap into politics,[63] and will be intensely interested to know whether or not he will get in, for the sake of anthropology at Cambridge I hope not.

Things here are going none too well. I got a fair amount of information in my first six weeks and was foolish enough to think that it would likely continue. Since then I have been getting material all the time, but it seems hard to get it on the stuff I want. I can get a collection of folk-tales and so on, but when I ask about the meanings and so forth the answers are so tinged with Xianity [Christianity] that I am tempted to swear. It will give you an idea of conditions here when I say that in the three months I have been on the job I have seen just one thing that could possibly be described as either religious or magical – and that was the throwing of a puppy in the river to make it a good bear dog.[64] I believe there has been nothing done of interest to me in this connection except one case of magical? [sic] healing; this has been prohibited by the government for years, (the whites assured me that it had all died out,) and I was not allowed to see it.[65] The surprising thing to me is the way social things have been lost.

I doubt if they were ever of much importance. WHRR would blame me for not getting more pedigrees, but the people don't seem to remember them or take much interest in the glories of their ancestors.[66] I have got a good many notes, though I am afraid that when written up they will look rather thin – however perhaps my last six weeks will be the best.

At present nearly everyone has gone off to work in the canneries, leaving, luckily for me, two old men who are useful informants.[67] The people are perfectly friendly now, and I thoroughly enjoy sitting down among a crowd of them and talking away. A good interpreter does not exist for the Bella Coola language, so I have learnt the amazing Chinook jargon. There are not enough words in it to be satisfactory, but eked out with English it serves fairly well. Even the old black magic man has consented to talk to me, though not on his work, in fact the only person I have had any serious difficulty with has been the missionary, because I work on Sunday when his flock returns from the canneries. He is afraid I am perverting their morals – if he heard some of the stories I have got from them he would think they had no morals to pervert. I would sympathize with the man were he not such an insufferable idiot, knowing nothing of the people he is supposed to look after.

H.I. Smith appeared a week or so ago, and his presence makes life here much pleasanter. He is working on the food [torn – the reading seems to be "plants and material"] culture of the Bella Coola [torn] we overlap a good deal.[68]

I wrote someone in Cambridge, WHRR I think, that the Toronto job had fallen through. I had a very nice letter from McMurrich that they were unable to start things owing to lack of funds, but that lectures by Currelly and Windle[69] had been put on the curriculum and they were optimistic for the future. In consequence I am in doubt as to what to do when this job is over. I hope the Canadian government will be able, and disposed, to give me a chance to write up my results, but I don't know. Last mail I had a letter from a W.D. Wallis,[70] a professor at Reed College, Portland, Oregon asking whether I would be interested in applying to teach anthropology there this coming winter. It would certainly give me experience, though whether teaching at a third rate American college, where a library and so forth would not exist, would be of much use either to anthropology or to me, is another question.[71] I am going to meet him in Seattle in August and talk things over. I must admit that the idea of a small college in the Western U.S. does not appeal to me. If nothing else seems promising I am tempted to take a holiday at home, return to Cambridge and have a try at African Colonial Service, always provided that no position for teaching or doing anthropological work is available within the Empire. However I worried you enough when I was in Cambridge, so should refrain now.

I wish Mrs. Haddon and yourself could take a holiday here; the wonderful climate and scenery would brace you up. The only blot on the landscape is the sight of the Indians crowded into a reserve, dirty, disease-ridden, their own pride lost, looked down on by all the white men (even the missionary), and trying to copy in a blind way the habits of the "superior" race which has done this. There is only one white man[72] in Bella Coola who takes an intelligent interest in them, and is not ashamed to give them practical help. This man helped me as an interpreter before I learnt Chinook, knows a tremendous lot about the Indians, but, I am afraid, will never have the energy to write anything about them. I persuaded him to write off a note on a tradition of fire-worshippers which I posted to WHRR a few weeks ago, in the hope that it might be useful for Folk-Lore.[73]

Please give my regards to Mrs. Haddon and to as many of my friends as you may see. I can hardly realise that it was just a year ago that I was writing the – Tripos there.

Yours very sincerely,
Mac

[F] *Bella Coola, BC*
17 June 1992

Dear Family,

One of the surprising things about Bella Coola is the way that time slips away, here is another week gone. As a matter of fact I am now

Captain Schooner and McIlwraith in a potato garden, talking anthropology, 6 June 1922. McIlwraith grew very fond of Captain Schooner, whom he regarded as the most knowledgeable of the Nuxalk elders he worked with. In turn, Schooner adopted McIlwraith by giving him some of his Nuxalk names, thus setting the stage for the anthropologist's participation in the winter ceremonials the following year.

busier than I have ever been. Into the bargain things are going just right, so I don't grumble even though time does not seem available for anything. My two old Indians are working famously. Schooner is an old fellow about 80, a devout pagan, scorning the missionaries and regretting the changes and loss to the culture of the Bella Coola. He is willing enough to talk, but often it is hard to follow him. He knows no English to eke out the Chinook, and has lost so many teeth that it is often hard to catch what he is saying. He gets excited when he talks to me, and plunges off into a whirl of language, often adding Bella Coola to his Chinook, which does not help me in the slightest. He has a great fondness for drink, and when a little fuddled by it becomes even more excited and boisterous. All told I find five hours a day with him a considerable strain mentally – also physically, as he is deaf and one has to shriek at him. The other man, Jim Pollard, is a different type. He has lived a good deal with whites and has the type of mind which would make a successful American financier. He has, thank goodness, finished with his own ancestral stories and I am able to get him talking on what I really

Jim Pollard in costume for the thunder dance, with Lame Charlie assisting, 3 June 1922. Although younger than most of McIlwraith's informants, Pollard possessed extensive knowledge of Nuxalk oral traditions and rituals. McIlwraith describes the thunder dance in a letter to his father dated 19 December 1923. It remains a popular part of Nuxalk ceremonials to this day. (See also photograph on page 103.)

want, social and religious practices.[74] I am always a little suspicious that his information may not be the whole truth, but at least it has the merit of being easily intelligible. With the two of them I am able to get in more than nine hours of work a day, which is quite all I can stand, in fact it leaves me no time to keep my notes in order, look up additional questions, and generally keep things straight. Jim Pollard is only here because his wife happens to be ill, and I go in constant dread that the good woman will either die or recover sufficiently to let him go off to a cannery. He has gone to one cannery today, and I sincerely hope he will have no luck in getting a boat.

Apart from these details life is very pleasant. The weather is on its best behaviour, the road over to the village is a mass of wild roses and raspberry bloom and the woods are a brilliant green. Smith has bought a disreputable horse and equally disreputable wagon, in which we ride over in state in the morning. We usually conspire to have lunch in the woods, and he goes back to the town-site about 5:30 p.m., while I have supper with me, and get back about 9:30 p.m. Then I usually get him to give me a bit of information, identify plants and so forth, which may have turned up in the course of my day's work, and then to bed. It is a great life and I will be sorry when it is finished.

I am awfully glad to hear that mother has decided to work in both the [Eastern Townships] and Quebec after leaving New York. I suppose Dorf. left last night.

Heaps of love,
Tom

[F] *Bella Coola, BC*
24 June 1922

Dear Family,

I always seem to put off writing letters until Saturday night, though for the life of me I don't see where I could have got time this last week – it has been rush all the time.

The more information I get, the more does it seem that I get confused and muddled, as a matter of fact it is a fiendishly complicated business. All my information is coming in as accounts of rites and ceremonies, not a single thing has been done since I got here[75] and to get this from old men via a mongrel jargon language is a brute. At times I feel disgruntled and annoyed at life in general, at other times I suppose I feel things might be worse. One thing I am glad of is that the Indians seem to regard me as rather a friend. With old Schooner and his family in particular I am free to go in, sit down, and chaff them along to my heart's content. Whatever the traditional, unemotional Indians may be, these are the reverse. They smile and laugh on the slightest excuse, and are as brimful of laughter as school-kids. It is pleasant to work with them. I get myself into awkward rows at times, as, e.g., when a worthy man has a row with another worthy man, and wishes to give the minister his version of it. Now the missionary is a more or less amiable idiot, who has been here for over a year and understands no Chinook, so I am requested to go along to interpret. I have no objections to interpreting though I find it a bit hard to keep my face straight when the missionary is cheerfully told how virtuous one of his listeners is. As a rule I know otherwise, however it is the job of an interpreter to interpret, and not to know too much.

Yesterday afternoon, Smith and I went off with an old fellow, Indian, who was looking at his bear traps. The fact that it is not the season for trapping was a mere detail, it is none of our business if they all break the law. We went away into the forest where there were plenty of signs of both bear and deer, but not much of anything to be seen. The mosquitoes found us with a vengeance – they are a brute if one gets to a place where there is no wind. The only spoil was an assortment of plants, bagged by Smith, and a porcupine shot by the Indian. They, the Indians, think that porcupine flesh is fine eating, as it may be for all of me. Anyway we helped him with the first part of its preparation, the skinning, done after the spines had been burnt off in a fire. The most interesting part of the whole trip was when I fell into the drink, thanks to the breaking of a log over which I was crossing. I got soaked to my waist, a minor detail in this brilliant sunshine.

Thanks very much, father, for the wall motto for Joshua. I have ceased to work with him, in fact am working with some of his enemies, so we had a row. I will wait till we are better friends before I give it to him, otherwise I know he would think I was trying to curry favour. It is just what I wanted, and will, I know, please the old sinner immensely. I am dead tired and have no news, so must stop.

Heaps of love,
Tom

[F] *Bella Coola*
June 30th 1922

Dear Family,

In some ways this last week has been the most interesting I have had in Bella Coola. The ceremonial life of the Indians all goes on in winter, and I have been cursing my luck that I have not been able to see anything. This last week I was able to see a dance, though I certainly did not appreciate its cause, which was the death of the chief's wife.[76] She was a daughter of old Schooner, one of the men I am always working with, and the poor old man felt pretty badly; it was his only daughter. For some unknown reason, he is grateful to me for coming to talk to him; it helps to keep him in good spirits. I maintain that such is just as much missionary work as any done by the paid missionary: he would not believe it, I know, but then he dislikes me, though it cannot possibly be with as much dislike as I hold for him.[77]

The actual burial was nothing very much. There is an Indian band[78] here and they were called on to perform. For the life of me I could not see that "Annie Laurie" was suitable to play over a dead Indian chieftainess, but the band's repertoire is limited, and their feelings were all right. The minister did the burial service, and prayed all in English, a language which about 4 Indians half understand. Then I was asked to chase him away, which I gladly did and then there were the usual funeral orations. However the big time was at night.

For some obscure reason they held the performances in a hall built by the Indians in white man's fashion, rather than in their own houses.[79] The result was not good, white man's lighting does not do for masked dancing. First of all food was given out to all, a present from Schooner. Then the choir gave three "cry sings" to the deceased. The choir was six old men, who beat a time on the floor and led the singing, while the women sang. It was the most mournful creepy thing I ever heard. The songs were of the early history of the people, whence they came and whither the dead would return. At intervals all through the wailing of the women could be heard.[80] Then a brother[81] of the deceased sang one of his own songs, parading around to do so with a blanket over his shoulders and waving a rattle. He had a fine voice and the effect was wonderful. Then the priests announced that the mystical ancestor was coming for her and outside could be heard the ghost whistles. Then in came a man entirely covered with a sheet and wearing a mask as eagle, raven and whale. He slowly went around the hall and those accompanying him blew eagle down over him. Then he disappeared and the whistling was heard outside. It was all wonderfully impressive. Then all the whites but

Bert Robson and I were requested to leave and the ceremonial distribution of goods took place.[82]

The whole ceremony to me was almost as impressive as the pipes over a grave, and I came away with a profound disgust for our so-called civilization which is so intolerant that it tries to stop such rites.[83] Pagan they may be, but what right have we to say that therefore they are wrong, and what right have we to abolish, with them, the rich life of a people whose only crime was that they lived in a country which we want? By the performance of these rites the people braced up and cheered up wonderfully, and I do not believe we have any justification to stop things which bring comfort to those who have lost friends and relatives. Christianity should not be forced down any person's throat via the law.[84]

Apart from this the week has been as usual. I am vilely busy, up to my neck in work, and getting information, though I hate to think of the contradictions and conflictions [sic] there will be in it, and of the job I will have to sort it out.

I nearly forgot that it was only last Sunday I had a letter from Cambridge telling of the death of Dr. Rivers.[85] I feel pretty cut up about it, no one ever had a kinder guide and teacher than I had in him. The poor man was taken ill at 3.00 p.m., and died at 7.00 the same night, as they tried to operate on him. I knew he was not strong, but had no idea that there was anything seriously wrong with him. I feel sorry too for Dr. Haddon who will have more work thrown on his already over-burdened shoulders. Rivers was one of the most brilliant men in Cambridge, and one who cannot be replaced.

This seems to be the end of my news this week and I certainly wish that the last item had not required chronicling.

Heaps and heaps of love,
Tom

[F] *Bella Coola, BC*
15 July '22

Dear Family,

The usual rush, only more so, in frantic efforts to get things cleaned up before my last weeks are over. The more information I get, the more I see there is to get, but I suppose that is inevitable. This last week has been a glorious medley, eating strawberries, assisting Indians to avoid the police, working like a slave, jumping on both sides of the fence with regard to the Indians I am working with. A most useful man got into a row at the Cannery and came back to Bella Coola, so I am working

[with] him at intervals with Schooner and Jim Pollard, both of whom are serious enemies of my new man. To say the least of it there are complications, and I listen cheerfully while each slams the other, and thus try to persuade them to get back to work. In some ways the most interesting work has been to stop a murder, not particularly out of respect for intended victim, but because a good Indian friend of mine was the intending murderer.[86] He suddenly decided that a relative of his had been poisoned, and wished to kill the man he suspected. Considering that the death was due to whisky I thought it was hardly diplomatic and managed to persuade him to this effect.

Until this week there had been no rain here since May and everything was burnt to pieces. It had been stiflingly hot though plenty of sun kept away the mosquitoes. Last week the weather broke, plenty of rain blew in and things are looking a lot fresher. The berry crop has been a failure, hay pretty poor, and on top of this a poor run of salmon. More of these came this last week, otherwise the valley people would have been hard hit.

I am absolutely falling asleep so must stop,

Heaps of love,
Tom

[F] *Bella Coola, BC*
28/7/22

Dear Family,

I was sorry that the wretched boat got away without a letter from me last week. I suddenly found that there was to be a native dance at the Indian village on Saturday night, the time I had planned to write, so had to dash off to it hastily, intending to write on my return. I prepared to do so, only to find that the miserable boat had arrived ahead of time, and had already gone out. I hope you were not too disappointed, I hate to do a thing like that, but though I try to be regular, accidents will happen. Dorothy will be in day after to-morrow, and then I plan to turn the letter-writing parts of the game over to her.

The most interesting event recently was that I went up the valley. I had been planning and intending to do so ever since my arrival, but always had to put it off for some reason, usually work. This time, however, I decided that work should go hang. Smith had been camped 35 miles up the valley for a couple of days, so I decided to go up and join him. Now the established way of doing such a journey in this country is on horse-back, but this had no attraction for me, so I borrowed a bicycle.

It was said to be the best machine in the valley, and it may well have been, at any rate it took me there and back, no mean feat considering the roads. None the less it had two serious defects, no strings to the saddle, and no brakes. This last would not have mattered except that I had so many hob-like nails in my boots that I was afraid to put them on my tire as a check, and accordingly had to walk down many hills when I did not coast violently and trust to luck, as I often did. However I got there, and back, without any trouble more serious than a strong disinclination to sit down on anything hard, a feeling which is just passing off now.

I left at 1.00 last Sunday, feeling like a mixture of fool and explorer. No one had ever ridden a bicycle so far into the interior, and no one had much idea what the road would be like from the bicycle point of view. The first part of the trip was fine, bar patches of sand and other patches of recently deposited river stones, neither of which are made for bicycles. Once past the Indian reserve the valley opens out a bit, and there is a fair sprinkling of farms. Most of them are small, very small, mere clearings in the forest. It is difficult to clear land in the valley, and energy of the Norwegians seems to have exhausted itself with the making of the small clearings, and they fall back on fishing in the summer to eke out a precarious living. 12 miles up I came to Hagensburg,[87] the second (and only other) town in the valley. It boasts a church, which Bella Coola does not,[88] and one store. As far as I know the church chiefly serves for revival meetings, the whole upper valley goes mad at intervals when they bring in some "square-head" revival man from the States.[89] It was the most glorious scenery, the comparatively narrow Bella Coola valley winding its way among a regular maze of mountains, many of them with snow-capped peaks and glaciers. After leaving Hburg the road turned inland in a horse-shoe to cross the Nusatsum River, a feeder of the Bella Coola. For about 4 miles in to the bridge and the same distance back there was not a clearing of any kind, merely the narrow road winding its way through the virgin forest. In places the road was tolerably good in others very bad, while the small bridges of more or less, chiefly less, smoothed logs shook all my interior to pieces. The bridge itself was about 100 feet over the Nusatsum, with a view on either side of the white roaring rapids, with snow peaks in the background. Once back to the valley of the Bella Coola a few farm houses again appeared, but getting fewer all the time. Most of the way one was winding through forest practically unscathed by the axe – and oh the roads. 25 miles up the road crossed the river, at Canoe Crossing, reminiscent of earlier days, and with a wonderful panorama of snow-peaks. From here on my real troubles with the road began, in fact I could barely go fast enough to avoid the mosquitoes which descended on me in hordes. Houses were few and far between, though once I passed a school, a primitive square building, perched in a precarious position between the mountain and the road. Never was such an ugly building in such a wonderful site. Most of the people up there are Seven Day Adventists, or some other queer sect, who moved up there to carry on their worship among the bears and mountains. After a bit I got into a patch of recently burnt timber, the usual forest fire started by some careless fool; this one was so recent that in several places trees were still smouldering. Smith was to be camped at Burnt Bridge, well named in this case as the bridge (one over an affluent of the Bella Coola) had been burnt out by this fire. My route instructions were therefore simple, go on the road till you are stopped by lack of a bridge. This I did, including a last stage of wheeling my bicycle up a two mile slope of mixed stones and sand.

Smith has an eye for scenery and on the way up I had been picturing to myself all the beautiful places, fully expecting to find him camped in such. But no, his camp was pitched right at the side of the road, in a part of the burnt land, without a piece of green for miles. He had got in at night, taken the first available spot, and stuck to it like a leech. To say the least of it, it was a funny camp. Smith is a queer bird, a thoroughly decent fellow, and all right if given his own time to do his own job. Unfortunately he has no trust in his own judgment, which, combined with an utter inability to see anyone else's point of view, and a desire to talk, – makes him a somewhat difficult person to get along with. He had taken with him as cook etc., a young Christensen, aged 11. Young Wilfred is a thoroughly nice kid, full of life and go when around the house, but what neither Smith nor I realised was that he would be knocked to pieces by homesickness and the absence of a flock of people around as is the case on the town-site. To make matters worse, the kid's stomach got out of order, and all combined he was down in the dumps, and about as useful around the camp as a white elephant. Poor old Smith could no more realise what was the trouble than he could fly, and his scientific talk did not help a kid of 11. I had to spend a few hours bucking up young Wilfred, and then to let Smith talk himself out on me, before I could get a word in edgewise to explain the why of the various troubles. Before we got to bed it was after 11:00, and then the *darned* mosquitoes ate most of me, and kept the rest of me awake till after 2.00 a.m.

I had somewhat rashly agreed to get up with Smith for a walk before breakfast, so had no excuse when he called me at 3.30 a.m. We did have a glorious walk, it was quite light, and we went away up the trail, over huge trees killed by the fire, then out of the burnt patch, and again into a stretch of magnificent timber. It was very different from the dense coastal underbrush, here was a land of jack-pine scrub.[90] We passed a temporary encampment of interior Indians en route home, very picturesque in the half-light, with not even a dog stirring. We watched the first rays of the sun on the snow-peaks, saw the eagles soaring around, and generally felt that life was worth living.

The plan for that day, Monday, was to accompany an interior Indian away up an old trail to a cave in the mountains where his people used to camp. We got there all right, after a pretty strenuous day, but found nothing worth going for. Across a narrow valley we could see another cave with what looked to be pictures on its walls. The only way to tell was to go there, so down, and up, I went. There was of course no path, and I had to climb a miserable slide, the sort of place that whenever one stepped a few stones went down and I never knew when a regular slide would not feel like taking me down with it. However at last I got up, only to find that the "pictures" were lichens, however, I had the finest views I had yet seen, both of the maze of mountains down the valley,

Harlan Smith, Andy Christensen, and Dorothy McIlwraith in front of one of the first houses built by Norwegian settlers near Hagensborg, July 1922. McIlwraith's sister Dorothy visited him in Bella Coola at the end of the first season of fieldwork. At this point, Andy Christensen, the son of his landlords, had already become his closest friend in Bella Coola. In the winter of 1922-3, McIlwraith helped Andy plan his marriage to Dorothy Clayton, the daughter of a former Hudson's Bay Company factor, and acted as best man at the wedding.

and also of the end of the valley in which we were, winding up to the plateau like surface above. Getting down was a brute of a business, and I was thankful to rejoin the others. It was 9.00 p.m. before we got back and had supper, a pretty strenuous day for all concerned.[91]

The real trouble was that the combined effects of the mountains and Wilfred had got on Smith's nerves, and he was in a hopeless state. I had to walk and talk it out of him, and I guess we would have gone on all night if we had not thought we had seen a bear in front of us in the road and diplomatically retired. We saw plenty of traces of both bears and porcupines when we were up the mountain, but nary a glimpse of either did I see.

I was so dead tired that night that even the mosquitoes did not keep me awake, but the brutes had their revenge by waking me at 3.00, and though I cursed and swotted [sic] simultaneously for three hours, I could not get to sleep again. In the morning (Tuesday), both Smith and young Wilfred were in better shape, and I was able to leave for Bella Coola without the expectations of disaster left behind. It took me most of the day to get down, and – I need hardly mention – I slept the sleep of the weary that night. Those were certainly the three hardest days I have put in for some time.

Since and before that I have been working like a nigger to get things more or less cleared up in my work. Loose ends are inevitable, but I want there to be as few of them as possible. I have certainly got a mass of material and I feel almost certain that they will employ me for several months to write it up, though whether in Hamilton or Ottawa I don't know. I have practically decided not to have anything to do with the Reed College people in Portland, it is too small an affair to give me decent teaching experience. I think the government may want me again next year to continue my work in Bella Coola, and if so, I feel much disposed to take a long holiday at home, merely doing work of my own, rather than to rush into something that will not be good in the long run.

I was glad to get, last week, mother's two letters from Quebec, and father's from Hamilton telling of her safe arrival home. It is fine that she has had a good trip.

Must stop now, heaps of love,
Tom

[C] *Bella Coola, BC*
July 30th 1922

Dr. E. Sapir,
Chief, Anthropological Division
Victoria Memorial Museum.

Dear Dr. Sapir,

In your letter of June 19th you asked me to write you, giving, in a general way, a statement of what I have collected in Bella Coola. My information can be placed under headings as follows —

Kinship System. Based on the family, including grandparents and grandchildren, with certain classificatory characteristics. The terms are almost forgotten and probably never played an important part in the lives of the people.

Marriage. Incest governed by relationship and rank. No compulsory marriage with a certain relative, but a strong tendency to marriage with any distant relative. The reasons for this seem to have been a desire to keep names in the same stock, and a feeling that it was proper to give back a woman to the family from which a mother or grandmother had been obtained: failure to do so caused friction. I have obtained accounts of the somewhat complicated exchange of presents between the two families (using the term in the restricted sense) at marriage. The family of the bride continues to give presents to the family of the bridegroom for years after the ceremony in order to "make clean the path of the offspring," or, as the Bella Coola also express it, "to buy back from the husband the wife and the children." Polygyny was not common and was limited to chiefs. Rather to my surprise I have also had accounts of polyandry, limited to the chiefs, in order that the woman's children might be powerful through having several fathers, who were never brothers.[92] Ceremonial "marriage" of infant children took place, followed by "buying back." This brought honour to the girl in question. Crests had nothing to do with marriage.

Rank. At Bella Coola and at Kimsquit there was a head chief, who had little authority. His name had been supreme at the time the first people came to this earth, and has been handed down since. Real authority rested with the man who had given the most potlatches, as a result of which he feared nothing and his opinion was almost always accepted. Anyone except a slave could give potlatches and become wealthy, although there was always a stigma unless his name and story had come down from heaven with the first people. Slaves had no rights and were outside the community although they could be initiated into the kusiut dance ceremonial.

Inheritance. An old man usually passed on to his children or nephews certain of his names (carrying with them privileges with regard to dances etc.), or intimated which of his family should use them after his death. If a man died without this willing there was frequently trouble between his children, only settled after long discussion. Personal property was usually destroyed at death except a few valuable objects given as presents to his friends. Property in land belonged to families, and was inherited both from father and mother, thus a man might have the right of hunting over numerous lands. Names, with privileges, also came from the mother's side of the family, leading to a multiplicity of crests. The whole system of inheritance was ill-defined, the wish of an old man or the ability of a prospective heir replacing any fixed system of law.

Death. Formerly the method of disposal was in trees though this method changed before the time of the white men.[93] Burial was in the contracted position, facing east. Personal property was either burnt or placed on the grave. On the night after death a masked figure representing the animal or bird used by the deceased's first ancestor (in the patrilineal line) to reach this earth descends to carry his body whence the first ancestors came. The life of the dead person returns up the path of his ancestors to Nusmata,[94] the original heavenly home of the people, the body goes to a land below where they live as transparent effigies of ourselves, the voice passes into the owl, and another portion into the wolf. The bodies of the dead in the world below must be fed by the living. Reincarnation is rare, although a child born with a hole in its ear is said to be some dead person returned to life. In the case of a chief, a potlatch is given several years after his death, at which the deceased returns as a masked figure representing one of his sisauk[95] stories in order to comfort his survivors. This is the central feature of the real potlatch, and can only be done if the family of the deceased is wealthy.

Sisauk Ceremonial. I mention this here because I was forced to refer to it in connection with death. It is one of the two divisions of the winter ceremonial. Sisauk dances are used on two occasions, at death, and at the elaborate distribution of presents – called ɬɩm in Bella Coola. The central feature of a ɬɩm is frequently the return of the dead, but in addition there is the bestowing of sisauk names on children with the recitation of their story, and the distribution, in a complicated manner, of presents to all guests. These presents are returnable, unless given to a poor man, but there is no trace of a fixed system of interest. At a ɬɩm a man uses his sisauk name, a name which came down from heaven with the first people. Only true Bella Coolas have sisauk names, and it is the performance of the sisauk – ɬɩm ceremonial which gives power to the chiefs. Most of the sisauk stories deal with the first peopling of the earth, others refer to strange experiences of distant ancestors. Each story is the individual property of some man. The masks used represent the early ancestors or other objects figuring in the stories.

Kusiut Ceremonial. This is the other division of the winter ceremonial, though, like the last, dances sometimes take place in summer. Membership in the kusiut is not as exclusive as the sisauk, although each kusiut must have a story-name. Such names were frequently given to slaves. Each name carries with it the power to perform some dance representing some action done, or object seen, by an ancestor. In almost all cases this original action or object was due to supernatural power (siut), and when a kusiut performs his dance the uninitiated believe that siut has descended on him. In all cases there is elaborate ritual, and a conspiracy of the kusiuts to deceive the uninitiated.[96] I have obtained accounts of twenty or thirty of these dances, the most important being – the eating of human flesh (similar to the hamatsa of the Kwakiutl),[97] the scratching of the body with the finger-nails, the breaking of property with stones, the beheading of the dancer, the casting of the dancer into the fire, or into water, the cutting of the stomach, the birth of the plants in the spring, and the progress of the supernatural canoe which brings the whole ceremonial to Bella Coola. The ritual of each dance lasts for a period varying from four days to one year.

Siut. Siut are the supernatural beings which regulate our actions. The supreme god, the sun, made the world and its inhabitants, but rarely interferes in the affairs of men. Many siut live in Nusmata, the heavenly house in which the Bella Coola were made and whence they will return at death. These siut sometimes come down to earth and are seen by men. Other siut live under the water, and the dead beneath the earth are siut. In the beginning the first people were half siut, and could talk to animals and birds. Since that time men have changed and lost their siut, but the animals are still siut. At the time of the winter ceremonial all siut from the universe flock to Nusmata for the dances there, and the spirits of all men and animals likewise leave this earth and go aloft. Sometimes siut bring new dances to this world. If a man sees siut he may obtain wonderful shamanistic power, or he may become lucky. The ability to see siut depends largely on the care with which the man has observed the laws of chastity, and ceremonial purifications. In certain kusiut dances the dancer is believed to go to Nusmata and interview siut.

Magic. The Bella Coola practise many rites which are in part magical, in part religious. Various "medicines" based on sympathetic magic[98] are used, especially at birth. In most cases no verbal prayer is made. The killing of people by magical use of hair, nail clippings etc. is firmly believed. Under this heading may be included a number of sexual tabus, food tabus, ceremonial washings and beatings, and other rites performed in the hope of obtaining supernatural power.

Privileges. These depend on the possession of names, with each of which is a privilege or duty. Some, such as types of house architecture, pass in families, but most are individual rights. They include such diverse powers as methods of hunting, uses of medicines, and protecting the river against anyone who would dare to break the laws with regard to polluting it during the salmon run. There are a few secret privileges, such as the ability to call on certain siut, and to use supernatural medicines.

Folk-lore. I have collected about 200 myths and stories. Some are personal property, being sisauk stories of the first people, others again are personal property as accounts of the origin of kusiut dances. Others are mere records of strange occurrences, wars, flood, fire, famine, how certain men went up to Nusmata, or visited siut under the earth or under the ocean. Others again deal with the doings of the first people and the exploits of the raven who travelled all over the world and taught the Bella Coola their arts and crafts. I have collected in this way a good deal of information about the relations of the various tribes with the Bella Coola, both as regards war and ceremonial life.

My information on any one of these subjects is not complete, but I think that on each I have enough information to make an intelligible account. I should very much like to return to Bella Coola to complete details and collect more facts, and especially to record the music and songs, some of which are in languages unknown to the Bella Coola. If there is any chance of my returning to Bella Coola I do not think it wise to put my material in shape for publication, but I would like the opportunity of sorting and arranging my information. I have been working with a number of informants, and as a result my notes are very badly arranged. If an arrangement could be made whereby I could be employed while putting my notes in order for future field work, I would be very pleased. I feel that to do this properly would need at least four months, but if the Department is unable, or unwilling, to employ me for this length of time, I would endeavour to write them up more rapidly though the result would be less satisfactory. As I wrote the Director, a good informant has recently become available, so I have remained in Bella Coola until the end of July. I presume this will be satisfactory to the Department in that I will be working until the end of my time, rather than drawing salary for ten idle days of my return to the east. I shall return to my home, 179 Duke St., Hamilton, Ont, and will be very glad to hear from you or the director whether an arrangement can be made to employ me while writing up my notes.

I trust you are having a satisfactory time among the Sarcee,[99] and are having less trouble with their language than I have had with Bella Coola.

Yours very sincerely,
T.F. McIlwraith

Editors' note: McIlwraith left Bella Coola on August 8th. From Vancouver he went to Seattle to meet Leslie Spier (a young anthropologist at the University of Washington), W.D. Wallis (from Portland), and Pliny Goddard (an American Museum of Natural History anthropologist who had paid a short visit to Bella Coola that July). Goddard was in the company of Franz Boas, with whom McIlwraith had had a rather unsatisfactory meeting in New York prior to undertaking his fieldwork. Their talk went much better this time. McIlwraith reported to Charles Newcombe in Victoria: "I had a very pleasant discussion with Boas on Bella Coola, although he asked me many questions I was unable to answer."[100] After this brief sojourn in Vancouver and Seattle, McIlwraith returned home to Hamilton to begin the large task of writing up his notes.

[H] *179 Duke St.*
Hamilton, Ontario
Aug. 29th 1922

Dear Dr. Haddon,

I am sorry that I have been so slow in answering your letters of June 23rd and July 6th, but you know the rush of the last month in the field when information comes in faster than it can be handled, and everything else is dropped.

Poor Rivers, I suppose that by now his loss has become part of your life, but I still find it almost impossible to think of Cambridge without him. I was broken up when I heard of his death, and it must have been a terrible shock to you who had worked with him for so long. I cannot help thinking that it is the way he would have chosen to go, quietly and quickly, without the torture of a long illness, but that consideration does not help those of us who are left to mourn his loss. I felt sorry that I was so far away from everything in Bella Coola where I could not even have the satisfaction of trying to help put his papers into shape, or perhaps might have been able to help you a little. The only thing I could think of doing was to plunge harder than ever into Bella Coola social organization, though Rivers will not be able to pull it to pieces for me. I hear that Elliot Smith[101] is literary executor, so shall write to him direct about a few minor points that Rivers had spoken to me with regard to the "History of Melanesian Society."[102] If there is any way in which I can be of help either to yourself or to Smith, please let me know, it would be a great pleasure to me to feel that I was doing something, no matter how small. I do not know whether you received reprints of the obituary notices you wrote, or if so whether they have been given away long ago, but if not, and you could spare me one, I would appreciate it very much indeed.

[The intervening four paragraphs of this letter deal with the results of the 1922 Anthropology Tripos at Cambridge and the appointment of Louis C.G. Clarke as curator of the university museum.]

It was more than fine of you to write Laufer[103] on my behalf, as always you are busy helping other people along and I am afraid that I am a perpetual source of trouble. I have had no answer from him as yet, he may be away. The job certainly sounds promising, if they would give a person a free hand. Rivers mentioned on several occasions the way the Field collectors had spoilt things in the Pacific by mere grabbing of specimens as curios, without getting information, and of course destroying things in the process. I would refuse, I hope, to sink to a curio-hunting hog, but it would be time enough to consider that if I were offered the job.

Meanwhile I am very comfortably fixed. I left Bella Coola on August 8th, and have been re-employed from the 25th in writing up my material. The financial end of the Civil Service has sanctioned my employment for six months if necessary, and meanwhile I have been told to go ahead for three. I have gathered a good deal of material and expect it will take me the whole six to put it into shape. Part of the time I shall be in Ottawa and part at home, which is, as you can imagine, very pleasant for me. If funds are available I think they will send me out again next summer, in which case it would take all the following winter to put my material into shape for publication. It is possible that Toronto will find that they can put through anthropology next year, I have no confidence in Currelly but McMurrich impressed me as a very capable and sound man. At any rate I am fixed up for the next six months after which anything might happen. I met Wallis, who worked under Marett[104] at Oxford and is lecturing on sociology in Reed College, Portland, Oregon, and talked things over with him. He was enthusiastic about the place, but from what he said, I was not. It is one of those very small, very low standard western American Universities, where the students are all drawn from local high-schools and know nothing. I would have had a good deal of lecturing on Sociology, whatever that might mean, and it seemed to me that the experience would have been at too high a price. It would have meant that with the work of getting up lectures I would have been unable to put my Bella Coola material into shape, with consequently no chance of returning to the field next year. Wallis pointed out that Reed was far above the standard of most American universities in that students were actually sent down without considering the financial loss of their fees. This struck me as a big joke, I hope I concealed my amusement.

On the whole I think I had a fairly successful time at Bella Coola. The whole life of the people has been broken down by our "civilization," and we have treated them in a manner that has many points of resemblance with the Germans in Belgium. They are disease-ridden, down-trodden, and treated as dogs, while for some insane reason the government has forbidden the potlatch[105] in which centres their whole life; it is the essential feature at all marriages, deaths, and winter ceremonial dances. There were about six old men who were unspoilt by the missionaries and I got on the best of terms with them. It was easy to become friends with them as they were so accustomed to white men who had no interest in anything Indian, that they were pleased with the change. I liked the people very much: they were cheerful, lazy, fairly reliable in most things except where time entered into the bargain, dirty, intelligent, kindly, and very proud of their own customs. When not working they would gather in small groups inside a house and pass the time gossiping, each family is intensely jealous of each of its neighbours, telling stories of doubtful decency, cursing at the rate of pay in the cannery, at the government, and at the Indian Agent, making fun of the missionary, and brewing a poisonous native wine.[106] There is nothing in which they are interested except a band which they have developed with the very slightest encouragement from the whites. No one has taken the trouble to teach them anything useful, in spite of their eagerness to learn, and their ideas of house-building and agriculture are limited to what they have seen white men doing – the result is not always a great success. Most of the Bella Coolas are fairly well-to-do, they fish for the cannery in the summer, if energetic, work for a few months logging and are able to earn in about 5 months all the money they need for the year. Being ordinary mortals they rest for the other 7 months of the year.

I found it depressing working with the survivors of a once numerous people and having my friends, the old Indians, lamenting the days that have gone, realising all the time too, that it was the white man who was responsible. The Bella Coola language is an absolute brute, but all the Indians speak a Chinook lingua franca which can be learnt in three weeks. Thanks to this I was able to get along without an interpreter. The Indian Agent never went near the Indian village unless there was trouble, while the missionary was too lazy to learn Chinook (in spite of the fact that only about three Indians spoke intelligible English), so my friends used to come to me for everything. I refused to answer medical questions, but made a shot at all others, especially theological ones. I have named babies (not to mention nursing the dirty and howling brats on all occasions), helped hide wine from the police, prevented a murder (out of respect for the intending murderer, NOT for the victim), helped in a potlatch (forbidden by law), taken part in horse-play in the village, helped old men with their salmon nets, put drunk Indians to bed, taken their part against the missionary, agreed emphatically that much in the white man's bible was wrong and inferior to their own religion, given my valuable (?) assistance to settling disputes, and done many other things that would be considered undignified by the majority of American anthropologists. In this kind of way I made myself popular with most of the Indians and they showed it. I was allowed to be present at the one potlatch given while I was there, I received three honourable and unpronounceable names, as well as a choice collection of foul nick-names by which I was called, and was given 4 masks with the request that I keep them forever as I was more to be trusted with them than the young Bella Coolas. My chief informant[107] was almost in tears when I left and proceeded to show his sorrow in a way that I could have dispensed with. He made a special brew of his native wine, locked the door of his house to keep out spectators, produced a single glass, and suggested that we drink each other's health. There was no way out of it without offending the old man, so we demolished the stuff – with at least a million germs. Unluckily it was stronger than I thought – enough said.

With the advantage of being on friendly terms with the people my chief difficulties were the infernal language, the decay of all the customs, and the trouble of getting the people to tell me what I want to know, rather than what they thought I ought to want to know. This last trouble was a brute as far as pedigrees were concerned, I fell down badly on that point. I won't try to give you any account of the material I collected. I had a mass of folk-lore thrown at me, and got a good deal about marriage with its great complexities and elaborate system of repayment by the wife's family to ensure a good position for the children, death with its complexities, winter ceremonial dances which are not dances at all but dramatic representations of experiences of ancestors, shamanism, the supreme god with his assistant supernatural powers who are everywhere, descent which is as involved as in the Kwakiutl but which seems to me to owe its complexities to the system of willing rather than to any merging of patrilineal and matrilineal institutions, the potlatch which is in essence the legal witnessing of the transfer of property or the carrying out of some dance, and a fairly large number of miscellaneous superstitions that can be most easily described as black magic and sympathetic magic. I got about 20 cats cradles and am sorry that I did not make an effort to get more, something else always seemed to be turning up to do. One of the most interesting things that I came across was non-fraternal polyandry among the chiefs, the first time I think that such has turned up for North America.[108]

From the 21st of June H.I. Smith[109] was working in Bella Coola. I found him a most agreeable man with whom to work, patient, painstaking, and the most unselfish colleague possible. He was working on the material culture of both Bella Coolas and Carriers, and of course our work overlapped to a considerable extent. My greatest stroke of luck in Bella Coola was coming in contact with one of the settlers there, a man named Robson. R. had been born and brought up on the coast, the son of a Hudson's Bay factor, and had a real understanding of, and sympathy with, the Indians. He had had sufficient interest to read Boas's account of "The Social Organization and Secret Societies of the Kwakiutl"[110] and seemed relieved when I told him that most of us were in his position of not being able to understand what Boas meant. R. volunteered to interpret for me while I was learning Chinook and did a great deal to allay the suspicions of the Bella Coola about me. His knowledge of the Indians on that part of the coast is wide but not sufficiently detailed for much use. I asked him to write a short folk-tale which he told to me and which struck me as interesting and perhaps important. I thought that Rivers would probably be less busy than you, so sent it to him for forwarding to the editor of "Folklore" if he thought fit. R. had a letter from Elliot Smith thanking him for it. I doubt if R. would have the patience to collect the necessary details to write much, or the energy to write material up if he did get it, but I thought it worth while getting him to send off this one note at any rate. He is a fine man and has quite enough education to write, but the rough life of the north does not give him much encouragement for that kind of work.

In the latter part of July Smith and I came across a broken Bella Coola box which we thought too good to lose but agreed that the museum in Ottawa would not have sense enough to appreciate. The bottom was lacking, but the lacing at the side was in position, a thing which I saw in few boxes in Bella Coola: almost all have white man's nails. We posted it off to you in the hope that it might be of some use for teaching purposes. I put inside a strip of cedar bark such as is used for baskets, and HIS sent a letter written by a Ulketcho Carrier Indian in the script taught to them by Father Morice.[111] We were unable to get a proper translation, but the meaning is to the effect that the writer has passed that way, serving as a notification to his later coming friends. In theory all objects collected by me should have been sent to Ottawa but I knew that they would fail to appreciate many things and especially duplicates. I brought a number of things with me which it would give me much pleasure to send either to you or to the Cambridge museum, if either would like them. Some of them are old and not in good condition, but none have been made to order. I shall enclose a list of them on a separate sheet, and if you would tick off any that are wanted, and return me the list I will send them, either to your house or the museum as you direct. It will be several months before they are ready for shipment as notes of what they are are buried in my other notes where it would take an archaeologist to find them at the moment. I suppose this is illegal, officially, so I would ask you not to have my name appear in any list of acquisitions. If it is necessary to have them entered at all it had better be as a gift from you (I would give them to you first so that would be literally all right), or as anonymous.[112]

Dr. Newcombe[113] of Victoria spent a week in Bella Coola and I enjoyed very much talking to him. He remembered you well, and told with great gusto of the time you scoured (?) Seattle for white dogs so that some Philippean [sic] Islanders might be able to give a ceremony.[114] Dr. Newcombe is very deaf now, but energetic as ever. He asked to be remembered to you and also to Potts.[115]

[Here follows a long paragraph concerning the possibility of *Man* publishing a 1562 Maya text as translated by R.L. Roys, a Vancouver scholar and friend of H.I. Smith.][116]

One of Smith's jobs was to make plaster casts of some rock carvings situated in a small valley entering the Bella Coola valley about 4 miles from the sea.[117] This place was the meeting-place of the chiefs from one of the Bella Coola villages, but the meaning of the pictographs is lost, other than a general idea of making something distinctive to show to the other chiefs. The carvings were pecked into the rock. HIS and I made a few crude tracings of the things with heel-ball, Reckitt's blue,[118] and other things. It was more in the nature of an experiment than anything else, and on my part to fill in a little time one day when I went with him to see what the things were like. I am enclosing them in the dim hope that they may be of some interest to someone in Cambridge sometime or other. Probably the best place for them would be a fire, if so please put them there.

I am afraid I have written a very long letter, but I shall probably have nothing else to record for some time, and I wanted to give you and Mrs. Haddon some idea of what I have been doing.

With kindest regard to all, and hopes that things are going well,

Yours very sincerely,
"Mac"

Left to right: T.F. McIlwraith, Willie Mack and son, Mary Mack, Joshua Moody, and Eliza Moody on the Bella Coola reserve, 25 June 1922. The costumes they are wearing are made up of an assemblage of elements used in different dances of the *kusiut* and *sisaok* secret societies. The central figure (possibly a young Clayton Mack), carries a bear's head, signifying a spiritual power impelling the dancer to eat human flesh in one variant on the cannibal ceremony of the *kusiut* society.

The Second Season, September 1923 to March 1924

For convenience the following identifactory symbols are used, printed at the heading of each letter, to identify their location: [C] Canadian Ethnology Service, Canadian Museum of Civilization; [F] Family; [H] Haddon Collection, Cambridge University Library; and [M] Cambridge Museum.

[F] *Namu, on SS* Camosun
8.00 PM, 22/9/23

Dear Dorfa,

My last letter I sent to father, so this is your turn, and anyway the *Camosun* seems more in your line. At the moment the donkey[1] is going strong as we seem to have brought millions of empty salmon cans to this cannery. If it had been the same all along the line our chances of reaching Bella Coola at all would have been slim, as it is we shall probably arrive about 3.99 [sic] a.m., ouch! Needless to say there is no change in the boat itself since last year. I bagged the deck cabin and was greeted by "Pat," "Wouldn't have that cabin on a bet, get soaked through whenever you come downstairs." I meekly asked, "Going to have rain all the time?" "Sure," says Pat. It was raining when we left Vancouver but since then it has been brilliant sunshine showing the mountains off splendidly. It certainly is the most glorious country imaginable. Today we have been messing around Rivers Inlet, and I keep wondering how the navigator ever remembers which turn he should take, it would beat me. Things are pretty quiet now that the salmon season is over, only about 25 passengers and not much freight. The passengers are the usual type, sans collar but not sans beard and dirt. Everyone friendly, yesterday we were hailed by a rowboat with two men, "I want to come aboard," so down we slowed and picked up one of them, a man whose gas boat had sprung a leak and been beached an hour earlier. As we came near Namu tonight we did some heavy whistling, and veered over towards a steamer that was going out: the captain from our bridge used his megaphone, "We have just had a wireless for you, go to Bella Bella for dried salmon," back comes a voice, "Hell, we were there yesterday." All this interests me tremendously. There are no Indians or Chinks aboard so there is not the ever present interest on the forward deck. Some of the officers are those who were on last year, a new captain, but the same second and third officers. The donkey man answers to the name of Kelly and keeps pretty busy; at Vancouver he was working in his Sunday clothes and I felt rather worried about them, however he is back to disreputable, but useful, duds and keeps the winch on the jump. A big Swede is the most interesting of the hands, strong as a horse and clumsy as a mule. No one of interest among the passengers, but one youth from up the Bella Coola valley, whom I met last year, and who gives the joyful information that a bath is installed at Christensens!

I have spent the two days very comfortably, doing plenty of sleeping and taking a few pictures with my new camera by way of practice.

Thursday night I had dinner with a Mr. Roys,[2] friend of Smith's who lives in Vancouver and who I met last year. He is an expert of Maya (ancient Mexico) and showed me the proof of an article dealing with some tests imposed on the priests.[3] They are in the nature of a symbolic examination, the high-priest asks for an impossibility, but the novice must bring what is meant. I chuckled at one of them, "Bring me the sun," is the command, and the novice brings a fried egg. I thought of the sun on SS, apparently [you] have been infringing an ancient copyright.

Don't think I have anything more to report, comfortable trip and I am looking forward to getting to Bella Coola and picking up the threads where they were dropped last year. Please send this letter on to father.

Heaps and heaps of love,
Tom

[F] *Bella Coola, BC*
26/9/23

Dear Father,

While I have my typewriter the question of whether to write to Dorothy or father is simple because I am going to use a carbon and send one copy to each.[4] If for any reason I cannot do this and want a letter to be forwarded in either direction I shall say so in the letter itself.

Well here I am, and the mountains are looking just the same, with the same old glaciers showing white and bright. Sunday morning I was wakened at 2.30 by the youth from Bella Coola who was on the boat and who was so excited at the sight of places that he knew that he had to come to me as the only one he could talk to, a sheer case of home-sickness after three weeks in Vancouver. We docked about 3.45, cold but no rain. Mike Christensen was on the wharf, his father being sick and Andy in the interior. He swore that he would not be long so instead of walking I waited for a ride in the truck and it was 5.[?] before I got up to the house, cold & bed seemed a superfluity, so we build the fire and brewed coffee in the kitchen. Smith appeared about 6.15 and proceeded to recount news steadily till eight. The worst item was the death of poor old Schooner, about three weeks ago.[5] I had a great liking for the poor old fellow, though I cannot help thinking that he had lived past the time he enjoyed and now did little but deplore the loss of old customs. It will make a great difference to me apart from the fact that I will miss him tremendously. Willie Mack, another important Indian has also died.[6]

Smith was bubbling over with a project. Last spring when I saw him in Ottawa he spoke of trying to have a national park established at Bella Coola but I paid little attention to him. However since then things have been moving and I found in Bella Coola a Miss Williams from the Department of Parks, Ottawa, sent out to report on the idea. She left wildly enthusiastic, and most optimistic about the chances of having it put through.[7] The idea is to take in all the south bank of the Bella Coola River and fiord from South Bentinck Arm to a point about 50 miles inland, and back from there far enough to take in all one side of South Bentinck. Certainly it would be a wonderful spot for a national park and things have gone so far that I almost think they will pull it off. Old Smith not so much asleep at the switch as he seemed. Miss Williams had been here a week, piloted by Smith, and reports a hectic but very pleasant week. Smith was as before, talking at great length; he has had a good summer, though just how his results will pan out is more than I can say.

Around the town site there a few changes. The Nicholascoonnay went on the rampage last fall, cut into the bank far enough so that the

Bryndelsons place is now canted forward at an angle of almost 45 degrees: it is a wonder to me that it did not collapse at the time but is still standing.[8] The bridge was carried away and the valley cut off from the wharf for two months, but a new one is in position now. The road up from the wharf is terrible. Much of the old one was carried away and the new seems to bump from root to root all the way. They have built a hall of sorts over near the school-house, but it could hardly be called a thing of wonder. The Christensens have rigged up a bath-room inside, above the old one next to the kitchen. It is not a wonderful place, but there is a real bath and it looks very pleasant to me. Mr. Christensen has been pretty ill for a week but apparently is getting better. The same old gang is around the house. I am in the room that was Smith's, and my old room is occupied by the school-teacher, who seems to be quite a decent kid from Victoria.[9] There is a new doctor in the town-site, Lt.-Col. in the war and said to be a very clever surgeon, but drunk all the time.[10]

The road to the Indian village was flooded out in the centre of the woods and there is now quite a creek flowing in the old part with dead salmon, after spawning, lying where I walked last year. The new road is rougher than blazes, much worse than that going to the wharf, and so rough than no one will drive over it except Vinny Clayton who is the proud owner of a Chevrolet. The Indian village shows few changes as far as houses are concerned, but of course Schooner's death makes a tremendous change. I was given the most flattering welcome there, more than I ever had anywhere I think from everyone, including a lot of Indians whom I did not know, or only knew slightly. Smith reports that they all kept asking for me.

Mrs. Clayton[11] was presiding in state over three grandchildren, Bert Robson's youngsters. Mrs. Robson was very ill last winter and has gone for a trip to the interior with Bert in hopes of making a final recovery. So much for the general news. I have been around the village a good deal, gathering the gossip and making plans to start work, which I plan to do to-morrow, taking lunch only with me.

There arrived, presumably on the same boat as myself, three tins, 50 in each, of Gold Flake cigarettes. They were posted in Hamilton but otherwise I have no clue to their sender. Whoever did so was a brick, especially to remember my favourite brand.

I think it is going to seem easy to drift back into the life here, my Chinook has come back and I think I am going to enjoy the winter. I have provisionally accepted an invitation for four or five days next week, to go out with a fellow in a gas boat after everything from ducks to grizzly bears. I want to work in all the odd trips like that possible this year. On Monday I went down as far as the entrance to south Bentinck, just for a trip. We saw one goat away up on the summit of one of the mountains.

All the love,
Tom

[C] *Bella Coola, BC*
29/9/23

Dear Dr. Sapir,

Your kind letter of Sept. 13 reached Bella Coola on the same boat as myself. As you can well imagine it was a great relief to get away from Hamilton where the strain had become almost unbearable. We were all thankful when the end came.[12]

I was very glad to hear that you had a good summer's work in Pennsylvania.[13] A broken tibia must have made things most unpleasant and uncomfortable, though I hope it was a clean fracture which will leave no ill-effects.

There have been some changes in Bella Coola since last I was here. My best informant is dead: a very fine old man whom I considered absolutely reliable. We were the best of friends and he always used his influence among the other Indians to help me on. His loss will make considerable difference to me here. I was given a most cordial welcome by nearly all, even several men with whom I had troubles last year have been smiling at me. So far (five days) I have done little more than pick up the threads of last year's work, verify some facts, and collect the gossip of the village. As usual this last appears to be promising as a death which took place over a month ago is attributed to black magic, and I am delving into the family dispute which is supposed to have prompted it.[14] I have arranged with three fairly good informants to work for me, so I expect little trouble except for the inevitable delays caused by lost horses, stolen canoes, etc. Time is of only minor interest to the Bella Coolas. I was very pleased to find that I had less difficulty in recording sounds than last year: I think your efforts with me last spring have had results.[15] Taking everything into account I think the prospects are good for a successful winter's work.

Yours very sincerely,
T.F. McIlwraith

[F] *Bella Coola, BC*
Oct. 6, 1923

Dear Father,

I am writing this on Saturday evening and there is a chance that the boat may come in early in which case it will be a short letter. If it ends in the middle of a paragraph that will be the reason.

I am just back from a gorgeous five days spent on a hunting trip. It was not a success as far as game was concerned, personally I got nothing and only one of the party bagged a small black bear, but it certainly was a good time. Last Sunday or thereabouts two of the fishery patrol officers announced that they were going after bear at Kwatna this week, would I come along? I went like a shot. How they worked it as part of their fishery patrol duties is more than I know or care about. The fishery patrol boat, "Merlin," is manned by two, Andrew Widstone a youth of about 22, and Johnny Nygaard, about 35. Both are Norwegians of this valley. They were going after anything from duck to grizzlies and suggested that I join them. The fourth in the party was an American from Denver, Howard by name, who came to Bella Coola a few weeks ago to hunt grizzlies, but had no success. They invited him to go along, and like I he accepted. It was last Sunday when plans were made. Then followed a somewhat hectic few hours. First of all I had to get a hunter's license from the policeman, then set about collecting arms. I borrowed my blankets from Bert Robson, a heavy rifle from one man (whom I had never before met), a shot-gun from another, and so forth. Never did a hunter set out under such borrowed plumage. The question of grub was simple, as they simply got double supplies and we paid for half of them, the we being Howard and self.

A truck took us and our supplies down to the wharf and about 10.00 on Monday morning the "Merlin" set off. She is a gasoline launch, 31 feet long, roofed in, with a small stove, a biggish engine, and that is about all. It was a fine day and everybody happy, not least of all myself to be trotting off in a small boat down the wonderful coast. Kwatna, where a small river runs in, is about 35 miles west of Bella Coola, the "Camosun" passes the entrance to it on her way in. All the way it was fine, and about five we pulled up at an old wharf belonging to a logging company that had once operated there. The first essential was supper, and the salmon that were jumping everywhere seemed to be the answer. So Johnny and I went out in the dingy, towed behind the boat all the way, with a troll. Half an hour and I had landed a couple of kohos,[16] one about 15 pounds and the other about 10. Back to a supper of salmon and potatoes which had been dug the same morning up the Bella Coola valley. By this time it was bed-time and the obvious answer seemed to be for one to sleep on the boat and three in the cabin on the wharf where we found a bed with a mattress. Who last had slept there was a minor detail. Howard slept on the "Merlin" and we three others slept on the bed, all that disturbed me being the row kicked up by the jumping salmon outside. Needless to say it was great.

Next morning it was planned to go up as far as the old logging camp, where there were two old Swede watchmen. It was said to be about two miles, but as no one knew the river we all piled into the dingy with our kit. As soon as we got into the river, Johnny, Howard and I walked to lighten the craft, and it was some walk. All the country had been forested and was a mass of fallen trees, scrub, and heaven knows what. By this time it was about 6.30 and the first sun was shining, everything wet as mischief. There were plenty of deer tracks, and a few bear, but we saw nothing. Even with only a rifle each we three were pretty well puffed by the time we reached the camp. My it was fine with the rising sun glinting on the barren mountain tops above the dark green that covered their flanks.

To my surprise I found a large camp, good wooden huts with sidewalk etc., and a railway. They said there was accommodation for 300 men. All this rather puzzled me till I learnt the why and wherefore. It seems that all this belongs to the Pacific Mills of Ocean Falls, a huge concern which has brought up enormous tracts of timber limits.[17] To hold these they must cut a certain amount of timber from each, which they have done. Accordingly at Kwatna, and elsewhere they have spent large sums of money, taken out some timber, and then closed up and gone on elsewhere. Apparently they find it more economical to buy their timber from hand loggers, but if at any time they want to go back they are ready to do so at a moment's notice. Meanwhile the camp is inhabited by two old Swedes. The railway has track on it for about three miles up the valley from the camp, where the logs were dumped into the river, and has been graded for another four. Several cars were just left standing on the track as well as three valuable donkey engines, all looking like very poor economy to me, but I suppose they knew their business.

From the Swedes, who welcomed us with welcome arms [sic], we learnt that there were plenty of bear in the valley, which we knew before, but they could give us little information as to where to find them. They also told us that there was a cabin about 8 miles up the valley with utensils in it, and that around there should be a good place. So we all set off up the track, carrying a little grub for the day. As far as the rails had been put down the country had been cleared of timber, and was nothing but a wilderness, fallen logs and second growth, with all that was pleasant being the mountains everywhere. We saw a fair number of bear signs, also deer, but saw nothing. Johnny and Andrew wanted to bring the "Merlin" up to camp on high tide, about 3.00 p.m., so they turned back, leaving Howard and me to locate the cabin. On we went, slowly, stopping at every sound, and getting deeper into the untouched forest. In most places the trail was quite good, but there were no bridges, and whenever there was a creek, and there were several, it meant scrambling down and wading through, unless one crossed on a rickety tree-trunk. The other drawback was that no windfalls had been cleared away, so that every fifty yards or so, one had to crawl under, or scramble over, a big four or five foot in diameter spruce. All this made walking none too easy.

About 12.30 we reached the end of the grade from where we were told there was a plain trail through to the cabin. We started off on it without any trouble, a narrow barely discernible track, winding through the devil's club, and other infernally difficult tangles. Somehow we missed the trail, wandered on in a maze of bear and deer tracks, and at length discovered that we could not even find our way back. It was a real case of being lost in the virgin forest. Then to add the final touch a pack of wolves began to howl, I forgot to mention that we had been passing a good many of their tracks, as well as those of deer and bear, both black and grizzly. Getting lost was a matter of no great difficulty as we had only to follow the river back to where our trail had come out on it after leaving the grade, but it meant some infernally hard walking, and a certain amount of swearing. However we did get back all right, after I, who had been poking on ahead, had seen what I had never met before, a ruffed grouse with its ruff all preened up parading before a couple of hens. From the trail we prospected on once more and this time found the cabin. It was a regular hunter's cabin, built of spruce shakes, split out with the axe and overlapping to shed the rain. Inside was a stove, an axe, a few cooking pots, and two beds of cedar boughs laid on strips of wood. We concluded that the signs were fairly auspicious for bear, however we had to be getting back to meet the others, so off we set. Again the same cautious advance with rifles ready as we might have happened to run into a grizzly anywhere on the trail, and they are said to be rather ugly customers. Again we saw nothing, and got back to the logging camp at dusk, after a somewhat strenuous day. Dinner of canned goods and potatoes, tasted fine too.

This was Tuesday. Troubles began right after dinner, when Howard and Johnny both felt ill. Apparently they had eaten something that had gone the wrong way. Tuesday night Andrew had collected something and spent the night vomiting. Yours truly was out at 5.30 looking for deer up the track, where there were plenty of signs, but I saw nothing. None of the others were on deck at all. Back for breakfast where we held a council of war. Neither Andrew nor Johnny had come armed with heavy bear rifles, so they decided to go up above after goat, while Howard and I went up to the cabin at the end of the rails where there were plenty of bear signs, almost as many as at the further cabin. There was no need to leave early, so Johnny and I went down to the mouth of the river, he after deer, and I after duck. Johnny saw nothing, while the ducks saw me, and as I missed the only shot that I had, it could not have been called a successful trip.

This was Wednesday. After dinner we parted company, Howard and I started off for up country. Among the Swedes' equipment was a hand-car, and they agreed to pack us up. So I wish you could have seen us; blankets, kit, two Swedes, rifles, Howard, and myself, all on a hand-car, worked by two men pulling handles like a rowing machine. I was balanced precariously on top of the truck, with the small scrub that had grown up between the ties whipping me in the face. We got up quite a good rate of speed and I began to wonder what would happen if we went off the track, when go off we did. Luckily for all concerned we did not tip over, it was a ta switch and we simply jogged off and stuck. Strangely enough one of our wheels went down between the switch and the main rail and the force of it bent one of the flanges of the hand-car so that it was the deuce of a job to get it out, the sort of thing that could never happen once in a thousand years, but did happen none the less. At last we managed to clear ourselves, and on we went to the first cabin. Here we sent the Swedes back and Howard and I set out to look for bear. This time we went up another branch grade, i.e. a place where timber had been cleared for the rails but they had never been laid. This was worse than the other for fallen trees and creeks, the latter smelling like blazes from the number of rotten salmon lying everywhere. They come up, spawn, and die, rising a smell that would wake the dead and furnishing food for the grizzlies. As before we saw a good many signs, but nothing else: it was a gorgeous afternoon and I for one enjoyed myself tremendously.

Then back to the cabin. Now the stove was supposed to be all right, ditto the wood, and Howard cheerfully started in to make the fire. Said fire must have seen us coming, it burnt brightly, then went out when our backs were turned, then it smoked sulkily, or again it simply refused to light. Of course everything in this country gets permeated with water, and I suppose that was it. Aided by a certain amount of swearing at last we got it going, got a meal, and turned in. Oh yes, we found we had no light and here Howard came to the rescue. Among the stuff in the cabin was a tin of grease of some kind, some of this we put in a saucer into which went a strip of my handkerchief and with a stone to prevent it from burning too fast we soon had quite a decent light. The cabin was of much the same type as that further up, hand split wood, and with no furniture save a rude wooden bench. I had no trouble sleeping that night, with the squirrels and deer scampering around.

Thursday morning we were off before daybreak, I up one branch of the grade and Howard the other. It was not raining but the woods were as wet as if there had just been a heavy storm, and soon I was soaked through, especially as to the feet as high as the knees where I had to wade through creeks full of salmon, alive, dead, and dying. One of the alive ones barged into me in one creek, worse than being bitten by a fish at the XII.[18] I went on cautiously, but saw nothing, though there were plenty of fresh tracks. By this time we had come to the conclusion that though there were bears in the country it was almost a matter of luck whether we struck one, with every creek filled with salmon, and countless berries on the hills there was nothing to bring them to any fixed point, and I felt as if it were a case of looking for a needle in a haystack, with the needle magnetized to avoid one. It was certainly great wandering around in the gloom and watching the first sun shining on the tops of the trees, though it seemed as if it could never penetrate to the depths were I was.

Howard got back about the same time as I, equally unsuccessful. Into the bargain he was feeling ill. So we got breakfast and then he decided that the only place for him was the camp and bed, while I determined to push on to the further cabin, and watch a sand-bar in the river near in the hope that I could find a bear or something on its way to drink either in the early morning or the evening. So about 12.00 on Thursday you could have seen me trekking off up the grade with my pack on my back, blankets etc. in it, and my rifle in my hand, past bear tracks, and getting further and further from other humans. I saw nothing before I reached the cabin, got a fire going, and cooked myself a meal. Then I went out and located a good spot on the river bank, a place where a huge tree had fallen down so that its roots rose to a height of about 20 ft. from the water, and from which I had a good view both up and down. Here I planned to squat from about 4.00 to dark. The place was about one quarter of a mile from the cabin and I had visions of finding my way back through the wilderness of devil's club with the light of my flash-light – and of getting lost, which would have been the devil. So I made preparations. In the cabin I found an old magazine, I wish I could say that it was "Short Stories," but alas it was only "Popular Mechanics," this I took with me and tore it up, leaving a trail of paper all along the trail, if you could define the route by which I had come as such. Then as it began to grow dusk I went out to my tree-root and sat down, endeavoring to "freeze." It was a pretty comfortable seat, but awful hard, and the "no-seeums" a minute kind of biting fly soon found me and began to eat me alive. The first item of interest were the eagles, three of them, two old birds and one young one, were established near at hand and objected noisily to my arrival. They gave me all kinds of views of them before they flew off. A few ravens were around, sitting in the tops of the enormous spruces and raising a din. After a time three mallards drifted downstream within 20 feet of where I was sitting. Three seemed to be a popular number and soon three mergansers did the same, feeding as they went, and entirely ignorant of my presence. A little later and the geese, Canada, went by, first three, then eight, and finally ten. All fine plump birds, some swimming lazily downstream, and occasionally diving for food, others waddling along the bank and getting something from among the stones. All this was sheer joy to me. It began to get dark and a mist rose from the water, gosh but it was beautiful. When it was so dark that I could not see the foresight of my rifle I went back, without having seen any game, though there had been tracks of deer, bear, and wolves on the shore beneath me.

It was a weird job picking my way by the glint of a flashlight through the woods. I was thankful enough for my paper trail before I reached the cabin. I got a fire going without trouble, and a candle gave me a certain amount of light. I wish you could have seen it: a tiny cabin lost amid the huge trees, no person of any kind nearer than eight miles, and there only five men, and me cooking supper in a trapper's shanty. The wolves began to howl as I was finishing supper and gave me quite a serenade as I rolled under the blankets and to sleep. This was Thursday night.

Friday morning I was around before daybreak and cautiously poking my nose out to the river's bank, but nothing to be seen. I waited until it was broad day, a slow business in the depth of the forest, and a dull day made it still slower. Again nothing to be seen, but to me the great joy was watching the sun shining on the banks of mist that were spread almost in formation up the sides of the mountains. Cooked breakfast and chopped some wood, then poked off up a little bear trail through the devil's club. Suddenly I heard a thud about 15 feet before me and caught one glimpse of a small black bear that had been grubbing ants behind a tree trunk. The first and last I saw of him was a streak as he crossed the path, then only a waving line of devil's club. I had heard that a bear could travel fast, now I believe it. As for a shot, such a thing was quite impossible, a streak was all that was to be seen. The country was certainly all in the bear's favour through there, and unless one happened to see a bear on one of the bars of the river there was practically no chance.

Towards noon when I was packed up and ready to get back it began to rain, not a gentle mist but a regular torrent. I had never been dry after leaving the camp, that is never below the knee, but now though my raincoat shed the rain I seemed to get wetter and wetter. I had thought the tide flats where I had chased ducks were wet, but they were dry in comparison to those woods, every branch was like a sponge and I had to brush through them all with a pack which really seemed heavy though it was only a light one. Through I plunged to the grade, and down it, climbing over or through windfalls every few yards, (so it seemed), each wetter and more difficult than the last. Two or three times I followed creeks down to the main river in hopes of seeing something, but though I was wading in water up to my hips at times, it seemed almost dry not having a pack to make me do contortions at every windfall. Finally a very damp individual reached the first cabin, where among other things we had left a tin of beans, which I ate solo and cold, being hungry. I might mention that I had eaten all the grub which I had taken with me. In this first cabin we had parked one blanket and a few other things, these I crammed into my pack and started off for the end of navigation on the railway, about half a mile away, where a slide had blocked the track for the hand-car. By this time the wet pack was really heavy and I had troubles all my own navigating the windfalls and was not sorry to see one of the Swedes with the hand-car, as arranged, to meet me. I found that working a hand-car is no easy work, brings in a lot of arm muscles that I did not know I possessed. So I returned to the camp, and got off as many of my wet clothes as I had substitutes for, which of course did not include my mittens, they had been wet for so long that I had forgotten all about them. The boys got me some hot grub, which tasted all right.

Andrew, Howard, and Johnny were all in camp, more or less better, but sickness and rain had interfered with their plan for a trip up above. However Johnny had been lucky and had killed quite a nice black bear right near camp. I went out again in the pouring rain just before dusk, but saw no deer.

That night Friday, I slept in state in the camp, and as before was out at dawn looking for deer, with the same no luck. We had breakfast with the Swedes, who seemed sorry to see us go, theirs is a lonely life, and got the "Merlin" downstream about 9.00 a.m. We stopped for an hour at an island off the mouth of the river where there was an old Indian cemetery, found the spot and a few old boxes, but nothing worth taking as specimens.[19] It was brilliantly fine to-day and it was a great trip up to Bella Coola, which we reached about 5.00 in time for a bath and a shave before supper. Both bath and shave were badly needed: I don't think that even I ever looked so tough, my beard is growing faster than it did last year, and the combination of wet and dirt had reduced my clothes to a wonderful state of grime. None the less it was a gorgeous trip from beginning to end.

No change in Bella Coola since last week. Last Saturday there was a gay time with a marriage, the adopted daughter of the Christensens' being married to one of the settlers.[20] Both were well known and liked in the valley and everybody rolled up in his or her Sunday best. The ceremony was held in the new hall, and afterwards a dance. Almost all the men in the valley started celebrating the night before and the amount of whiskey what must have been consumed made me think of army days. There were very few entirely sober, but everybody seemed to have a good time.

Well I have just about finished and the old "Camosun" has not yet whistled. Was very glad to get letters last week from Dorothy and Father. I have had no chance to attend to the insurance business enclosed by the latter, but will see that it is sent off without fail next week. Please send on the RCI magazine to me here, reading matter is hard to find in this neck of the woods. Was awfully pleased to hear from Dorothy that she had a good time both in Stanstead and was having one in Quebec.

I am too sleepy to write more even if there were anything to say, which there is not, except that I am thinking of both of you all the time, and am so thankful that we have one another.

All the love there is,
Tom

[H] *Bella Coola, BC*
13/10/23

Dear Miss Fegan,[21]

Thanks so much for forwarding to me Dr. Haddon's two letters from South Africa. It sounds very promising[22] and I am almost certain I shall have a shot for it, though, as I wrote Dr. Haddon, I want to finish up this present job and get my mss. in shape as a basis of some kind.

I got out to Bella Coola two weeks ago for the winter. Now that the canneries and logging camps have closed I expect little trouble with informants and interpreters, though I have no doubt there will be some woes, I am afraid that the law prohibiting the potlatch will prevent any Indian dances this winter, but I live in hopes. I am supposed to be taking part in one myself and it would be very funny if it should land me in jail.[23] The Indians gave me a most enthusiastic welcome; they are certainly a fine lot – at least the older people are, I have no use for the young and supposedly Christians.

I hope things are going well in Cambridge. If I should land the South African post it will be fine to see you all en route.

My very best regards,
"Mac"

P.S. I wrote this out in the woods where I usually take my lunch. Part of the latter, jam, got smeared on this sheet but I am really too lazy to rewrite it – please excuse me.

[F] *Bella Coola, BC*
18/10/23

Dear Father,

Now that I am back in Bella Coola and firmly established at work there appears to be, as last year, little to write about. The weather has broken at last and it now rains pretty heavily every day. The road to the Indian village, especially that part of it which was made new since last year is a sea of mud, very sticky, squidgy mud, and I am getting used to wading through it in the mornings with my rain-coat. I am the proud owner of a pair of gum boots, shod with spikes a la lumber man, they weigh like lead and are not handsome but keep my feet dry and if I ever kicked anyone with them I think it would be sure death. I don't think I have seen anything to equal the views, the trees on the lower slopes have turned to autumn tints, while above are belts of fleecy clouds, sometimes four distinct layers beneath the crest of the mountain. I have had far more trouble than I thought possible in getting people to talk to me, considering that they are all willing it is amazing the excuses which they can rake up, getting salmon, cutting fire-wood, sore throat that makes talking difficult: I think I have heard every possible one. The last few days things have been going better and I hope that it keeps up. I have been working in different houses where the meals are different, but all have one common characteristic – extreme badness.

Last Thursday I went up the valley to have supper with Mrs. Shulstead, she being the lady who came from Stanstead. Apparently I should have been able to spot who she was from the fact that she had a sister Mrs. Deacon, who visited her here last summer and who claimed that once upon a time she had known me. I imagine that said Mrs. Shulstead is some sort of a connection of the Flanders, but am not certain. She moved to Bella Coola last year, following the death of her husband in Ocean Falls. It seems that he had bought a farm here, he was a valley man, and they had planned to move here at the time of his death. So she came on anyway and is trying to run the farm with the assistance of a brother-in-law who appears to be an idiot. Anyways she has quite a decent house, and I had a good chicken dinner. Mrs. Shulstead struck me as decent but not especially interesting. The funniest thing was seeing a picture of some wedding group in Stanstead, with Uncle Sidney and Aunt Hattie visible, fancy a thing like that on the wall of a house in Bella Coola.

The next night there was a concert and dance here. The standard of the concert could not have been called high, though one man had what I should call a very pleasant voice. I met him the day before, a very tough looking specimen from up valley, dirty and unkempt, and at the time I was struck by the way he spoke, an educated voice. A few days later I heard he was an Oxford man, I wonder what twist of fate sent him here. What chiefly amused me about the concert was a turn given by a little girl of about six, who made a bow and started off, "My beautiful, my beautiful who standest proudly by, it was the schooner Hesperus, the breaking waves dashed high," and so on through the whole thing.[24] Visions of the days as was.

I fared rather well as far as mail was concerned last week, with two letters from father, one of which I suppose should have caught the mail preceding, and one from Dorothy.

[This is followed by personal family matters.]

Tom

[M] *Bella Coola, BC*
19/10/23

Dear Mr. Clarke,[25]

Thanks for your letter from New York: I most certainly remember the pleasure of meeting you both in Cambridge and Edinburgh.

Your letter puts me in rather a difficult position. As a Cambridge man, and one who worked under Dr. Haddon in the museum, I would be only too glad to collect specimens here. But unfortunately I have been given money to obtain specimens for the Ottawa Museum on the staff of which I am at present. Without their permission it would be impossible for me to send specimens elsewhere, much as I should like to do so. If you care to write to my chief, Dr. E. Sapir, asking whether it would be possible for me to collect for the Cambridge Museum, he might give the necessary permission, but I would not feel justified in asking for it, and if you should write I would ask you not to mention having first communicated with me. One of the disadvantages of my post is that it is a Civil Service position and as such I must be careful to obey a number of regulations which are annoying. There are very few ceremonial objects, masks, rattles etc. left in Bella Coola, so I am afraid there would be justification for objection from Ottawa in that the museum there would suffer if I purchased any of those available for Cambridge. I hope you realise how very sorry I am that I cannot see my way clear to do something for the Cambridge Museum.

The manner in which the ancient civilization has broken down here is truly deplorable. Really the only native objects in common use are a few baskets, a few spoons, sticks for drying salmon, and dug-out river

Interior back wall of Captain Schooner's house in Q̓omqo·ts, 1 August 1920. Harlan Smith purchased and removed this and many other carvings to the Victoria Memorial Museum in Ottawa in the early 1920s.

canoes. There is not even a single ocean going canoe left here. Many of the older people have a few boxes, a few coppers, some have masks, but I really believe there are only two rattles left in Bella Coola. The clothing used is entirely white man's work, even at the dances the blankets are white man's blankets decorated with mother-of-pearl buttons. Perhaps you would let me know (I shall be here till February) whether such objects as baskets, dried salmon and so forth would be of any use to you.

I have heard wonderful accounts of the way in which you have succeeded in getting things going at the museum. I have been more than delighted to hear of it, and certainly things were in a bad state of chaos when I was working there. Glad to hear that you have acquired more fine archaeological collections from Cambridgeshire.

I reached Bella Coola three weeks ago and have got fairly well into the work. My Indian friends gave me a most cordial welcome back, and I have been invited to take part in one of the dances this winter when a name is to be officially given me. I had several bestowed on me last year, but was not present to "dance" at the time.[26] My worst trouble is that my best informant is drunk on an average of three days out of four, and unless the old lady should be put in jail my chances of getting much information are slim. There is a good deal of sickness too that interferes, as well as the endless number of excuses for talking, "to-morrow," which would never come unless I almost carry a man off. However such troubles are inevitable and do not worry me much.

Glad you had a successful trip among the Zuni.[27]

Yours very sincerely,
T.F. McIlwraith

[F] *Bella Coola, BC*
26/10/23

Dear Father,

Another week gone, with nothing much to report. At long last I have got things going pretty well over at the Indian village and have two women working steadily for me. That is one of them works steadily, the other when she is not drunk, which is rather seldom. However she is a useful old dame when one can get hold of her. I had one stroke of luck in picking up my other worker, a surly old crone whom I had never had anything to do with. One day I was walking along the road when a dog, which I had often noticed as a surly, nasty looking brute came up behind me and tried to bite me. Luckily it jumped high up my leg and grabbed at the pocket line where my trousers happened to be flying loose so that all it caught was some loose change in my pocket on which I hope it broke its teeth. To say the least of it I was rather startled as, though I have often enough felt uncomfortable when dogs were yowling behind me I always have gone on the assumption that as long as I paid no attention to them they would pay no attention to me. I interviewed the female owner in a none too amiable frame of mind and was hardly soothed by her informing me that as the dog had been given a name and was a chief among dogs he thought he could bite anyone he liked.[28] I managed to cease to be angry to ask about the giving of the name to the dog, and since then I have been on the best of terms with the old woman and her husband, not to mention the ancient dog, and, alas, her much be-fleaed puppy that insists in jumping over me whenever I go to their house. However it is all in a life-time.

Last Saturday I was cut off from the Indian village by a flood. It had rained hard for three or four days and when I started out in the morning I found that there was a creek two or three feet deep over part of the road through the forest. It was the place where there was a sidewalk, and I went along this with water swirling beneath, until I came to a place where one plank had been carried away leaving a gap of ten feet. It would have meant wading up to my knees at least, followed by sitting all day in either a very hot or a very cold house, so I chucked the job for the day and by Monday things were back to normal. I had no idea that water could rise so fast, it was a branch of the Nicholasconnay that caused all the trouble.

The only attraction around the town-site that day was a trial, which I attended. It was the first time that I had ever been in a court, and I must say that it struck me as a huge joke. There were four prisoners, one charged with killing a doe, and the other three with being in possession of its meat. They were caught red-handed so there was no defence possible. The funny part was that one of the prisoners was the Norwegian minister from up the valley, a vile thunder and lightning individual. But the judge, a Norwegian JP, was the joke of jokes. He tried to read the charge, but seemed to have troubles of his own, especially when he read "protection of deer" as "protestation of deer" and had to be corrected by the policeman, the only person in the court who seemed to have any idea of correct procedure. In a place such as this one does not expect a learned judge but one does expect a man with some slight idea of common sense and dignity, two things that were entirely lacking.

Working over at the village I have been having my usual run of experiences. The funniest was one afternoon when I was working with two old women, neither of whom weighed less than 250, though both were short. One of them had been sweeping out her house and had thrown some rubbish onto the fire in her smoke house. She did not know that there were cartridges among the rubbish, and presently they began to explode, whereupon the old lady left her smoke-house, wisely, I thought, and came to talk to me. But one of the cartridges set fire to some old sacks and about an hour later we were roused by a very old man hobbling along and calling out something that was interpreted to me as fire. I dashed up the side-walk, only to find that the house was locked; while waiting I looked around and nearly collapsed. The two fat old women, one of whom was the owner of the house, were waddling and puffing up the walk like grampuses, behind them came two very old men feebly toddling along, a two year old baby whom one of the women had been tending was sitting on the sidewalk and yowling like a steam-engine, and about four dogs were messed up in the chaos. When the door was opened we soon threw out the burning junk and really there was no damage done. One of the things into which the fire had penetrated was a feather tick,[29] and I never knew how many feathers one of these could contain. Most of them, I think, got over me as I was toting it out. The Indians have been pretty decent to me, one old lady has given me a pair of knitted socks, and a pair of gloves, saying she was afraid that I would be cold in the winter. This last I am quite prepared to believe, anything much colder than my room in the early morning is hard to imagine. I have got an oil stove that soon heats up the place as soon as I can get up enough energy to light it. The cold weather has at least dried up the road through the forest to the Indian village which is one blessing.

[Personal comment.]

As usual was very glad to get your letter last mail (21st), dated Oct. 10, #5. By the way I spent one evening this week at the doctor's house, poor devil, rather a fine man I imagine till ruined by drink. He had one man in for the evening who really played the violin well, at least he played the pieces I liked, "Bonnie Dundee," "I'll tell my mother when I get home," "Bonny Mary of Argyll," and all the other old stand-bys. When the doctor heard I was from Hamilton he asked if I knew Ben Simpson, with whom he said he went to college. Carruthers is the doctor's name.

Much love,
Tom

[C] *Bella Coola, BC*
27/10/23

Dear Smith,

Very sorry about this delay in sending Harry Schooner's receipt, but he has not been back to Bella Coola – he is logging somewhere down South Bentinck, expected back at any time.

Things have been going pretty well with me. I have tried working with quite a number of different people, and am now fairly well fixed up with Mrs. Willie Mack[30] and Steamboat Annie. You see I am moving in high society.

Kindest regards to all,
Mac

[F] *Bella Coola, BC*
Nov. 11, 1923

Dear Father,

The boat is expected next Wednesday, but Sunday seems a suitable time to write letters so I will polish one off to you now. Since I got back from Ocean Falls there has been very little to report. I certainly did not go on that trip as a picnic but I was rather interested in seeing the place.[31] We left Wednesday morning at 5.45. The whole town is run by, and for, the company,[32] hence they have to provide meals for their early morning shifts at odd times. One of these is 5.00 a.m., and it was to this that we went, downstairs in the basement of the hotel. To say the least of it I did not think much of the company. I don't think I ever happened to be in such a mob of profanity in my life: Bella Coola appeared quite peaceful in contrast. If Andy and I had been alone with the runner of the boat on the way home it would have been a fine trip, but unluckily we had picked up two men who wanted to get back to Bella Coola and they rather hampered conversation, one being a half-breed French Indian logger, and the other some kind of comic from Wisconsin. We had to fight our way through a strong head wind all the way, in places where it had a full sweep only making about three miles an hour, and the boat certainly pitched and rolled in a wonderful way. I half expected to be sick and was thankful that I was not, and did not even feel squeamish. I managed to spend a good part of the day sleeping – on the hard floor beside the engine with various weird smells ranging over me – having had only about three hours sleep on the Monday and four on the Tuesday night. The rest of the time I was out on deck with the spray breaking over me, watching mountain after mountain sweep into view. It was a fine bright day, though cold as mischief. One thing that amused me was the label of the box on which I was sitting, obviously a box that had once contained whiskey –

> To His Majesty King George the Fifth,
> in right of the Province of British Columbia,
> Care Liquor Control Board, Vancouver.

It struck me as rather a long-winded way to describe the consignees.

Life here moves on as before. My chief trouble over at the village is the infernal amount of drunkenness, which wastes my time past all belief. I make definite arrangements to work with a certain man, and then lo and behold he appears helplessly drunk, and there is no chance of getting anyone else on the spur of the moment. A few nights ago I had what was really an awfully funny experience. In the evenings I am working with two sisters, both of them grandmothers, and both of them over 200 pounds. I knocked at the door as usual and announced who I was. There was no light in the place, and when I blundered in I felt as if an earthquake had struck me – one of the old dames had thrown both her arms around my neck, with her full weight on me, and cheerfully announced as she did so, "I'm drunk." How it was that the two of us did not land in a heap on the floor is a mystery to me, but someway I managed to pilot her to a chair and disentangle myself. Needless to say I had no luck that night.

In a way I am seeing more of the people around the town site than I did last year; they are certainly a queer assortment. Andy, whom Dorothy will remember, has changed a great deal since last year, and is really turning into what I consider an awfully fine fellow.[33] He and I have been thick as thieves since I arrived and it is decidedly pleasant to have someone around with whom I can talk. I cannot say that I think very highly of any of the rest of the family, though Mrs. Christensen has always been mighty decent to me. One of the other boarders is by no means a bad sort, though far from thrilling. The only other person at all sane around the town-site appears to be the school teacher, a kid from Victoria, who is rather lost in Bella Coola. The only amusement apparently are occasional dances and the community at large, headed by the school-teacher, is trying to teach me to dance. I think she has undertaken a hopeless task, but I rather wish that I could learn. There are rumours that a Badminton set is to be purchased, I hope this comes off.

There is an engineer from Victoria in the valley at present, Aldous by name. A few nights ago he was up talking to me in my room and the conversation drifted to Hamilton. He asked whether I knew a namesake of his there, a certain J.E.P. Aldous. I had no difficulty in pleading guilty. This man said that as far as he knew he was no relation but the name being so rare he had assumed that they must someway be connected, though I forgot to find out how this man heard of our Mr. Aldous's existence. This man is an Englishman of about 40, who has lived in Victoria for fifteen years or so. He struck me as a very decent sort.

Nothing else to report, I am keeping both busy and well, and life has no very serious drawbacks.

Much love, including
Aunt Jean,
Tom

[C] 12/11/23

Dr. E. Sapir,
Chief, Anthropological Division
Victoria Memorial Museum,
Ottawa,

Dear Dr. Sapir,

I should have answered your letter of Oct. 18th by the last boat, but unfortunately it arrived twelve hours ahead of schedule and caught me just as I was sitting down for an evening of solid letter writing. Perhaps you would send me the drawings of the string figures which Mr. Prud'homme[34] made for me; I do not suppose they will be of any real use to me here, but I should like to see what success he had had with them.

Thanks for your news from Ottawa. It was the first I had heard about Dr. Boas going to Bella Bella (other than that it was possible last spring). Two days ago one of my Indians told me that George Hunt was in Bella Bella collecting "stories"; I suppose Boas has sent him to clear the way.[35]

Things here have not been going as well as I should have liked. Most of the Indians were home when I arrived and I expected little trouble about getting informants, especially considering the cordial welcome they all gave me. But I have had a great many delays – firewood to be cut, salmon to be dried, and so on. Most of them have been logging and money is plentiful, accordingly forty cents an hour is no great attraction. Then there has been a good deal of sickness, and much heavy drinking. My best informant, a woman, gets drunk about twice a week, but she is so good when sober that I feel justified in keeping her on. All these combined have given me too much delay for my liking, but I really think they were inevitable. I have been able to clear up a number of points from last year, confirm several doubtful questions, and, of course, get a good deal of new material. I have been very strongly impressed by the clear vision in the Bella Coola mind between human beings on the one hand, and all other objects on the other, this second category being that of the supernatural ones. But what I did not realize until recently was that for a certain period during the winter dances a man is considered to have joined the ranks of the supernatural ones.

I certainly thought that I had brought employment forms with me, and was amazed to find that I was without them two weeks ago. Luckily I have been working with so many different Indians for odd periods that I have had no single man working for the equivalent of a month at full time each day – so I do not think any damage has been done by my oversight. I hope it did not inconvenience you to send them.

With kindest regards,
Yours very sincerely,
T.F. McIlwraith

[C] *Bella Coola, BC*
14/11/23

Dear Dr. Sapir,

Many thanks for the employment sheets which arrived a few minutes ago. I understand that Dr. McInnes is absent at present, accordingly I am sending them to you and would ask you to transmit them to whoever is in charge of such matters. I hope the forms are satisfactory. It is really impossible to fill in accurately the proposed period of employment depending, as it does, on whether the informant continues to give satisfaction.

Things have been going very well here for the last week or so, information piling in faster than I can handle. I am working over last year's material and have been able to clear up a considerable number of points which I had previously left in doubt. I am getting new information about souls, the supernatural creatures which are all around us, a second type of shaman, as well as more myths. Last year I thought (and perhaps hoped) that I had done something towards exhausting the supply of these, but they continue to come in almost as fast as ever. With the necessity of re-reading the manuscript I am unable to spend as long at the Indian village every day as I did last year, even though I am stretching my working day to about fourteen hours.

With best wishes,
yours very sincerely,
T.F. McIlwraith

[F] *Bella Coola, BC*
20/11/23

Dear Father,

Time is certainly flying and here is another week gone. I don't know what happened last Sunday, but someway I did not get any letters written, but as I am taking a half day off to-day it does not matter. I am working pretty hard these days though luckily the woman with whom I work at nights is going to Vancouver by the boat to-day and I am blowed if I book another night informant, life is too short. And ploughing over to the Indian village in the pitch dark is no joke.

For part of the time this week I have fallen back to work again with old Joshua. Last year when I was with him I needed an interpreter and there were a good many points about which I wanted more information. The old boy has been polite as they make him, butter would not melt in his mouth, and I have quite enjoyed working with him. He is certainly a clever man; I hardly expected to hear the following from any Indian, even Joshua. He told me that he had had a row with the missionary, and had ceased to go to church, then continued, "The Methodists say that the English Church is bad, the English Church that the Presbyterians are bad, they all say that the Catholics are bad, and the Jews likewise say all are bad, henceforth I shall have nothing to do with any of them but shall stick to the Bible alone." He is an infernal old hypocrite and I much doubt the truth of the last statement, but it certainly interested me a lot to hear an Indian say such a thing. Joshua has become disgusted at the feuds and jealousy of the Indian village and with the help of his son is clearing a farm up at the other end of the Indian reserve. It is heavy virgin bottom growth, and he is using fire as much as possible. I have been interested in seeing the patient way in which he plies brushwood around the bases of the trees and waits till in course of time it eats its way through and does what it would have taken two men with saws a day to accomplish. I am always a little uncertain which way the trees may fall and take up a strategic position behind some large standing tree, but it does not seem to worry Joshua in the slightest. I cut down one little 6 inch tree for him, but succeeded in having it fall in precisely the opposite direction to what was intended where it smashed a box which he wanted to keep, so I think that in future I had better let him do his own work. Within a few yards of where he is clearing there is a square hollow in the ground, obviously marking the site of an ancient underground house. Such are common in the interior and to a point some forty miles up the valley, but I believe they are unknown on this part of the coast. I spent half a day digging in it and unearthed some broken fire stones, which proved conclusively that it was a house. A large tree is growing from the stump of an old tree inside the house, so there is no telling how many years ago it was that people lived there. One day it was simply glorious in the woods, warm and bright I sat with my back against a log with the wood smoke drifting over me and wrote while Joshua talked to me, at intervals giving instruction to his son and at times piling on more brush-wood.

I think I mentioned that the whole community has been trying to teach me to dance, and last week I was reckless enough to go to a dance, the first I had been to since one at McGill in 1916. Needless to say I fell over my partners' feet, but nobody seemed to mind very much and I did not have too bad a time. They have a hall at the town-site now, and the whole community turned out. What amused me were the feuds and counter-feuds that were raging. They talk of the pleasures of a small dance where everybody knows everybody else, maybe, but at this one there were about four cliques, including several that would not speak to one another. It was funny. What with indignant partners, refusal to dance and so forth I was half expecting to see several free-fights break out, however none did.

This really seems to be all the news this week, except to say that last boat, after ten days interval, brought me a fine budget of mail, two letters both from Dorothy and father.

Ever so much love,
Tom

[F] *Bella Coola, BC*
27/11/23

Dear Father,

Another week has slipped away, gosh they are travelling fast. This one has been chiefly marked by the rain and mud, never in my young life have I seen anything to equal that. There is a patch in the middle of the road to the Indian village which all week has been about six inches deep in liquid ooze. All yesterday and to-day it poured, so that there were bets on in the town-site as to whether I would be able to get through. I sport gum-boots that come half-way to my knees, and had a beautiful time floundering through till I reached a place where the river had simply chosen the road as its course. There was a small bridge of which the planks were not nailed, and this was absolutely floating, each plank separately, in about three feet of water. By the time I had navigated this I thought all would be well but it ended in a patch where I had to wade with the water half way between knees and thighs, I do not think I ever remember quite such a cold sensation as when that water came oozing down into my shoes. Then came the "sidewalk"; this is an affair of single planks, placed end to end and resting, unnailed, on posts about three feet high. The water was lapping around the planks themselves, and at least two of them were floating clear, only held in position by the tightness of their fit at the ends, so that as I stepped on it was a case of manipulating with my feet to drive the planks into their place so that they rested on the posts. all this with a swift flowing stream at least three feet deep beside me so that a slip would mean at once a plunge into the icy cold. I was rather glad when I got over. Much to the amusement of the Indian village as a whole I declined point blank to sit all day in wet socks, instead stripped them off and hung them out to dry over the stove while I sat as near the latter as possible with my feet bare. I suppose it was not dignified, but at least it was sane.

Last Saturday night I went across to play bridge at Bert Robson's. It had rained for several days but the night was clear and never in all my life have I seen such moonlight. It was really bright as day coming back early Sunday morning, in fact one could have seen to read, with the moon, a shining orb reflecting on white fleecy clouds. The view from the bridge near Clayton's was past all belief, with the glaciers covered with new snow, and snow half-way down the slopes of the mountains, then the dark water rushing underneath, and the inky black trees on the lower slopes. As usual the road was a sea of mud through which I had to pilot the school teacher, who made up the fourth at bridge.

The only other dissipation this last week was a trip to Hagensburg, ten miles up the valley to attend, of all things, an auction sale of goods in aid of the blatant Methodist church which thrives there. How I ever consented to go to such a thing is more than I can fathom, but someway I let myself get into it with the Claytons and Andy. Going to one of such was allright, infact it was very amusing to see the old Norwegians, and their canny way of bidding, but two such affairs would be sudden death. The goods which they auctioned off ran from home-made candy, the only thing worth buying from my point of view, to socks, gloves, handkerchiefs, pillow-cases, and so forth. There was a short (luckily) programme, songs. The rabid Methodist minister presided and I forgave him a great deal for a remark he made after we had listened to a simply horrible affair given by the, so-called, choir, "As you all know the choir is crippled so I think it was brave of them to sing." So did I, not that I have any music in me, but it struck me as a wonderful remark for a chairman to make, though I really believe that our part in the back row were all that could see any humour in it. Coming back Vinny Clayton, who was driving, struck up 38 miles an hour in his Chevrolet, including a few slides on the sand: I am almost surprised that we are alive to tell the tale.

Other than this, absolutely no news this week, except that I am keeping amazingly well, and finding life none too bad, though somewhat strenuous.

[The letter concludes with the following handwritten paragraphs:]

As usual was very glad to get your letter also the "World's Work."[36] Am returning the form about the Saving Certificates, thanks for seeing about the same. I must admit I was very much interested in hearing that the Tigers[37] had won the Interprovincial, news of that kind simply does not belong here.

Could you do another chore for me? Bag me a $20.00 gold piece – or two tens – or four fives? Yankee gold would do just as well. I am negotiating for some gold Indian bracelets and must produce the equivalent in the metal.

Much love to Aunt Jean
and yourself,
Tom

[F] *Bella Coola, BC*
5/12/23

Dear Father,

This letter should reach you rather speedily as I am writing it on the morning of the boat's arrival, having been too busy all week to breathe, let along write letters. The Indians dances started last Friday, which has taken me over to the village every evening, getting back any time between eleven and three. All the time it has been pouring with rain my trench coat has not dried out for a week, but yours truly wears three pairs of socks, and gum-boots, so has managed to survive so far, with nothing worse than stomach-aches from Indian food. It has been a great time and I would not have missed the dances for anything.

To start with last Friday. The chiefs had held a meeting the night before at which some bright individual made the following remark, "Let us not be too depressed at Schooner's death, his son is with us, let him take his father's place." Now the "son" was me, but I happen to be rather popular at the moment so the suggestion was carried unanimously. Now Schooner's job was to say a few words as the people were eating, so various old Indians taught me what to say, though I must admit I am still ignorant of the meaning of the words.[38] Anyway about 7.00 p.m. all the Indians, about 200, gathered in the hall, along with several dogs, and a host of yowling children. I solemnly sat among the seven nobles at the top of the hall, no other white man present. After various delays the choir got to work, singing and beating time with sticks on the floor, and out pranced a lad dressed in an old blanket, and with cedar bark collar: he danced around with jumping steps in time to the music, while the women droned out their song. Then song after song was sung and several lads danced, one after the other as the proper song of each was used, also a few women. It was fairly impressive, and would have been decidedly so in an old house with a central fire but it looked out of place in a white man's type of hall with garish lamps. At last food was passed around, some twenty dish-pans filled with crab-apples mixed with elachen [sic] grease, the oil boiled from fish that have rotted for about two weeks.[39] The smell was almost enough to finish me, however one can only die but once, so I whittled a "spoon" from a piece of wood, sat on the floor and dipped into the common dish with six very dirty old men. I leave the taste of that stuff to your imagination.[40] Then an old boy hauled me off to the enclosure at the back where an old blue blanket decorated with mother-of-pearl buttons was put on me, also several cedar-barked collars, and as the last touch a very disreputable old woman came on the scene with her hands stained with soot and rubbed these over my face till I looked like a nigger. My sponsor stepped out and said that he had picked a successor to Schooner, to whom he was giving the name, xwots kmis,[41] whereupon I strolled forth and bellowed out my few remarks in my best Bella Coola. It was the first that most of those present knew of the affair and I believe I made quite a hit. Returned to the enclosure my sponsor picked up a rag from the floor, wiped the black off his own face with it (more or less) and then did the same for me: yours truly wondering all the time how many germs he was having rubbed off on him. More dancing of the same type, then a meal of tea, brewed in a coal oil-can and drunk by me from a cup supplied by some Indian, and hard tack. Then the usual "potlatch" at which I collected $1.00, and about five pounds of hard tack and soda biscuits. Some of the dancers performed alone, but usually there were three or four assistants who paraded around behind them, dancing at intervals, and yelling.[42] Somebody suggested that I be one of these, so again I donned the blankets, and collar, and stepped forth. I cannot say I performed brilliantly, hopping around in time to beating sticks, and remembering all the time to shake my head and wiggle my fingers is not as easy as it appears, but this being a joyous celebration no one minded, though for the first time in Bella Coola history the long droning cry which the women utter when a person dances, broke down because too many of them were laughing. Apparently I made a wonderful hit, at least I have been told that so long as there are dances in Bella Coola, so long will the night be remembered when xwots kmis danced, the first white man ever to take part in a Bella Coola ceremony.[43]

Next night was rather different. In the first place there was an elaborate attempt made to (theoretically) tie down a lad whose spirit impelled him to go aloft to heaven.[44] In this everyone took part, first circling around the lad and yelling, then it developed into a tug-of-war. I was in the centre of the howling bunch, and succeeded in planting my shod gum-boots very firmly on the [?] of an Indian, which finished his interest in the proceedings for the rest of the evening. That night I ate rice from the common wash-pan, and received apples and hard tack. But the final event almost finished me. It was decided that the best way for me to learn to dance a la Bella Coola would be for me to follow a good dancer. A youth was picked, and I was told to go out and follow whatever he did. I wore the usual blankets, and this time a mass of eagle down was put in my hair so that when I shook my head some of it kept drifting off.[45] Foolishly I failed to take off my gum-boots. At first it was not so bad, though I hardly distinguished myself by keeping time, but later the music got faster and faster till I was hopping like a jumping-jack, and revolving till I was almost dizzy. Then the darned youth sat down on his heels till his posterior almost touched the ground and in this position hopped around the hall. I tried nobly but I am not built that way, and my peace of mind was not improved by an old Indian dashing out and trying forcibly to thrust me down on my haunches. At intervals I was expected to growl and the two other assistants kept blowing (with showers of saliva) in my ears[46] while the ghost whistles were blown by a concealed lad.[47] It seemed to me that this went on for hours, anyway when it was over I was limp as a rag and do not think I have felt so horribly winded since the days of paper-chases at Highfield.[48] I thought I had made rather a fizzle of the affair, as indeed I did, but one can never tell how luck will turn out and next day an old woman said that she noticed my face was strained as I danced (small wonder), did I think that it was possible that the Bella Coola supernatural wanted to enter me? I replied truthfully that I did feel strange, and stopped, whereupon the news has spread through the village that apparently I am popular with the supernatural and I believe it will lead to my giving a dance of my own.

Other nights have been somewhat similar. I have not danced again, insisting that I be given a little coaching first, but I have again spoken, this time assuring the community that crab-apples and olachen grease are fine food and suiting my actions to my words eating a big spoonful of the stuff in full sight of the community, no chance to stuff it into my pocket as I had done on several previous occasions. Last night there were two masked figures, a talkative woman who acts as announcer for all the dancers[49] and the laugher of heaven.[50] Just as the latter appeared the masked announcer asked loudly whether xwots kmis were present, in came the laugher, chuckling and hee-hawing and wearing a mask of a laughing man. He strolled straight up to me, grabbed me by the coat as if to pull me from my seat, all the time laughing in a peculiar high-pitched cackle, then proceeded to pat both my cheeks with his hands. For the life of me I did not know what was the correct thing to do. As a result of these various things I have been given quantities of hard tack, peanuts, apples, and have dipped my spoon into various unpleasant looking (and tasting) messes. It is a great life, but if I do not contract a few diseases I shall be lucky.

Thanks as usual for your
letter, and very much love,
Tom

[H] *Bella Coola, BC*
9/12/23

Dear Mrs. Haddon,

[The letter opens with details of Mrs. McIlwraith's death and thanks for Mrs. Haddon's expression of sympathy.]

The government was decent enough to keep my position open for me so I got back to my dirty friends the Bella Coola Indians in September. Since then I have been so busy that I have hardly had time to think. This was a wonderful spot in summer, but in winter one must admit that it leaves much to be desired. It has now rained steadily for nine days and nights, so that the road over to the Indian village is in places under a foot or more of water, and everywhere covered with several inches of mud. Over and through this I plough every day and work with various Indians in their houses, all of which are hermetically sealed and blazingly hot from a stove, to the accompaniment of screaming babies, dogs

This photograph, apparently taken in March 1924, is hand-labelled "xwot knis (T.F. McIlwraith) in 'Cannibal' costume." The anthropologist is wearing a cedar bark collar from which hangs a number of weasel skins, a standard adornment in the *kusiut* ceremonials. The blanket is adorned with cedar bark hangings. It appears identical to a blanket shown as Plate 9 in Volume II of *The Bella Coola Indians* which has two wooden skulls hanging from the rear. These symbolize the corpses supposedly devoured by the cannibal (*BCI* II, 108). McIlwraith describes his performance of this dance, which involved the symbolic biting of a victim, in his 16 March 1924 letter to A.C. Haddon.

and cats, while the smells of dirt and food are rather appalling. Of course these trifles are mere details which lend background to the work, and I am getting some pretty good material these days, in spite of the fondness of my informants for strong drink. There have been a few Indian dances, pitiful remnants of the once important winter ceremonial, and at these I have been given a fairly important part, replacing an old man who last year adopted me and who has since died. In theory I have the right to kill anyone who makes a mistake in the ritual, but this part of my position I do [sic] think I shall use, and so far have confined myself to making ritual remarks in Bella Coola when the food is being distributed. I sit in state with the musicians at the top of the hall and solemnly take my share of the food from a dish-pan with six elderly Indian men. The favourite dish is fish-oil, boiled from fish which have been allowed to rot for two weeks, mixed with crab-apples, and my fate compels me to stand up, assure the audience that this is fine food and that they should eat a great deal of it, and set an example by wolfing down the mess, which tastes like nothing on earth. The other night I was called on to accompany a dancer, and my friends assured me that it would be easy as I had only to do what he did. Accordingly I donned blue blankets covered with mother-of-pearl buttons, three collars of dyed cedar bark, and had my face blackened with soot, and eagle feathers in my hair. But sad to say I had the misfortune to strike a fast tune, and nearly killed myself in my efforts to move my feet rapidly enough to keep in time with the beating sticks, all the time not forgetting to shake my hands, and my head, move in certain directions, growl at intervals, and allow two assistants to spit in my ears to soothe me after growling; the assumption being that I had collected some of the cannibal spirit of the dancer. I more or less survived until the dancer doubled himself on his haunches and in this position leapt around the hall like a kangaroo. I did my best but my legs were not built for that type of locomotion, and the result was not a success, in spite of one Indian trying to shove me down by brute strength. It is certainly an interesting life. So far there have been four dances, during which I have amassed one name, $1.00 in cash, a dozen apples, five pounds of hard-tack, and two of peanuts – not to mention the various unsavoury food which I have eaten on the spot. In hospitality and kindness the Bella Coolas could teach many white people valuable lessons.

I have written Dr. Haddon several times, so will add nothing further now, except once more to thank you for your letter. I am afraid I am too late to wish you a Merry Christmas, but this letter should reach you early in 1924, a year which will, I hope, bring to you and your family nothing but health, happiness and prosperity.

With very kindest regards
to you all,
Yours sincerely,
"Mac"
(T.F. McIlwraith)

[F] *Bella Coola, BC*
10/12/23

Dear Father,

There seems to be a strange fate around Bella Coola that runs me into the most amazing jobs, but this last week has really taken the cake. The funny part of it is that the two jobs are ones which I might conceivably have struck anywhere, but which practically I cannot imagine myself striking anywhere else. First of all I have accepted the position of best man at a wedding, and secondly I am teaching singing!!! I don't know which is the harder for me to imagine myself in.

To deal first with the wedding, which for two days I thought was going to be a secret affair with me and the clergyman as the only spectators. Andy Christensen, son of the household here, and Dorothy Clayton, daughter of the old Hudson's Bay factor are to be married, with me in support of Andy. The affair has been brewing for years, but when I was here last year the prospects looked very doubtful on the ground of the family's, Dorothy's, disapproval. This year they have come round, until when I arrived all was clear except for Mrs. Clayton giving her consent, without which I think they would have held back. Well a week ago last Sunday Andy plucked up courage to ask her, and she consented: that night Andy told me the news, being in the seventh heaven of delight. However they managed to keep it dark, no easy matter around here, in fact I think I was the only one outside the two families to know, and not all of each even had the information. At that time I had no idea that it was to be a speedy affair. The next event was last Wednesday when Andy came in to see me as I was reading in bed, usually either he drops into my room at night or vice versa, and began to talk about the weather. Finally he said he was going to bed, then, as if by an afterthought, said, "Got anything on next Saturday evening?" "No," says I. "Well, would you mind standing by and helping Dorothy and me get married." Being in bed I could not fall through the floor, but I'll admit it was rather a staggerer, having assumed that it would be an affair of the distant future. Nor was I more soothed by hearing his plan that I dress up as if to go over to play bridge at Robson's, and he to make his usual call at Clayton's, that Dorothy be met on the bridge, whence we adjourn to the missionary's. This plan certainly had its points in that it would avoid undue fuss, and of course I consented. I must admit that I had an uneasy wondering in the back of my mind what would happen when my fate would leave it to me to go ahead and tell the two families, feeling sure that if I was not killed by the one I would be by the other. I tried to put in a few words of fatherly advice about waiting so that at least the two families would be on the scene, but Andy was in no mood for any advice of that kind, nor was Dorothy when I saw her the next day. However on Friday they talked it over and decided to wait for a bit, and let the families know, but they still expect to have it either before or soon after Christmas. And I am still in the role of best man. It may be too late, but would you post out to me my blue suit, which is somewhere in the house, I must at least try to look reasonably respectable. Needless to say this is for father, not Dorothy.

Now for the singing proposition. The Indians are getting up some kind of a Christmas tree entertainment at which their band is to perform as of yore, and at which there will be both whites and Indians present, with the programme likewise supplied by both. Two old Indian men, each the owner of a good voice, judged by native standards, had the brilliant thought that they would learn and sing a Christmas song in English. Would I teach them one? Well, I wish them to think I am reasonably infallible, so I said I would, though I took the precaution of telling them that I did not have a wonderful voice and that if they could find a better instructor I would not feel offended. But they wanted me, so, in a barn in the village, you can hear me any day gently singing, "Good King Wenselaus," [sic] to two old Indians.[51] What the performance will be like is more than I care to think, but I think I am safe in that the chaos, and I anticipate nothing else, will be ascribed to the failure of the Indians to pick up the white man's music, and not to their poor instructor. For two days I was threatened with even worse, in that they wanted me to sing a song in Bella Coola. Again I accepted, though the vision of me standing up in public and singing before an audience including whites, was rather rich, especially as the whole valley knows of my musical voice, as Andy and I regularly rouse the Christensen household by singing a duet in the morning to annoy the community. However I think my two Indians have decided that it would be better for me to make a speech, with which sage counsel I quite agree, still it would have been a rag.

Almost equally surprising is the fact that I have been raked in to help coach the youngsters on the town-site for a programme which they are to give at a Christmas tree entertainment. There are the usual piffling playlets, but I drew the line at equally stupid recitations, conned Dorothy's huge poetry book, with the result that one kid is to say, "He thought he saw a kangaroo, that ground a coffee-mill," and another, "My father calls me William, my mother calls me Will," and two other nonsensical pieces that have nothing to do with Christmas.

There is really nothing else to report this week, except that last night it snowed so that there was six inches on the ground this morning and everything looked fine, then it proceeded to melt to-day, so that when I came back from the village the road was almost beyond even my energy, in fact I fell twice in getting through.

Much love, as always
Tom

[F] *Bella Coola, BC*
19/12/23

Dear Father,

The supply of news this week is very small, though as usual there are a few items of interest. I must admit that I am tremendously interested in the approaching marriage of Andy Christensen and Dorothy Clayton. Things are not going smoothly, and it is a new job for me to have to [do] what little I can to smooth matters out. About a week ago they decided to do the deed on the 22nd, sans trousseau and with a borrowed ring if necessary, with only the two families and me present. But since then Mrs. Clayton has put down her foot on such a speedy affair, and I have been called in to play bridge on various evenings to clear Dorothy's brother out of the way, carry messages back and forth, as well as make futile suggestions as to methods of persuading the old lady. Except for Mrs. Clayton and the two concerned I am the only one with any notion that the affair is to be soon, and I am more than mildly interested, the first time I have been in such a mess. As far as matters now stand I think it is an even break whether the affair comes off on Saturday: they may do it even if Mrs. Clayton remains firm. Anyway Andy pours out his woes to me at night, and I see Dorothy almost every day over at the village and hear her version of the affair, and generally act as messenger and intermediary. I will probably finish up with a broken neck or something.

Last Wednesday I landed myself into another job that I have never met. The doctor here is slowly dying from drink and dope, and everyone, including himself hopes that it will be swiftly. He lives at the hospital with a worthless individual by the name of Scotty. On Tuesday evening Scotty was over at the Indian village hopelessly drunk, and I saw him start back for home. Wednesday night about 11.30 Andy was in talking with me and casually asked where Scotty was staying, that he had not been home all day. I jumped up and told him that he had started for home and was not at the village, so without more ado we both began to put on our boots, a drunk man missing for 24 hours on a road in this country means death in the mud. We collected Mr. Christensen and went up to the hospital. The doctor was lying downstairs with bottles of extract beside him, too far gone to get to bed, the fire out and, having had no food all day. Needless to say he was drunk and helpless. We carried him up to bed, in a room that was filthy and smelt of foul drugs and dirt, a place that almost sickened me; I have never seen such a wreck of what was once a man – Service's line, "The beast I am, and the man I used to be," struck me pretty strongly.[52] Then we looked for tracks, found that the buggy had been back, hence Scotty, and tracks that he had set off on horse-back. That seemed to show that at least he had not died in the mud between village and town-site, so all we could do was feed a colt which otherwise would have starved to death, and come back to the house. Next morning Andy and I went up, built a fire and cooked the doctor breakfast, as well as telephoning in all directions for Scotty and notifying the policeman, who knew all about it but did not seem to think it was up to him to take any steps. Later on in the day Scotty came back, having worked off his blind, and things are going on as before. But what a ruin for a once clever man. I certainly hope he dies soon.

The Indian dances have started again, and last Monday there was quite an affair. Largely through my incessant urging they have decided to keep out all whites except the Claytons and myself, and up till last Monday I had been the only white man present at any one of the shows. Several weeks ago I had arranged with the Indians that whenever there was to be a good show I was to bring Miss Scott, the school-teacher who stays at Christensens, to it. So at 6.30 we set off and ploughed through the mud, which nearly finished her though I am used to it. I think she rather regretted her rashness when we got to the door and it was a case of pushing through a bunch of noisy Indian youths to a seat at the side of the hall, a hall filled with some 300 Indians, not to mention dogs and cats. After the usual delay out came two masked figures, the Laughers, who parade around the hall with fiercely grinning masks and who laugh in a disguised voice in a way which is really almost uncanny. They have the right to go to anyone and make funny remarks, at which the community laughs. The first time I saw it done the figure came to me and with the usual weird laughter grabbed me by the arms and went through the motions of trying to haul me out onto the floor. Well, these two creatures went through their stunts with various people, and then headed for the place where Miss Scott and I were sitting. I thought of course that it was for me, and Miss Scott moved a couple of feet away to give them a clear space. Instead of this the figure started his laughing stunts in her face and grabbed her arm as if trying to pull her out onto the floor. Wild amusement on the part of the audience, combined with considerable annoyance on the part of me. I interfered without much success, and the affair lasted for only about a minute. It was supposed to be a compliment for my guest, regarding her as one of the community, but whatever the motive I could have wished it otherwise. Luckily Miss Scott is one of the best sports I have ever met and thought it was a joke, so no harm was done. There were two dances put on that night, both of them really good, though of course the effect was spoilt by the whiteman's hall. One was the dance of Thunder,[53] a masked figure with hooked nose and scowling features. He wore twigs in his mask on which were eagle feathers, and a long cloak covered with painted boards. Around he danced in wild contortions, in time to the beating of sticks while the women droned. Then he returned with a rattle effect, the thunder, and danced wildly, while in the curtained space at the back people rattled stones in coal-oil cans to imitate the reverberations of thunder. It was really quite good. Afterwards out came Rain,[54] a masked figure carrying a bucket of water, with which he soused as many of the audience who did not get their coats up quickly enough. Then two more masked figures, The Defamer,[55] a supernatural creature who claims to be superior to Thunder and insists that whatever the latter does is wrong, and a supernatural dancer, who acts as if he were going to show the people a wonderful dance, but runs away after a few short beats. All this was repeated twice. Then came a dance which few of the Indians had ever seen, the Fort Rupert cannibal dance,[56] the theory being that a supernatural creature has entered into the performer impelling him to eat human flesh. The dancer performed very well, dancing in time to the beating of sticks and going through the motions of lifting to his mouth corpses and throwing them away with a scowl of disgust after he had bitten them. Then came the supernatural being that was the cause of it all,[57] a masked figure wearing a mask about three feet long, and with cedar bark clothing that covered him entirely. He went round in wonderful style with this, snapping beak and wild contortions. It was really quite impressive.[58] I certainly enjoyed seeing it, so did Miss Scott, I think, though I continue to be thankful that she saw the funny side of being the butt of an Indian ceremony.

Last night they had a long affair, I was in the hall for over five hours and returned very weary. It was chiefly marriages, each of which must be validated by the transmission of money, an endless affair.[59] There were a few dances, in one of which I took part, and did better than before, and a few masked figures. As a result I received a name, giving me that right to bite people,[60] one dollar, and six hard tack. Also a cup of tea. It is quite a life. The most amusing is however yet to come, on the Christmas Tree celebration next Monday night when there is to be a mixed Indian and white audience, and a mixed programme. I am to sing (so-called) in Bella Coola!!! Luckily it is a short affair, six lines only, and I believe the tune does not much matter. I hate to think of the amusement of the white community who have heard my musical voice more than once, especially in the morning when Andy and I sing in unison to wake the household. Then I have to make a speech, which is going to be awkward as I don't mind saying things individually to Indians which it would never do to say with the missionary or Indian Agent present,[61] and how I can continue to say them in their presence is rather a mystery. I must use a certain amount of Bella Coola which no one but the Indians will understand.

[The following appears in handwriting:]

No letter from you this last week, but the Xmas cards, direct from Toronto, did arrive. Of course it is too late now and at first I thought I would send them back, but decided to keep them and use here.

I sent off to A.J. a pair of much busted socks: I wonder if she would mind re-knitting them as the sock situation is getting serious within. I wear three pairs at a time here and they are always wet at night.

Much love to you both.
Tom

[F] *Bella Coola, BC*
24/12/23

Dear Father,

Gosh but there is a rush around this place at Christmas, though precisely what there has been to do is rather a mystery. Anyway I have been up till two or three in the morning for the last ten days, and it is now almost midnight. Sad to say there have been Indian dances every night, which has meant that I have not got back to the town site till one or so and then there come letters to write and odd jobs. The most insane thing

I let myself in for was the filling of stockings for everyone around the house, about a dozen people. We collected junk of all kinds, tried to label them appropriately, tied them up nicely, and they are at present stored under my bed. It was a fool thing to do, especially as it meant that I only got to bed about 4.30 yesterday morning.

Jim Pollard in thunder mask, 3 June 1922. Pollard served as the master of ceremonies for the 1923-4 winter ceremonials. The thunder dance was among the most important *kusiut* ceremonies and remains enormously popular with the Nuxalk to this day.

I have just got back from the entertainment, Christmas tree entertainment, at the Indian village. The programme consisted of the band and me. The thought of singing in public was almost enough, but at the last minute I found that my sponsor had decided it would be a good idea if I danced first, a sort of a circular shuffle that luckily was not hard to do. Anyway the chairman announced that I was to sing, and on I came, wearing a long blanket covered with designs in mother-of-pearl buttons and a head-dress of grizzly bear claws and weasel skins.[62] To say the least of it I felt a fool. Then in cold blood I had to start dancing in more or less time to the hand clapping of two old Indians and at the end sing. I was really half afraid that I would be rattled into forgetting the proper sequence of grunts that comprised the song, but luckily I did not. Then I had to make a speech, using enough Bella Coola to disguise the meaning as far as the whites were concerned. I managed to remember most of the things that I intended to say, and I certainly got a fine round of applause from the Indians. It was decidedly worth it, but I simply did not dare look at the faces of the white people in case I started to laugh. I suppose they thought I was several kinds of an idiot all rolled into one, which was the truth I suppose, but it did not worry me in the slightest.

My other job, that of best man, has not yet come off. It was to have been on the 22nd, and I trotted over to interview the missionary and fix things up, but the day before they decided to wait until the furniture for the house arrived. This should get in on the 26th, in which case the ceremony will be on the 29th. It has been an absolutely new experience for me, this chasing around with conferences and counter-conferences. But for me they would have gone though with the ceremony without telling anyone, and I think they have been eternally glad since that they did not.

This scrawl has been written at intervals, now it is the 26th, and the boat is due any minute. I spent Xmas at the Clayton's, excellent dinner and a tree for the youngsters, followed by six hours of solid bridge. I got back to the town-site at 1.30 where we built a fire and sat talking till 4.30, and as I was up at 8.30 I am feeling a trifle weary to-day.

Must stop now,
with all the love there is,
Tom

[C] *Bella Coola, BC*
26/12/23

Dr. E. Sapir,
Chief, Anthropological Division
Victoria Memorial Museum

Dear Dr. Sapir,

I am enclosing employment forms in duplicate for another Indian, perhaps you would be kind enough to forward them to the proper destination.

I was very glad to get your letter of Nov. 22nd, and also the drawings made by Mr. Prud'homme. The latter appear to be entirely satisfactory. With regard to your letter, though of course I am sorry to hear that there is no possibility of my obtaining a position on the permanent staff, yet I am by no means surprised. It was kind of you to make an effort on my behalf and I certainly appreciate it. Not only does this kind of field work appeal to me, but I feel that it is excellent training, and accordingly I would be glad to do more work of the same type next year. Above everything I hope it will be possible for me to write up my results. Though in actual quantity I shall not obtain as much information this year as I did last summer, yet it will require a good deal of time to combine and put in literary form the two seasons' work. I feel that six months could profitably be spent on this. If, following this, it would be possible for me to go on another field trip next winter I would be very glad to do so. Of course I understand the financial and other difficulties.

Since last writing you I have been having a very successful time. Information has been coming in splendidly – my only trouble being that there are only 24 hours in each day, and a few are needed for sleep. I have gone through in great detail the whole question of chieftainship and marriage, which in Bella Coola are closely connected. Though I have collected much new information it bears out what I found last year, that a man's importance in the community depends more on the number of times which he has given a ɬɪm (potlatch) than on his ancestral name. The holder of even one of the highest names is a person of no consequence unless he has shown himself worthy of it by the distribution of goods. I have found the key to the system of marriage (in the old days) among distant relations, a matter which puzzled me last year. At marriage a certain portion of bride's father's ancestral story (smaiusta) is transmitted to the husband, e.g. the right to carve or paint a raven on a food box. Unless repurchased this remains in the husband's family, but as the smaiusta is transmitted it is always remembered that a part of it is in another family and a son, grandson, or other descendant of the wife's father will seek to regain it by marrying a woman of the other family. As the Bella Coolas express it a man always "hunts" when marrying to get back pieces of his smaiustas.[63]

For the last six weeks there have been dances every night. I thought I was busy last year, but it was nothing compared with the present. I am in the Indian hall from six at night to midnight, 1.00, 2.00, or 3.00 a.m., and it interferes very seriously with my work. Of course I get some information every night, but not enough to compensate for the time spent. Strangely enough the dances are being performed in better style than they have been for several years, through my assistance. Each dancer has his own song, usually made by the choir for the occasion. In the old days there were a number of men who did little but remember the words of these songs, and whisper them to the announcer who called out the words line by line. But now there is only one old man who tries to combine the duties of "rememberer," and announcer.[64] Things went badly until he asked me to join the choir, and I am now given the words of each song and whisper them to the announcer at the right moment. This has given me a wonderful insight into the manner of making the songs, and also the way they are sung, but it is rather annoying when I want to watch a dancer to have the announcer's elbow jammed into my ribs with an urgent call for the next few words. Speeches have been made thanking me for my help, and I have certainly become popular. I have danced myself four or five times, and have stepped into the shoes of an old man who last year adopted me and has since died. As a result I have made ritual speeches in Bella Coola and have the (theoretical) right to kill anyone who errs in the ritual. All this is satisfactory, but it takes valuable time, not to mention energy. As all the Indians are at the dances, however, I could do no work elsewhere even if I so desired.

May I extend the usual compliments of the season.

Yours very sincerely,
T.F. McIlwraith

[F] *Bella Coola, BC*
1/1/24

Dear Father,

Happy New Year, etc. When I think of the changes that 1923 brought I cannot help wondering what will follow this year, but whatever may come it can be nothing as terrible as the last year. But there is nothing to be said about that.

This has been a dull week here, most of the whites spending their time running around in a semi-drunk condition: apparently Christmas keeps up for weeks here. The biggest change is that it has turned cold – really cold. Up to Christmas it had never been really cold, in fact it was so mild that walking was quite comfortable. But on the 27th it turned icy, with a sweeping gale from the east. The thermometer has been hovering between zero and a few below, but with the wind it has seemed far worse. I parade around with three sweaters, an undercoat, two overcoats, and a fur cap, so I have not felt the cold, while by keeping my oil stove constantly on the go I manage to keep my room fairly comfortable. This house is not built for a cold snap, so they have to keep the water running all the time to avoid freezing the pipes, and someone has to stay up all night to keep a fire in the kitchen. It is far from pleasant and I hope the cold snap does not run its usual three weeks.

The worst is at night of course and the Indians dances still continue. I have been given rather a funny job. Each dancer has his song which is made by the choir only a few hours before his dance, and which is bellowed forth line by line while the people sing. These songs are repeated night after night and it is a brute for the man whose duty it is to remember these to do so, often thirty or forty songs. In the old days there would have been three or four of these men sitting by the announcer to whisper to him what he should call forth: now there is only one man who combines in himself the duties of announcer and remembrancer. This individual got the happy inspiration of having me write down the words and be ready to whisper them to him whenever he poked me in the ribs. So I am an established member of the choir, and when I walk in the evening go straight up to the head of the hall and greet the choir with, "Hello, fellow-singers." Some of the Indians of course do not like it a bit, but the combined announcer-remembrancer made a speech to them saying how much I was helping him, and they could do nothing. There is really no doubt but that the dances are going off in better shape through my help, but it makes me chuckle inwardly when I find myself bellowing out, "No, watch your step, there are six lines to the assikotl,"[65] or whatever the particular thing may be. I have even been known to step into the breach and act as leader of the choir myself. I come away every night with my just share of whatever is being distributed, usually hard tack, though last night it was two bottles of pop and a tin of pineapple, as well as bread and biscuits. The most useful thing was the headdress in which I danced on Christmas, a thing I was really glad to get. Luckily recently the supply of olachen grease has run low, and the chief thing I have been eating is stew, not too bad either, but oh the germs. However I still continue to thrive.

I have not yet had to act as best man, but the date is definitely fixed now for the 3rd. The two families are to be there and everything in due and proper order with supper, wedding cake and the rest. I have found myself rather amused when trying to look surprised at hearing that the marriage was to take place so soon, and to look surprised and pleased at being asked to be best man. Considering the wheels within wheels I maintain it is funny.

Andy is going to live in a small house over near the Claytons': His leaving will make it unpleasantly lonely here. Of course one has no right to expect to meet decent people in a frontier settlement of this kind, but Andy certainly is decent and we have been pretty good friends. The only other person on the town-site whom I have enjoyed knocking around with was a Miss Scott, the school teacher who was staying here. We used to horrify the community by playing crib till all hours of the night and then foraging for food in the kitchen till all hours of the morning. Bananas and cream consumed at 2.00 a.m. are not so bad. But Miss Scott left for good last boat, and with Andy moving away in a couple of days I shall sink back to a hermit's life, and probably get more work done than when there was something else to do.

[The following appears in handwriting:]

There was no letter from you last week, but another very pleasant Christmas parcel, that with the bed-room slippers and the hard candies. For both of them, many thanks. They could not have come at a more welcome time with this brute of a cold snap.

Much love to Aunt Jean
and yourself,
Tom

[F] *Bella Coola, BC*
6/1/24

Dear Father,

First of all I will explain why I got no letter off last week. In part it was my own fault in that I was so busy I left it till the last minute, and only sat down to write my weekly batch of letters on the Wednesday morning. Then the wretched boat came in very early, leaving me with a couple to polish off, so I asked Mr. Christensen to let me know the last thing before he left for the boat. This he promised to do and I went up to my room. After a while I became suspicious and went down to find that he had left for the boat long ago, so I had to tear down to the wharf where I arrived in time to see the boat leaving. I cursed the worthy Mr. C. in several languages, but that did not seem to help matters. The really annoying part of it was that I had a number of letters finished, including the one to you, but was waiting to put in all at the same time. I certainly was peeved, but there was nothing to do.

I have spent a good deal of energy this last week in getting Andy and Dorothy married, which took place last Thursday. Everything all OK. I had the haziest notions of what constituted the duties of a best man, but have a feeling that I did several which are not customary. The time was 6.00 p.m. and I decided that I must take the day off, and in the morning went over to the village to interview the missionary. He reported that all was clear and that he would be ready, and all I did there was rustle up an Indian to cut wood for the church, as the wedding was to be in the Indian church. Then I went over to the Claytons' where everybody was in a state of chaos, and the bride was somewhat perturbed because her dress had not come, a hat but no dress. Considering that the first plan had been to have the wedding without any trimmings of any kind, or guests, this really was no serious matter. I collected a meal there and then announced that I was going back to scrub Andy, whereupon Dorothy asked me to see that he cleaned his fingernails, and I borrowed a nail brush from her for this purpose. Needless to say I was chuckling violently. Arrived here at 2.00 and collected Andy who was pretending to be cool and collected, without much success. I was rather doubtful as to what I was to do with him for the next three hours, and decided the best thing was to manicure his finger nails. So we took possession of the bath-room for an hour and three quarters while I literally scrubbed his hands and then doctored up his finger nails to the best of my ability. Gosh it was funny. At intervals various members of the family wanted to get in to wash and I proceeded to tell them what was happening. Andy spent most of the time cursing a blue steak at me, and at intervals assuring me that though he might curse he really appreciated all I was doing for him, I think he did too. The manicuring finished I trotted him into my room where we got dressed, and I have never seen my room in such a mess as when we finished, not only discarded clothes, but cigarette stubs and wrapping paper scattered everywhere. I hate to say how many times Andy asked me whether I had the ring all right. Also he kept asking me other questions about what he was to do and so forth, all of which I answered without hesitation, which called forth from Andy, "I don't believe you know a damn thing more about this job than I do, but it is hellish comforting to have you confident." The lack of affection around this household had always struck me, but never so noticeably as last Thursday; Andy's father came in once to see how we were getting along, but his mother seemed to regard the whole affair as rather a bore, while all through Andy talked to no one but me. We got through all right and at 5.00 went downstairs to be gazed upon by the community.

The scheme was that the party from here drive over, drop Andy and me at the Indian village, and then go on over to Clayton's to collect the people from there. From here there were just Mr. and Mrs. Christensen, Andy's sister Dora who was to be bridesmaid, and an objectionable youth named Jorgen who drove the team. From Clayton's there were to come the bride, her mother, a married brother and his wife, a ditto sister and her husband, and another brother. Well, when Andy and I arrived at the church, which Mr. Peat had sworn would be all ready, we found there was fire, but no lights. We went to the house where Mrs. Peat was full of apologies, that Mr. Peat had been delayed and was just dressing would be along in a minute. We waited 12 minutes for the wretched man, during which time what curses Andy did not hurl at the heads of all missionaries and Mr. Peat in particular, I did. It was really damnable, at last he appeared in a semi-dressed condition and gave us the keys to the church. We were still struggling with the lights when up drove the sleigh from the Claytons', whereupon both Andy and I swore heartily. I dashed out and sent them off for a walk – in the bitterly cold wind, and when they came back five minutes later all was ready, including a (rightly) very apologetic Mr. Peat. In this stage of the game I was accused of looking much more worried than Andy. There were only two disasters in the ceremony itself, Mr. Peat getting twisted in both the names of Andy and Dorothy and I had to correct him. But neither Andy nor I dropped the ring, nor did anyone faint, though Dorothy looked decidedly worried. Then we all drove back to the Claytons' where it seemed as if it took hours to fill up the register,[66] all the while Andy and Dorothy looking more than happy, and yours truly trying to help matters along by chasing the rest of the community into the dining-room. Then we had supper, quite a nice cold supper, and I proposed the health of the bride and groom in coffee as Mr. and Mrs. Peat were present.

So far all had gone off OK, but now there was an inevitable period of wondering what to do next. They put on the gramophone and we danced a bit, and at last Mr. and Mrs. Peat beat it. Then I proposed the health of the bride and groom in port. Meanwhile the first disaster had occurred, in that the worthy Jorgen had broken into Andy's suitcase and pinched a bottle of whisky and one of rum, on which he had got decidedly drunk. One of the bride's brothers and her brother-in-law had done the same, and I began to look worried. I have a strong suspicion that I was very officious, and before the evening was over I hauled out the three of them, which perhaps hardly comes into the role of best man. I packed off Jorgen with Mr. and Mrs. Christensen to the town-site, but later came a telephone that he was bringing back a bunch to congratulate the bride and groom. I knew what that would mean so I arranged to get Andy and his wife out the back door and up to their house, a nice little house about 100 yards from Mrs. Clayton's. It was nearly 11.00 before they arrived, whereupon Dorothy and Andy disappeared, leaving me to act as host, dish out cigars and chocolates, and see that no one became too drunk. It was a merry mess all right: about six of the girls had come from the town-site and wanted to dance, most of the men were too far gone to be able to do so, so unfortunate me had to dance every time as well as supervise matters. I was rather thankful when I get the bunch back to the town-site at 2.00 a.m. Best man in Bella Coola is no easy job, I suppose I should have been diplomatic, but I was peeved. I had supper with Andy and Dorothy last night, their first guest and their first meal other than in the kitchen, both obviously self-conscious, but rather a pleasant meal. I think they are both glad that they waited as long as they did.

Otherwise little to report this week. The cold snap has broken and given place to heavy rain; hardly an improvement. The dances are still on, and I am over every night. A few nights ago I danced again, and was told that I did it very well, had quite got the hang of it, but no one realized that night I did not have a stomach ache from eating rotten fish-oil. Last night I disgraced myself by refusing the food, putrid salmon eggs, the smell of which nearly made me sick, and I am not over-fastidious. I will be thankful when the dances are over. One of the most interesting was a dramatic representation of a man whose supernatural spirit caused him to bite himself.[67] He did it fairly well, sinking his teeth into a sack of paint hidden in a mass of cedar bark on his arm, so that the "blood" squirted over the floor. The only unnatural touch was the lad's grandmother going around afterwards on hands and knees with a gunny-sack and scrubbing up the blood. I continue to sit in state among the choir men, and consider that I am well enough established that I can be rude to Indians whom I do not like, a thing which I have long wanted to do but have not dared.

I am still eating Christmas candy and food, and cleaning up debris from my room, having literally had no time to do so for weeks. I received from the household here the usual variety of gifts which we were exchanging right and left, other people's old shaving kits, boot brushes, etc., gentle insinuations about my personal appearance in this [?]. Two were, I maintain, funny: a broken mirror with the label, "Oh, man, thou art vanity fair," and my ancient and honourable bedroom slippers which I had been wearing around with a yawning cavern in each toe returned to me neatly repaired with a patch of bright red cloth over each toe and "Merry Xmas" inked on. I am glad that I am busy as with Andy's departure there is no one left to talk to here; both of the other Christensen boys being away from home and I disliking the two youths who do odd chores around here.

[The letter ends with handwritten paragraphs mostly dealing with family issues but also with the following news about Bella Coola:]

If you like you can give Ben Simpson the latest news of Dr. Carruthers. He grew steadily worse here until on the 26th they sent him down to Vancouver. He had to be carried on the boat and it was doubtful whether he would stand the journey; only his favourite dope, vanilla extract, saved him on the trip. But we had a telegram telling of his death in a Vancouver hospital last Friday, a brilliant man killed through drink and not leaving a single friend in Bella Coola. His children had been sent down before and went, I believe, to a grandmother in Halifax.

I forgot whether I ever told you that I used the Xmas cards, one with each present which I gave to the Indians. It was an awful waste, but probably pleased them, so all was to the good.

Much love to Aunt Jean
and yourself.
Tom

[C] *Bella Coola, BC*
7/1/24

Dear Smith,

I have delayed answering your letters of Nov. 8 and 27 expecting to have Harry Schooner back every day. But the wretched man stayed at the Falls until just before Xmas with the result I have only now been able to fix up the receipt. I enclose it, and trust it is satisfactory. I have left the date blank thinking that probably you would prefer to fill in a time suitable to yourself. I am sorry that I kept you waiting so long but it was unavoidable.

I wish I could give you a picture of life in Bella Coola in winter, but you know the place and how the life is made up of a number of small incidents, each in itself of no interest but all combined give life here its charms. First I will give you the news of the whites, as being easier to recount.

Andy and Dorothy were married on the 3rd. A very quiet wedding in the Indian church with only the two families and one or two friends present, 14 in all including the bride and groom and Peat. I was best man and had a hectic time running things. They are living in the little house that was Charlie Lord's and appear to be deliriously happy. I had supper with them on Saturday, their first guest, and was much amused at their self-consciousness. I am sure they will be very happy, and I know I hope so, as they are both damn decent.

The other news of the whites is that the doctor is dead and Tanton[68] in the insane asylum at Westminster. Dr. Carruthers has been going from bad to worse all the time, constant use of dope and vanilla extract has been his downfall, until he was unfit to look after himself and was chased from the hospital for fear that he would set fire to the place. On the 26th of December he was sent below, had to be carried onto the boat, but though he stood the journey a telegram soon after said that he had died in Vancouver. As for Tanton: he went below at the time the doctor did, went straight to Victoria where he created a disturbance in the parliament buildings, I suppose recounting the murders in Bella Coola, anyway he was shipped straight to Westminster. Had this been done months ago it would have saved a lot of trouble.

Now for the Indians. My chief trouble is that too many people want to talk to me, combined with the heat and the stink of the houses. Working in winter has its drawbacks from the point of view of comfort. But the greatest time-killer has been the dances, which have taken place nightly for the last six weeks. Luckily (or unluckily) I have an official place in the choir: the words of the songs are given to me when composed, then when they are to be sung I am established by Jim Pollard and whisper them to him to call out when necessary. It is damnably hard work, sitting in poor light and glueing my eyes to my book to follow where they are as the songs vary a bit from my written text, and if I let my mind wander for a moment I am sure to get an elbow in my ribs and a frantic call for the words. The dances are really going off better than they would were I not present and several speeches of gratitude have been made to me, while I take my just share of whatever is being distributed. Of course I glean some information in this way but the dances have so altered from the old style that I do not get enough to compensate me for sitting from 6.00 to midnight or later every night. But there is no help for it; I have an official name and position in the community, and it would be disastrous should I stay away. When the food comes round I sit with the other sing-men and dip my spoon into the common dish-pan on the floor and try to look as if I were enjoying Olachen grease and crab-apples, soapollalie,[69] or whatever the dish may be. I hate to think of the germs but I am not dead yet. One night I made a "speech," about a dozen words, in Bella Coola telling the people how much I like olachen grease, and to back up my remarks stood up and swallowed several spoonsful [sic] of the vile mess in the centre of the hall. I hate to say how close I was to being sick afterwards. Then I have danced four or five times, the first occasion I made a damn fool of myself, you have no idea how hard it is to keep time to the beating of the sticks, especially when one has a stomach ache from olachen grease, but a few nights ago I did the alxotła[70] (hamatsa) in what was said to be fairly good style. Thanks to these performances I feel that I am fairly well established with the community, so much so that I have had the pleasure of bawling out several Indians whom I dislike, a thing which last year I never dared to do. Needless to say with six hours a night in the hall I have not had time to sleep, let alone eat.

At the moment I am working with Jim Pollard and Joshua – can you appreciate what this means? I have been surprised to find how good the latter has been when I could handle him direct without an interpreter, but he needs a lot of taffying. Thank goodness I have been able to choke him off his biblical allusions, though he told me that my remarks about the bible were, "like a butcher knife in his heart." Never mind, I sent him back to the dances in which he was taking a fairly prominent part until he got sore at one of the Kings and departed. Jim is pretty good as long as I can keep him in a good temper by telling him how wonderful he is, and at the same time let him know that I can get along without him.

Quite the funniest affair was on Christmas Eve when there was a Xmas tree in the hall, presided over by Peat, the band played and there was a mixed audience, all the Indians, and many of the whites. Yours truly the under-signed, melodious voice and all, sang a song in Bella Coola. Only four of the Indians and one of the whites knew what was to happen, and there was a gasp when Peat announced that I was to sing and I came prancing in attired in an old blanket and a headdress of grizzly bear claws and weasel skins. Thus attired I first danced while Jim Pollard and Reuben Schooner beat time for me, then I hopped forward, said a few words in Bella Coola about the song which I was to sing, fixed my eyes firmly on the roof to keep from laughing and sang to the best (or the worst) of my ability. I have been known to recite at concerts and so forth on a good many occasions but I never got such applause in my life as I did then. As an encore I made a speech, telling them how glad I was to have received a name, to have joined the choir etc., and how sorry I was to learn of Schooner's and Willie Mack's death, finishing up by giving valuable advice about preserving their ancestral duties. Needless to say I put in enough Bella Coola that the whites could not understand what I was talking about. Then I subsided to my seat feeling that I had done a good night's work. Needless to say the whites thought I was a damn fool, but they do anyway, especially as I have quarreled with almost all the community, but as long as the Indians were pleased I did not care, and they were pleased.

Glad to hear from your letter that the prospects of the park are good. In spite of the fact that for the last two months it has rained hard every day except for one week when it was bitterly cold, I do not envy you in Ottawa. I am soaked through most of the time but in spite of it keep well and flourishing.

Kindest regards to your family and any other of my friends there, not forgetting Rhoades.

Yours very sincerely,
T.F. McIlwraith
wina[71]
Xwot̓sɛkmis

[This is followed by two lines in Nuxalk. Unfortunately, the handwriting is too faint to make out the words.]

[F] *Bella Coola, BC*
13/1/24

Dear Father,

At length and finally the Indian dances are over, at least I hope they are, and I am getting far enough back to normal to be writing a letter on Sunday. I have taken this as an absolutely lazy day, woke up at 8.30 and lay in bed reading until 11.00. I could have wished some food, but one cannot have everything in this world, so I breakfasted on my private supply of apples. I must admit that my first meal this morning was at 2.15, in the kitchen. I introduced Mah-Jong to the Robsons last week, and they at once became mad on it, with the result that I am in constant demand. Last night we played from 7.00 to 1.30, at the end of which I was over 6000 down. I must admit that I prefer bridge, but I have a feeling that henceforth my chances of getting any here are almost nil. Of course I like Mah-Jong too, but bridge is the game of games to me. The rest of to-day I have spent in manoeuvering a hot bath and reading, which is just about all there is to do here, though I am thankful to have time to keep my notes in more or less shape. With neither Miss Scott nor any of the Christensen boys here this place, the household, has ceased to be anything except dull.

In the old days each Indian dance went on for four successive nights, on the last of which there were masked figures representing the supernatural beings with whom the person for whom the performance was being given was connected. This year there have been only one or two nights on which masks have been used with the intention of having a large final night when all the masks would be used together, an innovation. This came off last Tuesday and was not bad. At the top of the Indian hall there is a platform which can be shut off by two sheet-like curtains decorated with paintings. To this enclosure went various old Indians carrying bundles, and of course I was there too. Inside everyone was opening his bundle and hauling out masks, blankets, collars and other ceremonial objects, and then requesting his neighbours not to step on them. There was not enough room for all who wanted to get in – let alone their belongings – and there was no one with authority to direct anyone else. Never in my life have I seen such a confusion, and everyone excited, never believe anyone who says an Indian is not capable of excitement. Several were half tipsy, which added to the chaos, while one woman was hopelessly drunk, was lying down on the only bench and wailing, while her husband tried to keep people from sitting on her. Add to this that there was not enough lighting, not enough pins to hold the blankets in place, no unanimity of opinion as to which event should come off first, and each man trying to bag a good dancer to use his mask, and trying to teach said dancer how to perform in it – it was an inferno. Through it all they showed no sign of anger, I was the only one to get somewhat peeved when half a dozen Indians asked me to do different things at the same time, and forgot to explain how they wanted them done. It was the first time since I have hit Bella Coola that I have met what got very near to rudeness, through people being too busy and too excited to attend to me. The sanest of the performances were the two clowns who hung onto their paraphernalia like grim death and went out at intervals to keep the people amused. The worst complexity was a dance representing the supernatural maker of pounded cedar bark, who needed a masked choir.[72] To get these six people, all of whom had other jobs as well, rounded up and ready at the same time was a work of art. Then the curtain had to be raised to display a wooden salmon[73] which was supposed to raise its fins, unluckily at the last moment it was discovered that the fins would not work, frenzied appeal to the best carpenter who righted matters, and someone began to haul the curtain – I point out, yelling at the top of my voice to make myself heard in the din, that the drunken woman will have to be moved or the audience will see her, we do so, again the curtain prepares to rise, only to discover that one of the women who was to sing in the chorus describing what it is all about and who should have been displayed hovering over the salmon had in reality rushed away to see after her grandson who had a fight with another lad. Then there was chaos over a cradle like mask over which a woman was to sing a lullaby, she being the representation of the supernatural being who gives birth to all the animals. I finally found a quiet corner on top of some sacks filled with heaven knows what, a seat which I shared with one Steamboat Annie, a woman of about fifty whom I know to have led a somewhat hectic life but who is more or less of a friend of mine. Annie was rather drunk and insisted on telling me about everything in whispers (not that anyone could hear what anyone else was saying in the din), and to make sure that only I heard what she was saying she used to wrap both her arms around my neck and stick her mouth actually into my ear. Gosh it was funny. Everyone had told me that I must wear a mask, but it was Annie who wrapped a blanket around me, and thrust a far from beautiful wooden mask over my head. There were eye-holes, but they seemed to be somewhere near my ears, anyway it was only when I turned my head on one side and squinted that I could see anything, but as I was only to parade around the hall and had a guide (to protect the audience from supernatural me), this was no matter. I was a supernatural mosquito![74] and as such had to keep up a constant buzz and carry a small stick which at intervals I was expected to thrust in my mouth and rush at one of the audience and stick in the stick – as the jabber of a mosquito. This seemed simple except that I could not find the mouth of the mask, however I hummed nobly, and jabbed at four or five people. One of them was a girl of about 12 (I could not see enough to tell whom I was going to strike) and nearly chuckled outright when I saw an absolute look of terror on her face as I rushed at her; this job of mine certainly is a queer one. Thunder with his attendant rain and the other supernaturals called to his performance, was there, and also the Fort Rupert cannibal dancer's masked spirit, the two dances which I had seen several weeks earlier. In a way the most spectacular was that of the Hao-haos,[75] four huge bird like creatures which I have assured the inquisitive Joshua are known to the white men, as pterodactyls. They performed rather well, in fact the whole show was really worth seeing. When I wanted to watch anything I used to slip around the end of the curtain and hide behind a stove, from where I had a wonderful view, albeit a dirty one. When the whites had left (all had been invited) we, the Indians who had been taking part, sat on the stage and ate peanuts, and discoursed volubly about the affair. It was a night to be remembered.

The next night they went to quite another kind of affair. Some Fort Rupert Indians had been staying here for a week and the Bella Coolas wanted to display to them our skill, and accordingly ran a band concert. It was decreed that it should be a farewell "good time," so in addition to the band various Indians sang or told stories. I did both, gave them an old Bella Coola story in Chinook and capped it by "singing" (their word not mine) the accompanying song, four lines long. Later on they bagged for me a headdress with 19 weasel skins, a rattle, a blanket, and an apron covered with puffin beaks which rattled when I moved, and thus attired I danced till I was pink in the face and then sang another song. As a last touch I gave them the Tiger football yell[76] at the top of my voice, and made a sensation by being able to make more noise than their official announcer. Whenever I find myself doing fool things of this kind I cannot help wondering whether I am still quite sane, but the madness of it appeals to me, and it certainly helps my popularity with Indians. They are to give a concert next Saturday night, for whites and Indians, and the band leader asked me to sing a song in English. I managed to persuade him that I would prefer to sing in Bella Coola, and if encored to recite in English. They called on me for a speech in English on Xmas Eve, and as the simplest way of dodging I recited. I was caught unprepared that time and on the spur of the moment attempted "The Highwayman,"[77] and had a terrible time trying to make myself heard above the crying of babies. Next time we choose something shorter.

No letter from you last week, but the photographs turned up O.K. Cunningham[78] certainly made a fine job of them. Thanks very much for having him do the job. I suppose we can claim the negatives – if so I wish you would get them – they will be useful if I ever want other copies or to have lantern slides made. Much love to Aunt Jean and yourself.

Tom

[C] *Bella Coola, BC*
15/1/24

Dr. E. Sapir,
Chief, Anthropological Division
Victoria Memorial museum,
Ottawa,

Dear Dr. Sapir,

I received your letter of Dec. 31 by the last boat. Thank you for letting me know in such good time what the prospects for next year are. Your letter really answered all the points which I mentioned in a letter which I wrote you about Jan. 2nd. I have never been optimistic about the possibility of obtaining a permanent post on the museum staff, for the present at any rate, but I had hoped that it might be possible for me to undertake another field trip next winter, however I see that there is no chance of that. There is one point in your letter which I feel sure must be a mistake – "That during the fiscal year 1923-1924 you devote four months on the preparation of the Bella Coola report for publication and that we remunerate you at the rate of $140.00 per month." Is the fiscal year beginning April 1924 not meant? Assuming this to be the case, I presume I could start work on April 1st. I shall do my utmost to complete my report within four months, but I am honestly doubtful

Willie Mack's sons playing with a mask collected by Harlan Smith, now in the Canadian Museum of Civilization, 18 August 1923.

whether this will be possible. As soon as I hear from you that it will be satisfactory if I work at my manuscript through April, May, June, and July I shall start looking for a job next winter. I have enjoyed very much working on the museum staff, and I feel sure that the field experience which I have obtained will be most useful to me.

Information is coming in a most satisfactory manner at present, my chief trouble being to keep track of last year's manuscript so that there will be as few loose ends as possible. During the dances I found it utterly impossible to do so, with the result that I must admit I am at the present rather confused as to how much I have yet to clear up. Then there are always new things cropping up, especially the supernatural creatures which give a man his kusiut dance. Almost every informant regards his own as one of the most important, and there must be fifty or more of the creatures, each giving a different dance. I am deliberately putting off the collection of phonograph records until near the end of my stay and concentrating my efforts on getting an account as clear as possible of everything else. I hope this will meet with your approval. One reason that I am doing so is that most of my people are very proud of their ability to sing, so that if I once started I know I would have endless trouble getting them to do anything else. Naturally no report can ever be complete, but when I finish here at the end of February I think I will be able to turn in a manuscript that will be worth publishing. This year I have found far less difficulty in recording sounds than I did last year. There are some glides which worry me a good deal, and I am suspicious that I must be missing some glottal stops: I have plenty of glottalized consonants, but I cannot find a great many stops, while in the songs they seem to be almost entirely absent.

Many thanks for your three reprints which reached me by the last boat. "The Social Organization of the West Coast Tribes"[79] appeals to me particularly, though I must admit that I have not yet found time to read it.

With regard to the meeting of the British Association in Toronto.[80] I knew of it of course, and had hoped to be present. If I am to work at the manuscript until the end of July I am sure this will be possible. I should like to read a paper on "Aspects of the Potlatch among the Bella Coola," dealing with the various types, the feeling with regard to repayment of debts, its significance in the lives of the people and so forth, rather than giving a description of the actual ceremonies. Does this seem satisfactory? I hope such a paper will have a better fate than one which I read at the Edinburgh meeting in 1921, a paper which called down on my head the wrath of Sir William Ridgeway.[81]

Would you be good enough to send me a book of receipt forms, G.S. 81.

May I extend the usual compliments of the season.

Yours very sincerely,
T.F. McIlwraith

[M] *Bella Coola, BC*
16/1/24

Dear Mr. Clarke,

I have delayed answering your letter of Nov. 11th in the hope of hearing from Dr. Sapir that I might be allowed to collect officially for you. But he has not mentioned the subject to me, from which I suppose he replied direct to you that such would be against all the laws of the land.[82] I am sorry, but I know you will understand my position. As a matter of fact I have been able to obtain very few specimens, partly, it is true, through my unwillingness to take away many of the few which remain; practically no new ceremonial objects are being made, and any losses curtail the already too much curtailed sacred life to that extent. If anything can be done quietly and unofficially you may be sure I shall do it.

Glad to hear that you have been making satisfactory progress with the museum. You must have been almost in despair at times with fine specimens but no labels. Even in the short time I was working there on African specimens I found enough of such difficulties to last for years. I keep hoping that some day I shall be back in Cambridge, if only for a visit, and I know that I will be entirely lost in the museum.

I have been having a fairly satisfactory season here, somewhat hampered (and certainly made unpleasant) by abominable weather, and still more by my best informants insisting on getting drunk at the wrong time. The ceremonial dances lasted for six weeks this winter, only concluded last week, and I had a fine opportunity to get an insight into them, in their present degraded condition, through acting as prompter to the choir. The texts of the songs were given to me, and I used to sit with my note-book waiting for a jab in the ribs and a frantic appeal from the choir leader for the next line of the song that was being sung. This kept me from 6.00 p.m. until midnight nightly for six weeks, fiendishly trying work, but interesting, and what information I did obtain in this way was certainly correct. Through this, I was able to dance five or six times, and was entrusted with the task of wearing one of the masks, I was a supernatural mosquito! Although everything has so broken down here the older men remember a great deal of what was done twenty years ago: they're willing to talk and I only wish I could work even longer hours than I have been doing.

[A final paragraph deals with notes and books left in storage at the museum.]

Hope all will continue to go well in the museum this year.

Yours very sincerely,
T.F. McIlwraith

[F] *Bella Coola, BC*
22/1/24

Dear Father,

Another week has rushed away with nothing much to report. I have been learning a few odd details of things that I did not understand in the dances. One of these concerned me; the night of the concert affair before the Fort Rupert Indians parted I was run in to dance and sing a song – as I know I reported. At the time I noticed that when I had finished three old women got up and paraded across to the guests and there deposited various articles of clothing, but it was not until a few days ago that I got the point. In all dances here presents must be given to the spectators to validate what is being done, to the Bella Coola mind it would be unthinkable to give a dance without paying the audience for attending, and henceforth they are witnesses both of the dance having been done and of any names etc. that may have been transmitted. Well I thought of course that as this was almost like a white man's affair, with the band, that I was out of all such matters, but apparently I had sung what had been a cradle song of one of the women, so she thought it must be validated, accordingly the old dame announced that she had adopted me for my song, and stripped off her hat, a sweater coat and her dress to pay the guests for listening to me.[83] Personally I am quite prepared to admit that anyone who listens to me trying to sing should be paid for so doing, but why an elderly lady should have to cough up seems a trifle obscure.

There was another rather funny meal that I found myself landed for near the end of things, the stuff called soapollallie, which was the dope that nearly finished Mrs. Hills last year. The consignment for the choir, including me, arrived in a tin pail with a grubby urchin aged about ten to stir it. The theory being that unless constantly stirred it would lose its stiffness, accordingly said urchin kept stirring with his whole arm and fist in the mess. Round and round went his arm, and when he with-drew it to give us a chance to get in our spatulae there was always a lot sticking to it which he used to lick off and then plunge the fist once more in the pail.[84] It's all in the game, but oh you germs!

Saturday night they gave a band concert. Now even the Indians realise that nothing but band gets monotonous, really it is enough to deafen a person for a week, and they wanted to get a few whites to help out with something. They got one lady to bang the piano, but the only other volunteer was myself. They had tried to teach me a fairly long Bella Coola song (it was a love song of all things) but luckily I failed to get near enough the tune to satisfy even their easily satisfied natures, so at the last moment I was taught another, almost tuneless and shorter. The missionary was chairman and when he announced that the next item was a song from Mr. McIlwraith I heard rather a gasp from the whites, however up I wandered and bellowed forth, albeit decidedly shaky as to the words, while the tune was somewhere in the next block at least. I was also supposed to recite, and the wretched missionary kept hauling me back, and of all the infernal jobs trying to recite above the din of howling babies is a brute. Of course all this adds tremendously to my popularity among the Indians, which is what I want, and I am to be taken up the valley to a concert which they are giving next week as well as to Ocean Falls the following Saturday. I hit one stroke of luck last Saturday, they raffled a gramophone for the benefit of the band, and I won the affair. It does not look to be worth anything but should at least be the equivalent of the fifty cents I paid for it. There are said to be four records with it but as yet I have not seen them, nor have I been able to get the machine over to the town-site.

I have a feeling that another gramophone at the house here would be rather a mixed blessing. They have one tin can affair here but the greatest noise making affair is myself. Started as a means of getting Andy out of bed in the morning, and ever since then I have made a point of singing loudly on all occasions. The last week one Charlie Wood has been here: he is a boy I knew last year and who was here for a week or so when I first blew in this time. We are really quite good pals and he has a voice about the equal of my own with the result that the two of us have been raising the very deuce all around here for the last six days. He goes up to the interior in a few days and there will then be peace for a week or so. They had a dance here the end of last week; not only did I attend it but I had a good time, and it ended with Charlie and me running things and generally raising cain. As several times mentioned before, strange things happen in Bella Coola, but nowhere else could I imagine myself keeping things going at a dance.

Otherwise, nothing to report. The weather has been fairly mild with the roads sloppy for the last two days. Charlie and I have been over playing bridge several nights, and on one I never imagined that there could be such moonlight, it was literally as light as day at 1.00 a.m. Things are going pretty well as far as information is concerned, but at times I get worried when I think of what I have yet to cover before the end of February, however we will do what we can.

[The following handwritten note appears at the end of the letter:]

Many thanks for the gold, I hope to be able to use it, and if so will be awfully glad to get it. I sent Dorothy one bracelet, but there has been no time as yet for a report. They are hard to get but are things which I think are well worth chasing.

Two very excellent pairs of (I think) re-knit over socks came last boat. Please thank Aunt Jean as usual. Thanks to her the situation is now saved, especially as my boots are now water-proof once more.

Much love to Aunt Jean
and yourself.
Tom

[F] *Bella Coola, BC*
29/1/24

Dear Father,

A most uninteresting week has slipped away. I am now getting to the sort of last lap, seeing a huge pile of stuff in front of me and wondering how much I can get done. Recently information has been coming in fine shape and I think I will be able to put in a good report. I must admit that I have by no means gone at things as hard as I did last year, at first the "pep" was not in me, and then there cropped up several affairs around the town site that took up some of my time, including Andy's wedding. The wretched Indian dances, though they gave me a lot of information, took up the [fiend's?] own amount of time, but such things will be. I think I am rather lucky to have got through this much of the winter at any rate without being at all sick, the constant rain and other details gave me plenty of excuse.

Though the official dances are over and the supernatural has departed from Bella Coola there is an occasional "good time" dance. Last night was one of these, and it nearly finished me, especially as I began it on a meal of none too fresh fish eggs, dried in the sun last summer and packed around for miles by Stick Indians,[85] the said fish-eggs being now boiled up and made more palatable by the addition of sugar and raisins. I said I was not hungry and ate but little. The first part of the show was a mourning song for Schooner, and afterwards all kinds of dances, the idea being to rejoice the hearts of his sons by giving them a good time. The chief drawback was that the leader of the choir was drunk, so drunk that he insisted on running everything without ever stopping to remember that no one else in the crowd knew what might happen to be in his mind at the moment, even if he did which was unlikely. I was hailed to dance (applause on the part of the audience), and found myself rigged up in various articles of ancient ceremonial attire and armed with a rattle, being almost violently pulled out into the centre of the hall by a drunken Indian whose face is normally far from handsome, but who when drunk looks like the devil itself. No one had remembered to tell me how to dance, or rather they changed the tune at the last minute, however I endeavoured to look happy and hopped around in my stocking feet till I was breathless, to the intense amusement of the audience. Dignified it was not and I was inclined to feel peeved but it is all in the game. Then I sang a Bella Coola song for which I got a tremendous round of applause, and the evening ended with beef stew and tea – including the inevitable germs, I have no doubt.

Absolutely the only other item of interest this last week has been the arrival of the new doctor, one Richardson by name. For once the fates have smiled on Bella Coola and I feel sure this is a first rate man, or at least far and away better than one has any right to expect in this place. He is an old man, fond of hunting and fishing, hence willing to chuck up a city practice to come to Bella Coola where he can take life easy. Further he plays a respectable hand of bridge as Bert Robson, one of the Christensen boys, and I found the other night.

Last Friday I went to a dance about four miles up the valley. It was held in one of the Norwegian's houses, music supplied by piano and fiddle. I managed to have a fairly good time (strange though it sounds). On almost all occasions there is a shortage of ladies here, and the wild scraps for partners amuses me.

Otherwise absolutely nothing in creation to report. It has rained most of the week, not that that worries me very much.

Tom

[F] *Bella Coola, BC*
6/2/24

Dear Father,

Here ends what has without doubt been the dullest week since I hit Bella Coola, absolutely nothing of interest to report anywhere. No Indian dances, no nothing. Andy and Charlie Wood are still in the interior, will not be back till Sunday, and this house is a quiet place. I have been driven to talking to the school-teacher next door, a most respectable fish who was born in Guelph and knows the name Goldie. But the most peculiar link with eastern Ontario is an old man named Ball who has been in from Ocean Falls teaching the Indian band. He is a very good musician, and has travelled all over the world, among other details having instructed the band of the King of Siam. He is a most dogmatic variety of Cockney, a type which I dislike, but in course of conversation it turned out that he had led the Bowmanville band in 1873-4-5 [sic], when it played at Hamilton and other places around at fireman's entertainments and other things of that kind. It is a small world after all.

The work is coming along pretty well, though I have still plenty to do. I have not yet decided whether I shall leave here the last boat of February or the first boat of March, but it will be one or the other. What happens next remains to be seen. I shall be busy till the first of August writing up, and am to give a paper at the British Association in Toronto sometime in August, after that I have the haziest notions in the wide world where I shall wander. But it will be time enough to think of such matters when I get back east. If you want to write me at the last minute it might be a good plan to send it care of the Turpin's [sic] in Vancouver, with a covering letter saying that I shall call to get it; I may spend a few days in Vancouver and Victoria before going east.

The weather here has been wonderfully mild, so mild that last Sunday I was able to go out for a walk without a coat. Even the rain has more or less stopped, which suits me.

Absolutely nothing more except that I am flourishing and am busy as the deuce.

Much love to Aunt Jean
and yourself,
Tom

[C] *Bella Coola, BC*
7/2/24

Dear Dr. Sapir,

I am enclosing another employment sheet (in duplicate). Would you be kind enough, as before, to forward it to the proper authorities? I hope this will be my last regular informant.

As I enter my last month I find that my information is rounding out satisfactorily. At times I am perturbed by new information on subjects which I thought I had cleaned up, but in most cases it has turned out to be of little importance. I know, of course, that it is hopeless to expect completeness in any ethnological work, but I believe I shall be fairly well satisfied when it is time for me to leave in the first week of March.

Please excuse the brevity of this note: it is written after a very tiring day.

Yours very sincerely,
T.F. McIlwraith

[F] *Bella Coola, BC*
19/2/24

Dear Father,

Unless I should happen to get a letter from Ottawa to-morrow telling me to leave the following week (which is most unlikely) it will be two weeks from to-morrow that I shake the mud of Bella Coola from my boots. While I think of it, if you want to write me at Vancouver, and there will be time for an answer to this letter to reach me, send it to general delivery at the PO and I shall prospect for same there. In some ways I shall be glad to leave here, to get away from the mess and the monotony, but I must admit that I have enjoyed this winter more than I thought possible. I think I have got all that could be got out of it, both from the point of view of work and general amusement of life. Among other things which I shall have to get accustomed to when I get back to the city will be shaving every day and NOT singing on all occasions, as I do here, much to the annoyance of the community at large.

I certainly had a strenuous and most unpleasant two days last week with the man whose nerves simply ceased to exist. I have never seen a man so go to pieces and hope he managed to stand the trip all right. A letter was brought to him on the boat which by no means reassured him, but there was no excuse for a man becoming a lunatic: the next time that such happens I am going to be somewhere else, life is too short.[86]

For the last ten days I have lived in an atmosphere of gramophones. I had sent to me from Ottawa, in fact it arrived before me, a recording machine with which to collect Indian music. I knew if I ever let my dirty friends know that I possessed such they would all want to sing so I only opened the boxes ten days ago. Disaster number one was when I had the affair transplanted to the Indian village only to find that there was no horn with it, a brilliant error on the part of someone in Ottawa. I sent out the kids of the village and soon was deluged with horns, but not one could I find that would fit. This was getting serious but at last I came across a gramophone of much the same type that had been stored in an attic for ten years. It had a horn but it would not fit mine. The only thing to do was to have a general swapping of parts, which I did, with the result that most of the government machine is in pieces, but enough of them fitted so that I was able to patch up the ancient machine. Since then all goes well. I have parked the machine in a man's house over at the village and am limiting myself to getting songs from him, which saves me a lot of trouble as long as his voice holds out. But it is one cheerful job. Every song must also be written down in text with a translation, which is much more wearying, both to me and the Indian, than the mechanical part of putting on the machine and letting it do the work. So far I have collected 59 songs, comprising 26 four minute records. By the end of this week I expect to have collected all that I want which will give me one week to clean up odd details, and then exit me from Bella Coola.

Otherwise there is no news. The weather has not been too bad, a certain amount of rain of course, but no more cold weather, and the roads have not been as bad as they were before Christmas. There has been a little snow but not enough to do any damage. Andy and Charlie Wood got back from the interior with a big pile of fur a week ago last Sunday. I went up in the truck as far as Hagensburg to meet them and rode one of the horses down. Never again! The stirrups were not of the right length and I innocently thought it would not be worth while changing them, which would have meant a lot of work. But I was stiff as a board for days after. Charlie went out to the Falls last boat, and I think Andy and Dorothy are going down to Vancouver for a trip to-morrow, which will mean an amazingly quiet last two weeks.

[The letter concludes with a handwritten note:]

Please thank Aunt Jean very much for a pair of re-knits, my sock supply is now in wonderful shape, thanks to her.

Thanks for sending on the "Times." I must admit I have barely time to look at it, but I pass it on to the community who enjoy the pictures.

Very much love,
Tom

[F] *Bella Coola, BC*
26/2/24

Dear Father,

[The first two paragraphs concern family matters and McIlwraith's itinerary home.]

This week has been terribly dull. Andy and Dorothy went down to Vancouver last boat for a holiday, and I have been busy cleaning up odd items of information with the Indians. I think I am going to be able to put in a really good report, though I hate to think of the work ahead of me in writing up my material. Most of this last week I have been working the gramophone over-time, with the result that I have now collected 104 songs, comprising 44 four minute records, which is not so bad, but the amount of trouble transcribing the texts and getting them translated is a brute.

I am sending one handsome (?) picture of myself, a relic of the trip to Kwatna. Dorothy likewise is receiving one, so you or Aunt Jean had better hang on to this work of art. The camera is working fine: I sent off some other snaps to Dorothy this week and suppose she will pass them on to you. I took a batch of the people etc. around here and am ordering 194 prints for various people by this boat, quite a job to keep the orders and accounts straight.

Absolutely nothing else to report, except that the weather has been fairly decent, mild and not too much rain, and that I am flourishing, although busy. Last night I survived an amazing noise making affair, staged in the house here, two gramophones, playing different tunes at the same time, one man playing the piano and singing a third song, and myself trying to sing down the combined noise making efforts with another song. The row was terrible.

This will probably be my last letter from Bella Coola, as I expect to write direct from the boat next time.

Much love to Aunt Jean
and yourself,
Tom

[C] *Bella Coola, BC*
4/3/24

Dr. E. Sapir,
Chief, Anthropological Division,
Victoria Memorial Museum,
Ottawa,

Dear Dr. Sapir,

Now that it is time to leave Bella Coola I presume I should give you a brief summary of my results.

The larger part of my material deals with the two types of winter ceremonial, the kusiut and sısaok. Last year I collected a large mass of material concerning the actual rites of the former, this year I have been able to add considerably to this, especially with regard to the songs used and the significance of the whole, both in the eyes of the initiated and the uninitiated. Almost every adult of the tribe has had his own dance, depending on the supernatural being with which an ancestor had come in contact. It would be practically impossible to collect details of all these, but I feel that I understand the whole system fairly well, in fact that I know more about it than do any of the Bella Coolas except the singers. I was made a kusiut last November and joined the singers as prompter, the texts of the songs having been given to me. In this way I really took a leading part in this year's rites; they are mere shadows of what they used to be, but even so I gained a very real insight into the manner in which they are carried out.

I am less satisfied with my sısaok material. Largely this is due to recent "borrowings" of rites from the Bella Bellas: by "recent" I mean within the last hundred years, with the result that there is much confusion among the older people as to the proper rites. Further the sısaok ceremonial is wrapped up with marriage and chieftainship, and the system of marriage likewise has undergone a radical change within one hundred years.[87] Add to this the fact that an individual's own wishes can alter appreciably the normal marriage arrangements, with the result that in Bella Coola the whole sısaok ceremonial is exceedingly fluid and evasive. I feel that some of my material is good, in fact I think I have a fair comprehension of the sentiments of the people on such matters, but I realise that it is going to be very hard to explain the system when writing up my material. Somewhat loosely connected with sısaok rites are a number of non-sacred dances, about which I knew nothing last year. I feel that they may be important as linking Bella Coola rites with those of other tribes. Rank and social organization might be mentioned here; I think my material on both topics is fairly good.

Religion has been satisfactory. I have a clear conception of the peopling of the earth under instructions from the supreme god, and of the house above where he dwells with the supernatural ones. Rites and dances take place there of which those performed on earth are copies. I spent a certain amount of time investigating the three "souls" (I use the term for lack of a better one) with which each mortal is endowed at birth and which enable him to cross the chasm which, according to Bella Coola ideas, separates success from failure.[88] I have collected a great deal of material ranging from direct prayers to the supreme god to purely magical rites. These play an important part in the lives of the people and I feel very well satisfied with my material on this subject. Last year's material on shamanism was fairly satisfactory though I have been able to add a certain amount to it.

I have done comparatively little on folk-lore, feeling that those tales collected by Boas, combined with what I took last year, would be enough to illustrate the Bella Coola types and that it would be more valuable for me to concentrate on the social life. I think I must have taken about fifty tales this year, but they do not vary greatly from last year's types.

Thanks to your instruction last spring I have had less trouble recording sounds than I did last year. I know that my work in this respect leaves a great deal to be desired, but it is certainly as accurate as care and attention could make it.

I left the collection of songs until the end of my stay, and had a very strenuous time during the last two weeks to deter would-be singers who had forgotten most of the words of the songs which they wished to sing. I have collected about 120 songs, making up about fifty four-minute records.[89] In each case I have written down the text and translation, though in many cases it was utterly impossible to obtain a literal word by word translation. As far as I know every type of Bella Coola song has been recorded. I hope this is satisfactory. What may be considered a fault in my records in that I have relied largely on a single individual. He is regarded by the Bella Coolas as their best singer and was the only man who did not keep forgetting the words of the songs. Under the circumstances I thought it best to use him almost entirely.[90]

The collection of museum specimens was more difficult than I expected. I found that it was going to interfere with the willingness of my people to discuss the secret parts of certain rites, so I made no great effort. I am shipping one box of specimens to you,[91] and also the two cases, one of the gramophone and the other of records. I had assumed that everything necessary would have been sent from Ottawa with the gramophone, accordingly did not unpack the cases until ready for use about three weeks ago. Then I found that there was no horn. I made one of tin which answered the purpose. I mention this to explain why there is no horn in the outfit sent back. The three boxes are addressed to you, which is correct, I hope. Each record is numbered on the cover and on the box itself, while I have marked a cross on the covers of a number of records which I ruined – usually due to an Indian forgetting the words of a song.

Now that I have put my notes together I find that I have nearly as many as last year. I shall do my best to combine everything and put the two sets in shape but, speaking frankly, I think it will be impossible to do so within four months. Without question there will be gaps in my report, but on the whole I feel fairly well satisfied. As far as possible I have left no loose ends, making a point of cleaning up as I went along, even at the cost of annoying an informant eager to broach some new subject. The Indians have treated me in an exceedingly decent way, I think I had only two enemies in the village, while I really think that most of them liked me, at least they used to ask my advice on all kinds of subjects in a way that was flattering, though most embarrassing. I think they were sorry to see me go, and in many ways I was sorry to leave. It has been a most interesting winter, rather marred by incessant rain which has made living conditions disagreeable, but I was most comfortable housed among the Norwegians on the town-site, who, in their way, treated me as well as did the Indians.

I have heard nothing further from you as to whether it will be on April 1st when I am to start writing up my results, but I assume this to be the case. I am leaving Bella Coola on the 5th and, as it would be impossible in any case for me to reach Hamilton by the 10th, when my period of employment terminates, I suppose there would be no difficulty if I remain in Vancouver for a few days.

I am sending in to you clearance sheets for those Indians for whom I had previously sent employment forms.

Having heard nothing to the contrary I suppose I shall be allowed to write up my material in Hamilton as last year. My address would be, as before, 179 Duke St. I should like to consult you about certain points, and perhaps it would be possible for me to visit Ottawa in the early part of April when I have started up my material.

Yours very sincerely,
T.F. McIlwraith

P.S. I have always forgotten to tell you that the Bella Coola name ä'łqun-täm[92] has been legally conferred on you – as my chief. I protested, not having been given as exalted a name myself, but the community wished to honour you, "for sending me to Bella Coola." I am assured by friends that you would feel highly flattered.[93]
T.F.M.

[F] *S.S. "Venture"*
7/3/24

Dear Father,

Well Bella Coola and I have parted company and sometime this evening we hit Vancouver. The worthy "Cam sun" [sic] does not make the trip in winter, the idea being that she is not strong enough to stand the gales across the sound, but this craft is very much of the same type, and the same style of passengers. We left Bella Coola at 3.45 on Wednesday, and spent most of yesterday messing around loading salmon in Rivers Inlet. The weather has been fine, brilliant sun-shine to-day. In fact all through February there has not been much to worry about in that respect, quite a reasonable amount of sun-shine. Everybody reports that the

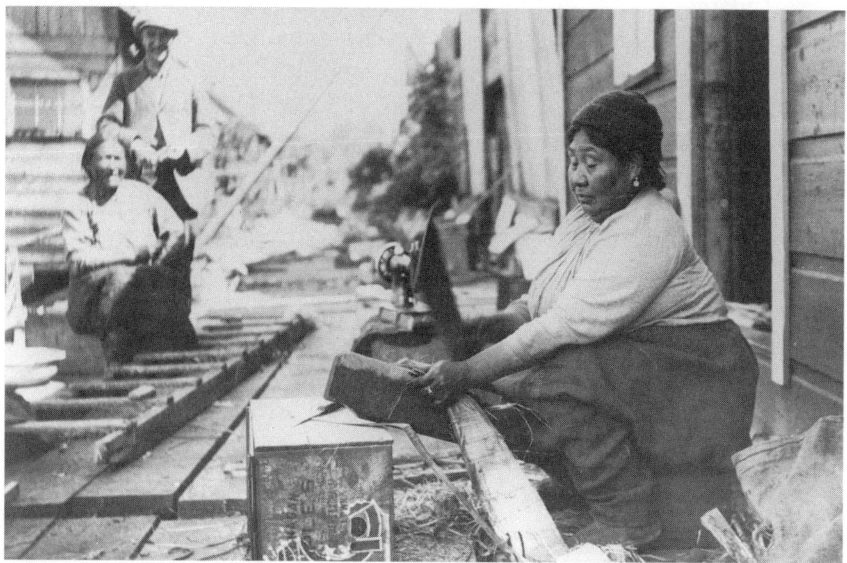

Mrs. Captain Schooner hacking red cedar bark in Q̓omqo·ts, with Likwum and T.F. McIlwraith in the background, 6 June 1922. The Nuxalk traditionally used cedar to make baskets, mats, and ceremonial blankets and adornments. Details on the preparation and use of cedar bark can be found in *BCI* II, 540-2.

weather below is very fine and, if all is well, I intend to spend a few days at any rate knocking around between Vancouver and Victoria. I had hopes that Dorothy and Andy would be down for another week, but they came in on this boat, resplendent in new clothes, a Ford Coupe, and a puppy. The truck was a bit late so they met us half way to the town-site, and I piled out to be driven down by them, and spent all the time cursing them fluently for not staying down below – with the Ford. Bert Robson is in Vancouver and I shall probably see something of him, but otherwise I don't seem to know anyone to knock around with, and knocking around alone is not all that might be.

Needless to say I left Bella Coola in a state of rush and chaos, finishing packing at 5.15 on the Wednesday morning, the boat being expected about 9.00. I must admit that I did not start this final spasm of packing until 3.00 a.m. as there was a dance which continued till after 2.00. It was a good dance at that. Leaving anywhere is rotten and I certainly hated the actual clearing out of Bella Coola where I have had a far more pleasant winter than I ever expected. With one exception the Indians were sorry to see me go, we have got on even better this year than we did last. This time there was no one of them of whom I thought as much as I did of old Schooner last year, but none the less I am carrying away a great many pleasant memories, and had a minimum of trouble. Some of the people around the town-site were, I think, glad to see the last of me, but I had made some pretty good friends there too, and I think the Christensen family was sorry to see me pull out. They certainly treated me awfully well, I was never in a place where I found it so easy to fit into the scheme of things and rag around with the bunch, but it is high time that I get back to civilisation before I forget how to behave in a place where one shaves regularly and does not wear clothes that would disgrace a respectable tramp. Last year I did not seem to have time to enter into the life of the place, but this year I certainly was in the thick of Bella Coola.

It seems foolish to write any more at the moment, I will send you a line from Vancouver as soon as I make up my mind what next.

Much love to Aunt Jean
and yourself,
Tom

[H] *31 John St., South*
Hamilton, Ont.
16/3/24

Dear Dr. Haddon,

Thanks very much indeed for your letter of 3rd, Feb., which reached me as I was leaving Bella Coola. I was decidedly pleased to hear that your trip to Australia had had the gratifying result of starting anthropology at Sydney.[94] You certainly start things wherever you go, and it will be fine if things get going in Australia. For personal reasons too I was pleased to hear that there were good chances of at least one position becoming vacant: the government is keeping me on until the first of August, but after that I see few chances of a permanent post in Canada. I will watch "Science,"[95] when I get east, for advertisements, but if you should happen to notice when a post was advertised I would be extremely grateful if you would post to me a clipping of it, as "Science" is sometimes hard to obtain here. Unless something unexpected should be available in the east I would certainly apply for a post anywhere.

I was sorry to hear that Mrs. Haddon will not be coming to Toronto in August. I had been looking forward to seeing you both, but it will be a great pleasure to talk things over with you. I wish I could have asked you to spend some time in Hamilton, but alas I have no home now so that is impossible.[96]

I have had an amazingly good season in Bella Coola, and think I have the material for a good report. When I reached there last October I found that my best informant had died since the preceding year, but I had a very cordial welcome from the Indians. I continued going around from Indian to Indian and collecting information of all kinds, but the interesting time came with the ceremonial dances in November. These are a mere shadow of the old rites, most disappointing from the spectator's point of view. They are held in a wooden hall built in the white man's fashion, illuminated with gasoline lamps, and heated with box stoves. But the rites are, as the Bella Coolas themselves say, pictures of what was done long ago with the social significance still maintained. I found that the rites helped me to understand many things, though I kept sighing for the old houses and the central fire. In the old days there were certain men whose duty it was to remember the words of the songs, these they whispered to an announcer who called them out line by line. At the present time there is only one man capable of performing these jobs, and he found that the two tasks were too much for him. So he asked me to write down the texts of the songs and sit in the choir ready to whisper the words to him if he got confused when announcing. This suited me famously, so I was duly installed as a member of the choir. Judging by the amount of prompting which I had to do I think they were lucky to have had me, at any rate I listened to various speeches of gratitude for the way in which I was helping out the ancient ritual. There were draw-backs; on many occasions the dances and songs were repeated without change, and it became deadly monotonous to sit from 6.00 p.m. to midnight or later, under the constant strain of prompting, with no information coming in, especially when it meant a two mile trudge to bed over a road about one foot deep in mud, and in pouring rain and inky blackness. Also the food proposition was difficult: of course I dipped my spoon into the common dish-pan and have painful recollections of the stomach ache that followed a mixture of fish-eggs, sugar, and currants. The favourite dish, rancid fish-oil and crab-apples, at first was unpleasant.

My first position in the kusiut society, one of the branches of the winter organization, had been held by an old man who had adopted me the previous year and had since died. The elders thought it fitting that his "son" (yours truly) should succeed, so I was solemnly given a name which carried with it the right to kill anyone who made a mistake in the ritual, and the duty of tasting all foods and telling the people to eat. After a while they got tired of listening to me and this part of my function lapsed. Then I became a cannibal and bit (theoretically) a man. The cannibal dance is a brute. I think you would have laughed had you seen me trying to keep time to the frenzied stick beating of the choir, and at the same time shake my hands, growl, move my head, and a few other details. Nor was I helped by the fear that my collar was going to fall off, while two old men spitting in my ears added to the reality of the show. I failed miserably when trying to sit on my haunches and jump around the room. I knew that this would lower my reputation, but luckily an old woman who spoke to me about it the next day added that she had noticed that my face appeared strange when I was dancing, could it be that the supernatural beings had tried to communicate with me when I was dancing? I replied truthfully that I had never felt the same as I had the preceding night (a stomach ache from rotten fish-eggs was the real reason), and the word went round that something had come to me, and my reputation soared. All told I danced about six times and once was entrusted with a mask, as a mosquito. My job was to parade around humming and at intervals rush at a spectator and jab him or her with a short stick, the sting of the insect. Unluckily the mask did not fit so that I could not see where I was going: one of the people whom I stung was a girl of about ten, whom I would not have chosen had I been able to see my victims until actually jabbing, and the expression of fear on her face and the way she cowered against her mother made me chuckle.

I also became a member of the other branch of the winter ceremonial, and as such used to dance with a rattle and a headdress of grizzly claws and weasel skins. Further it entailed singing in Bella Coola. Now I have no voice and have never been known to get within miles of a tune, however no one seemed to mind. These dances were usually held on "non-sacred" nights with much merriment. One night I was given a wonderful round of applause for a song which I had learnt quickly without getting the meaning. Next day I found it was a most suggestive love-song. Perhaps it is just as well that some of my Cambridge friends could neither see nor understand that performance.

Each dance was followed by a potlatch, strictly forbidden by law.[97] As a government official I found considerable amusement in receiving my share of whatever was being distributed, as well as helping with pencil and paper to figure out how much each should get. More than once it was due to me that certain individuals were given presents. These duties gave me a great insight into the way in which dances are run at the present time, so much so that more than once I have found fault with the leader of the choir for mistakes in the texts of his songs – much to the amusement of the other Indians. When I left I think that most of the Indians were really sorry to see me go, at any rate there were tears from two old women who had adopted me and protestations of eternal friendship from several of the old men.

On the whole I think my notes are fairly satisfactory. I had two men who were really good on magic and religion, and have some good material on these subjects. Either the Bella Coolas have more of this than other BC tribes, or it has been overlooked. Social organization is not going to be so good: in Bella Coola the personal prestige of a man who has given many potlatches is so great that he can do almost anything with the result that fixed laws are neither made nor respected. The same applies to chieftainship, where everything is most fluid and evasive. My material on the dances, and folk-lore, is fairly satisfactory, and, taking all in all, I feel fairly well satisfied. Among other things I made gramophone records of over 100 songs, with texts; I might mention that this job nearly deafened me when I had half the village trying to demonstrate to me their vocal skill. It also caused a fairly serious row between one of my best friends and his wife, she unfortunately came into the house when he was singing a love song which he had made for another woman. I could not understand what she called her husband, and me, but from her tone, her remarks must have been far from flattering.

I was fiendishly busy all the time I was in Bella Coola, but someway found time to get thoroughly into the life of the whites as well as the Indians. I must admit that I found the life of a frontier settlement in winter most interesting. I went to a number of the dances where there were always at least two men to every woman, and the struggles that ensued were more amusing than any novel. There were several very nice families in the valley and I made one or two really good friends among the rough but essentially decent people. Among other jobs which fell to me were those of best man, in Bella Coola this entailed scrubbing the groom's fingers, making as many of the rougher element drunk as possible the night before, and moving heaven and earth to see that they did not get drunk at the ceremony itself. As a stranger I was regarded as neutral and was called on to settle matrimonial disputes and give advice to parents as to how to keep at a distance too ardent suitors of their daughters. The most unpleasant job was when the doctor became helpless from dope and drink so that I had to set a boy's leg and take him out to hospital 60 miles away, in a 30 foot motorboat. It meant travelling all night, and at two a.m. the wretched engine broke down, leaving us drifting in a storm down a fiord with precipitous rocky shores. The other two men on the boat were working furiously at the engine with me on deck lying over the crippled youngster as the only way to keep the wind from whipping away his blankets. I was thankful to reach the hospital at Ocean Falls and could see the funny side of being refused admission to the only hotel as I did not look sufficiently respectable.[98] It was, I think, the most interesting winter I ever spent, but it was strenuous, for six weeks I think I averaged four and one half hours sleep a night. Luckily there was only one week of cold weather, but from the middle of Nov. until February it rained without stop and the roads became past belief. But I was comfortably quartered in a Norwegian boarding-house and was about the only person, white or Indian, in Bella Coola who did not fall sick sometime or other during the winter.

I expect to leave for the east to-morrow. I have about 500,000 words of notes (the two seasons work) to get into mss. form before the beginning of August, and I am afraid it is going to be impossible.

I posted to you a basket in process of construction and a tump line which I picked up on the reserve near Victoria.[99] It was impossible to pack them as I would have liked, but I hope they reach you, though they're of little value. I am enclosing a number of snap-shots, in which you may be interested, including some which I took last year and am sorry to say had never posted. H.I. Smith took a great many excellent photographs, with the result that I merely used my own camera for odd things, it seemed better to use my time on grubbing information.

Please remember me most cordially to Mrs. Haddon, and any other of my Cambridge friends whom you happen to see,

Yours very sincerely,
Mac.

P.S. In reading over this letter it seems to contain nothing but "I, I, I." Please excuse the over-stressing of the personal element.

Bella Coola Manuscripts

MAGAZINE SECTION. THE TORONTO SUNDAY WORLD, AUGUST 10, 1924. PAGE TWENTY-ONE.

At Home with the Bella Coola Indians

Government Anthropologist Finds Romance in Studying History of Earliest Canadians and Present Customs of Their Descendants

The following article was written for The Sunday World by a Professor of Anthropology, who was commissioned by the Dominion Government to make a study at first-hand of the life and traditions of the small tribe of Indians living in the Bella Coola River District, British Columbia. The professor will lecture on the same subject during the present convention in Toronto of the British Association for the Advancement of Science.

Top picture shows Tallio Charlie, a Bella Coola Indian, wearing a wooden mask representing the "How-how", a mythological bird of enormous size. The lower photograph is a view of the Bella Coola river.

A river canoe made from a cedar tree. It is hollowed out with adzes and fire. Such canoes are poled up the rapid rivers.

Jim Pollard and Lame Charlie, members of the Bella Coola Choir.

General view of the Indian Village, Bella Coola.

"At Home with the Bella Coola Indians," as the article originally appeared in the *Toronto Sunday World*, 10 August 1924. Harlan I. Smith's marvellous photographs are accompanied by a sensational, and highly inaccurate, portrayal of the anthropologist witnessing the Nuxalk winter ceremonials.

At Home with the Bella Coola Indians

By Thomas Forsyth McIlwraith

Editors' Note: The following article was published in the *Toronto Sunday World* newspaper on 10 August 1924, in part to publicize the upcoming meetings of the British Association for the Advancement of Science that were to be held in Toronto that year. It is identical to the original manuscript version except for a change in title (formerly it was "Among British Columbia Indians") and the addition of the first two paragraphs. For reasons unknown, McIlwraith is not identified by name as the author of the article but incorrectly as a "Professor of Anthropology" (he was still a year away from obtaining a position at the University of Toronto). An annotated version of this article was previously published in *BC Studies* (Barker 1987).

GOVERNMENT ANTHROPOLOGIST FINDS ROMANCE IN STUDYING HISTORY OF EARLIEST CANADIANS AND PRESENT CUSTOMS OF THEIR DESCENDANTS.

The following article was written for The Sunday World by a Professor of Anthropology, who was commissioned by the Dominion Government to make a study at first-hand of the life and traditions of the small tribe of Indians living in the Bella Coola River District, British Columbia. The professor will lecture on the same subject during the present convention in Toronto of the British Association for the Advancement of Science.

ROMANCE, even in this busy twentieth century Canada of ours is still to be found by anyone willing to leave the beaten trails for the northland where pioneers are even now blazing the way for future settlements.

Adventure, hope of gain, love of the untouched spaces where Nature still holds sway, all these tempt the foot-steps of the wanderer. Though the casual traveller may or may not have unusual experiences, these come in the daily work of government anthropologists who are striving to record the life of the Indian as it was before the white man came. The customs and beliefs of these first Canadians are of supreme interest not only to historians but to scientists who, as they work in all parts of the world upon the problems of man's mental evolution, find this can be most readily investigated by comparing the habits of primitive men. Nor is it too much to hope that in Canada, as in other parts of the world, it will be found that the easiest way to educate the native is to build on the foundation of his own culture rather than to attempt to bridge, too abruptly, the huge gap between his civilization, whatever it may be, and our own.

NO Indian is able to sit down and give a logical and detailed account of his social or religious beliefs. How, then, can the investigator study these? Romance lies in penetrating to the vision of a people whose outlook on life is as different from ours as would be that of the ancient Britons were we able to speak with them across the chasm of time.

Two years ago an anthropologist landed in Bella Coola, at the head of a long fiord penetrating far into the mainland of British Columbia, some three hundred miles north of Vancouver. Here it was that Mackenzie first reached the Pacific after his momentous journey across the continent. Then, as now, the snow-capped mountains rose in rugged grandeur surrounding the Bella Coola River as it winds, snakelike in many rapids to the sea. Then, as now, the clouds must have formed fleecy belts around the barren peaks as if resting on a solid mass of conifers, while high in the sky floated the ever-present eagle. At that time Indians came swarming forth from their houses to gaze at the white man whom they thought a spirit returned from the other world; now their decendants [sic] buy clothing and goods in white man's stores, and are more interested in his prices than in any queries about his celestial origin.

In Bella Coola there is now a community of thrifty Norwegian settlers who some thirty years ago carved out their houses in the virgin forest where previously the Hudson's Bay Company's post had been the only mark of the white man. These Scandinavians work in the salmon canneries in the summer, raise their own fruit and vegetables on their farms and live happy, contented lives far removed from the turmoil of cities. The anthropologist soon established himself with a hospitable Norwegian family, but to make friends with the Indians was another matter.

THE descendants of the once numerous Bella Coola tribe, now reduced to some three hundred individuals, live on a reserve about a mile and a half from the Norwegian town-site. He would be a rash individual who would dare to refer to the twenty or thirty houses as a "village." The investigator walked over to the Indian settlement through the huge cedars, rather wondering how to commence conversation. It was March, and the long row of Indian houses, built in the white man's style with many queer relics of native art, looked bleak and uninviting as it faced a sea of mud. Nor did an occasional Bella Coola, dressed in shoddy white man's clothes, seem a promising subject. Only yapping curs welcomed the stranger.

Early travellers have described the groups of noisy Indians clustered around the central fire in some big, log-built house where dried salmon hung from the smoke-grimed rafters, giving the pervasive smell that lingers in one's memory of the Northwest Coast. Instead of this, our anthropologist found each family living in its own small house, and the strains of "Tipperary" from a creaking gramophone did not suggest that this would be a favourable place for investigations.

A colleague had advised him to talk with one Joshua, whose house was easily found. Joshua turned out to be a smiling Indian of about sixty, who readily interrupted his carpentry at the sight of a visitor. Conversation was difficult with a man who knew some twenty words of English.

"What you come for?" asked the Indian bluntly.

To explain the quest of an anthropologist seemed impossible in broken English, so the investigator tried flattery:—

"To talk with you, Joshua."

"Then you one velly [very] wise man," was the somewhat disconcerting answer.

The first problem was that of language. Bella Coola is spoken only by the members of that tribe, and though some of the younger men know a considerable amount of English, they are ignorant of the ancient practices of their people and therefore useless as informants. Nor were they of much use as interpreters, because the old men, scornful of the younger for having forgotten their own mode of life, felt indignant at having to explain these matters to them. So the investigator fell back on the Chinook jargon which serves as a lingua franca up and down the coast.

Its history dates back to the early trading posts of Oregon where the pioneers carried on conversation with the natives in a mixture of their own language, eked out with French and English. As posts were established further north, Chinook Indians were taken along with the whites as interpreters, until in course of time this "jargon" evolved. Some two-fifths of the words are Chinook in origin, another two-fifths belong to Indian languages of the west coast of Vancouver Island, and the remainder is degraded French or English. The history of British Columbia is implanted in this jargon; an Englishman is still a "King George man," as the traders in the reign of George III called themselves; and an American is a "Boston man," that city being the home of the early Yankee adventurers.

A FEW weeks served our anthropologist to master Chinook, which simplified the collection of information. Like all Indians, intensely proud of myths describing the adventures of his own ancestors in the Golden Age, Joshua was only too willing to talk when convinced that his listener was genuinely interested, and not disposed to treat what was sacred to him with amused contempt. The words of the old Indian began to open to his hearer conceptions of the manner in which the natives regard their country and their life.

"See that mountain over yonder. That was where Kaliakis came to earth in the beginning of time, when the supreme god made him in his house above and sent him down to this world as an eagle. He doffed his eagle cloak; it floated back to the land above, where we were all created. When I was a young man, and strong, I wished to show my friends this history, so I made an eagle mask and called them to my house. The ghost whistles sounded; the eagle entered; we said that it was my father who had returned to pay a fleeting visit to his children; the young men believed and were afraid."

Steeped in the lore of his people and endowed with a graphic power of description, Joshua was in many ways an ideal informant. Philosophically and religiously minded he had been among the first to embrace Christianity, and did so with a fervour that many white men might envy. To him the Old Testament was a living reality, the events described therein were such as he expected to occur at any time as he had carried with him from his old religion the firm belief in the omnipresence of the supernatural. Nothing was an accident; a sudden thought was a vision, and more than once did the investigator have to sit patiently when Joshua interrupted a conversation by saying that a vision had come to him. He would then stand silent in the corner of his house hoping for some divine revelation, and always sadly saying that its failure to appear must have been due to his own frailty.

The Indians live in an atmosphere of the supernatural; not only are the forests tenanted by mythological animals, which Joshua admitted he had never seen, though he had heard them, but the birds, the animals, and the fish, all are capable of assuming supernatural form. Long ago, in the Golden Age, when man was more powerful than at present, he was able to penetrate the disguise of the animals, but now, alas, mortals have no such ability. Bella Coola mythology has many points of resemblance to that of the ancient Norsemen. But we Anglo-Saxons consider ourselves advanced beyond the point of belief in such tales, while the Indians consider they have degenerated, and that is why such experiences are no longer to be expected. None the less, the older Bella Coola firmly believe that supernatural animals still exist could one have the power to see them.

NEWS that a white man was collecting stories from Joshua soon spread through the village. At first it was only a matter of interest, but when it became known that Joshua's information was to be published in a book and so preserved for posterity, jealousy was aroused.

"Why should the adventures of Joshua's ancestors be recorded and not ours?" ran the comments.

At times this desire to talk became embarrassing. It was found that the best results could be obtained by working with one man at a time, yet if Joshua were neglected he intimated plainly that he would regard it as a slight to his veracity and would have nothing more to do with the investigator. Tact, flattery, and a willingness to exchange jokes on all occasions soothed this difficulty, for the British Columbian Indian has a merry disposition.

After a time it was found advisable to work with Captain Schooner, one of the few surviving heathen. Dirty and unkempt, this old man lived in the old village, among the ruins of the native houses. In his younger days he had been assistant to the Hudson's Bay Company's factor, who had placed the greatest confidence in him. Now, in the evening of his life, he was glad to talk on the days that had been, but always with a touch of sadness at the decay of his people and the abandonment of their rich ceremonial life. There were no chiefs among the Bella Coola, but Schooner had been a man of influence and was well versed in ancient practices. The investigator found him a gentleman in the truest sense of the word, a man of honour, and a very real friend. Schooner, for his part, was wont to speak of the anthropologist as his son. Ready to help on any occasion, the old man provided information about many ancient rites, so that much of the value of the investigator's report is due to his friendship with Captain Schooner, Komanukwila.

By mid-summer the anthropologist had collected a huge amount of notes requiring analysis and correlation impossible in the field. Much remained to be done, especially with regard to the ceremonial dances and feasts held only during the winter. So he returned to the east, but last October found him back again in Bella Coola.

But there was one change. Schooner was dead. His spirit had gone to the land where he felt sure there would be an abundance of salmon and berries, and where the spectre of change would not be forever before his eyes as it was in his beloved Bella Coola.

Joshua and the other Indian friends of the investigator welcomed him cordially and invited him to be present at the dances which were to start the next month. These are dramatic representations of mythical experiences of an ancestor of the performer, and, as such, the right to perform one is an Indian's most valued possession. As the elders discussed the coming ceremonies they asked one another who was to take Schooner's place.

"Why not his son?" said one man.

SO the investigator found himself, by popular consent, established as a leader in the ceremonial dances. In the old days these used to take place in a native house, illumined only by the flickering light of the central fire; now they are held in a hall built in the white man's style and furnished with kerosene lamps. Even so it was intensely interesting to watch the Indians drift in by ones and twos with their wives, their children, and their dogs, even the latter apparently taking a keen interest in what was to come.

"Music" was provided by six old men who sat at the head of the hall and beat on the floor with short sticks, accompanying the beating with a song. The tune and text they had composed previously, and when they began to sing the performer appeared from an enclosure behind them. His face was blackened with soot; eagle down was in his hair; around his neck was a collar of cedar-bark; and from his blanket hung an apron decorated with bear claws. The women droned in a peculiar high-pitched key, and while the choir beat time and sang the dancer paced to and fro in time to the music, his hands shaking furiously. Long, long ago, an ancestor had seen some supernatural being act thus and ever since it had been the prerogative of a member of this family to do the same, a social matter entirely independent of religion. To the watcher it was easy to visualize how it must have seemed a scant thirty years ago when such ceremonies were held in the old-fashioned type of house, and a large number of uninitiated persons did not understand the meaning of the dance, so regarded it with awe.

"Then, indeed," say the Indians, "was there power to our dances."

In those days the goal of a man's ambition was to dramatize an ancestral myth, to invite people from far and near to see it, and to recompense them for their attendance by lavish gifts of dried salmon, dried berries, mountain goat wool, deer skins, copper plaques and such like. Thus did a man spread the fame of his name up and down the coast and attain a position of influence. Nowadays, lacking the distribution of presents, the dances are mere shadows of what they were formerly; but if a white man can gain the Indian viewpoint it is not difficult to provide the missing setting.

The investigator had been instructed in his duties. He was to make a ritual speech in the Bella Coola tongue, inviting the guests to partake of the food provided, and to eat the first mouthful himself. As the meal was brought in, he was led to the enclosure at the back of the hall where he donned such a ceremonial costume as the dancer's, inwardly wondering from how many diseases the Indian suffered who had last worn it. His face was blackened with soot. Meanwhile one of the elders had announced that Schooner's successor would appear, a statement which caused considerable speculation among the audience.

Out came the disguised white man!

"It is Weena!" ran the cry, for that was the Indian name of the investigator.

THE Bella Coola language abounds in "kicks," but the anthropologist managed to splutter through his ritual speech and then joined the singers, from whose dish, a tin wash-pan, he was to take the first mouthful from a large wooden spoon painted like a whale. Alas, the food was a mixture of rancid fish-oil and crab-apples! Closing his eyes and hoping that he would not be ill on the spot he swallowed a mouthful. It tasted as it smelt, horrible. But details of this kind must be experienced by any anthropologist as part of the day's work. Though he never grew to like this Indian delicacy, after a few meals the investigator was able to eat it without experiencing the stomach-ache which followed his first taste.

The ceremonial life of the Bella Coola is crowded into six weeks in the early part of winter, the time when formerly food was most plentiful. Soon after six every night the Indians would gather in the hall to watch the performer of the evening. After the latter had done his part the singers would take charge of events and beat out the tune of some man or woman who had danced in previous years, whereupon he or she would perform again. Sometimes an assistant would dance in some other part of the hall; but never with any interplay of movement between the two. As for any dancing together of men and women, that would be unthinkable; in fact the Bella Coola regard the white man's dance as indecent!

In the old days, the position of a singer was one of high honour; several men would devote their attention to remembering the proper text which one of their number would call out line by line to the audience who were expected to join in. Last winter there was only one old man, Jim Pollard, capable of doing this, and even he found it was too great a strain to hold all the texts in his mind. So he appealed to the anthropologist;—

"Would Weena write down the texts in his note-book and join the choir as prompter?"

The investigator who previously had found difficulty in obtaining the much-desired texts promptly accepted.

IT was a strange occupation. Night after night as the Indians were assembling, the anthropologist would enter the hall, nod to friend after friend, and take his seat among the singers at the head of the hall. There he sat from six till midnight or later nightly for six weeks, his eyes glued on his note-book as a dance was taking place, waiting for the frequent nudge in the ribs signifying that Jim Pollard had forgotten the next line. The Indians soon took his presence as a matter of course; in fact speeches were made thanking him for his help.

Insight into the dances was at times dearly bought. The atmosphere of the hall was stifling, and the constant repetition of the same dance, night after night, monotonous. Sometimes the investigator was asked to dance to assist the leading performer, and he has painful recollections of the first time that he did so, following a feast of fish-oil and crab-apples. Feeling none too comfortable in his ceremonial costume, he found it extraordinarily difficult to keep shaking his hands, jerking his head, and growling, without losing time with his feet to the frenzied beating of sticks on the floor. Still worse was it when the music changed and he tried to squat on his haunches and in this posture leap about the floor like a kangaroo. After about ten minutes of this he was reduced to a limp rag.

To represent the mythical beings seen by an ancestor, on occasions grotesquely carved wooden masks were used and the Indians wearing these danced with considerable dramatic effect. The investigator once took part in such a performance, disguising himself as a supernatural mosquito! He was expected to hop lightly around the hall, but found the holes of his mask so far above his eyes as to make hopping difficult, also uncomfortable when he collided with a stove.

AS the older Indians die so will it become increasingly difficult to study the lives of these earliest Canadians. That such lore is of interest and importance to scientists is shown by the existence of a flourishing anthropological section of the British Association. At the coming meeting in Toronto, several papers will be read by Canadian anthropologists on Indian beliefs and practices. To the casual listener such records may appear dull, but if he uses his imagination, he can sense not only the life of the Indians, but the conditions under which the information has been painstakingly collected.

Certain Aspects of the Potlatch among the Bella Coola

by T.F. McIlwraith

Editors' note: This conference paper was read on 12 August 1924 at the British Association for the Advancement of Science meetings in Toronto.

A few years ago, when I was studying anthropology at Cambridge University, one ceremony that all students found difficult to understand was the potlatch. This was due not to lack of information on the subject but, rather, to the extreme voluminousness of the accounts, which tended to obscure the fundamentals behind a mass of comparatively unimportant detail. Accordingly, I have thought it might be of interest to our English guests to hear something about the principles of the potlatch as it is carried out among the Bella Coola. As most of you are aware, these Indians constitute an isolated group of Salish-speaking people in central British Columbia, some three hundred miles north of Vancouver. Their culture is of the coastal type, although many of its features appear to be only weak imitations of those observed among the Kwakiutl to the south or the Tsimshian to the north in that province. In Bella Coola the potlatch lacks many of the excrescences found among the Kwakiutl, but the fundamentals appear to be the same. On account of the comparative simplicity of the ritual in Bella Coola, the subject can, perhaps, be more easily studied there than elsewhere on the coast.

In scientific and popular writings alike, the term "potlatch" has been applied both to the ceremonial distribution of presents, which is a feature of so many rites of the Indians of British Columbia, and to the rites themselves. Among the Bella Coola, whether it be a dance, the bestowal of a name, initiation into a secret society, a marriage, or the assumption of a hereditary prerogative, no ceremony is valid without the distribution of presents. Every Bella Coola ceremony is, therefore, a potlatch. But as one of these is regarded as the most important, the aim of every ambitious man, the term potlatch will be limited to this rite alone, the *ɬɩm*.

What do the Indians believe to be its origin?

Every Bella Coola is, or should be, able to recount how, in the beginning of time, the supreme god in his house in the land above caused ancestors to be created who were then sent down to populate the earth. A creation myth of this type is a man's most cherished possession. Most myths describe the adventures of these first people, how they prospered in the Bella Coola country so that they were able to invite to their homes guests from far and near and show what they had achieved through the assistance either of the supreme god or some other supernatural being. By so doing they were carrying out the wishes of the deity as recorded in many myths. He told most of these first people that if they accumulated much wealth, in those days chiefly food, there was danger that the first obtained would rot, hence they should regularly give away the earliest supply. The Bella Coola term for "to become rotten" is ɬ l [sic], from which the Indians state that the word ɬɩm, potlatch, has been derived. Whether or not this is actually the origin of the word is open to doubt, but it is significant that, to the native, the term potlatch means "a giving away of long accumulated goods which otherwise might rot."

By the splendour of his gifts each of the first people able to give a potlatch spread the fame of his name to the towns from which his guests had assembled. In course of time those who had first given potlatches died, but, when their sons assumed their fathers' names, each endeavoured to uphold the traditions of his parent by inviting guests from a distance and bestowing on them valuable gifts. At such a ceremony the family history – that is, the family myth – was recounted, so that the donor of a potlatch not only increased his own prestige but incorporated himself with the traditions of his parent. That is the essence of the potlatch as carried out today.

What are its consequences?

In the first place the donor spreads far and wide the fame of his name and also the myth with which it is incorporated. A name, though legally endorsed by presents to neighbours, can only be made "heavy," or "firm," by lavish expenditure at a potlatch. In this way a man upholds the prestige of his ancestors, a source of intense pride and gratification.

More important still, it elevates the donor himself. With the proper carrying out of the complicated ritual, and the knowledge that his name has become known among different tribes, a man experiences a feeling of mental superiority that enables him to take a leading part in the affairs of his community. In Bella Coola a chief is a person whose influence is paramount owing to his success in giving potlatches. The advice of such a man is generally followed, though he has no judicial or executive authority. In fact a chief's own feeling of mental superiority is accepted by the community. If several chiefs in one village have given potlatches, he who has given most is generally the person of greatest importance, although often a man of forceful character who has held, for example, five potlatches will be regarded with greater respect than one of lesser weight, even if he has given six. The whole system is exceedingly fluid, as might be expected where chieftainship depends on individual prowess. In theory, the man who bears the name of the first person to occupy a village, at the time the earth was settled, should be chief in that village. If he has been able to hold the necessary potlatches to give weight to his possession of the name the fact that he is a legal descendant of the first chief will add a certain amount to his prestige, but unless he has been able to do so his influence will be slight.

What are the requisites for giving a potlatch?

The first is the possession of an ancestral myth containing a name or names. Probably every Bella Coola has this requisite. A man's family may not be the proud owner of one of the myths dealing with the first settlement of this earth, but, if not, he will at least own some ancient myth the fame of which he can increase by a potlatch. Sometimes the possessor of a most dignified name, one of those given by the supreme god to a person sent down to this earth at the beginning of time, will choose to elevate an earth-made name in preference. Thus, in Bella Coola, there is no class of nobles, such as exists among some of the northern tribes. The slight feeling of deference shown to those who hold the names of the earliest inhabitants of earth, the first chiefs, is subordinated to the genuine respect shown to the successful givers of potlatches. The descendant of one of the first people has the potential right to be a chief, but unless he can give potlatches he fails to gain a position of eminence.

The second requisite is some occasion for giving a potlatch. Like the preceding, this is never lacking. The potlatch consists of a number of closely associated rites, any one of which will serve as a reason for the ceremony. The most important feature is the return of a dead ancestor, or ancestors, to visit the living. It is obvious that this reason is available to anyone at any time.

The third requisite is wealth. Unless a man has the necessary goods with which to make presents he cannot invite guests, no matter how important may be his ancestral myths and names. He may be able to amass some of this wealth by his own labour, but unless he is assisted by his family it is virtually impossible for a man to succeed. The Bella Coola say that a man cannot become a chief except through the large payments made by a woman's family when they return the bride-price with interest. In other words, no man can succeed without the support of his wife. In choosing a mate he is guided almost entirely by the ability of her family to give him financial support.

The fourth requisite is supernatural assistance. To the Bella Coola this is quite as important as the preceding. One man may work very hard but his efforts are never crowned with success, whereas a neighbour will gain in every venture. This is due to the guiding spirit, the ability given by the supreme god to the latter. By prayer, ceremonial chastity, and other means a man may strengthen his own supernaturally given powers, but if these are entirely lacking he can never hope to rise to the position of chief.

Potlatches are always held in the autumn, the time when formerly food was most abundant. After consulting with his own and his wife's relatives the intending donor concludes that he has sufficient wealth to carry out the coveted ceremony. He next decides which myth, embodying which name, he will use. Almost all of these contain some prerogative with regard to the construction or decoration of his house. This entails the destruction of the old edifice preparatory to rebuilding. Some evening the donor invites his neighbours to his house. He outlines in general terms his ancestral myth and then distributes valuable presents of food. There is no stipulated amount, but the more bestowed, the greater is the respect shown to him by all. It is the privilege of a chief to be generous; thus does he show his chief-like nature. Following the distribution of food, a number of young men rush into the house with a battering-ram: a sham fight ensues during which the walls are broken. Then the intending donor allots to the carpenters different tasks in connection with the rebuilding. Finally, the supernatural element of the potlatch is first made manifest by a whistling from without, which those who are uninitiated to certain dances that accompany a potlatch believe to be the voice of a presiding deity. In reality the noise is made by a hidden accomplice of the donor.

A few days later messengers are sent to invite guests from neighbouring tribes. They carry whistles, which ensure them safe-conduct from hostile raiders. The potlatch, with its associated rites, appears to form a ceremonial bond among the coastal tribes. Bella Coola mythology contains many tales of the dire fate that befell those who failed to respect the safe-conduct afforded to envoys or to guests.

The donor uses his own discretion concerning those whom he invites. First he selects those whose guest he has been himself on like occasions, next those he wishes to honour by offering hospitality, and third, those whom he wishes to shame by the munificence of his display. Although it is not obligatory upon a man to accept an invitation, it is customary to do so.

On the arrival of guests at Bella Coola they give presents to the donor and his friends and, in return, receive small gifts. Then follows a complicated series of dances of a type limited to potlatches. Those who participate constitute what is practically a secret society, and it is at a potlatch that new members are initiated and receive their names, each of which is embodied in some ancestral myth. It would be tedious to describe in detail a ceremonial that may last for a week or more. Enormous quantities of food are given away, as thus the donor demonstrates his lofty spirit. The guests admire the totem-pole, the wall paintings, some peculiar feature of house construction, or whatever may be the prerogative that the donor has derived from a myth. The culminating feature is the entry of a masked figure representing a dead ancestor. The sound of whistling is heard from without, which those who are members of the secret society tell the uninitiated is the voice of a supernatural being. A breathless silence ensues as an elder goes out, and the whistling is continued as if in conversation with the mortal. The latter returns.

"It is Kaliakes," he calls out, or whatever may be the name of one of the donor's dead relatives. "He has returned to visit us."

Next, amid intense excitement, a masked figure enters. It is disguised under a blanket or skin covered with eagle down, and on the head is the mask of an eagle, raven, bear, or some other animal or bird. The Bella Coola belief with regard to this is that in the beginning of time the supreme god sent down the first people to earth, each in animal or bird form. On reaching Bella Coola they became men and women while the cloaks, if they may be so described, floated back to the land above. When a person dies his soul travels back from generation to generation until it reaches the spot where the first ancestor came to earth; there it assumes the form in which he arrived, and in this guise returns to the celestial land. This belief is so firmly rooted that the uninitiated do not suspect that the figure before them is not the recently deceased, appearing in the form in which he resides aloft. After circling the central fire the figure withdraws, whereupon renewed whistling marks his departure for the land above.

The guests have now seen the donor's prerogatives with respect to house construction and the form in which one of his relatives is living in the land above; they have heard his ancestral myth and the name that he has taken for himself from it; and they have witnessed a number of dances and the initiation of novices into the secret society. All these rites must be validated by presents. The principle of their distribution is the same at every ceremony, whether it be a mere dance or a true potlatch.

In each case there are three separate distributions, each of which is distinct in function. The first is a payment; the second validates the ceremony, whatever it may have been; the third is an investment.

These must be considered in detail.

The first gifts constitute the pay of those who have worked for the donor: the carpenters who made the masks and those who built or decorated the house; the bards who composed songs for the occasion and the members of the choir who sang them; the messengers who invited the guests – all these must be recompensed. Although goods so distributed are payments for services rendered, the Bella Coola never regard them as such but, rather, as presents made by the chief. There is no idea of bargaining between employee and employer. The carpenter or singer accepts what is given him without showing either pleasure or displeasure: a large present shows the importance and power of the donor, a small one displays his weakness. Gifts of this type are not returnable, either directly or indirectly.

The second distribution of goods is made to all the guests, irrespective of rank. It is these that validate the ceremony, the recipients becoming, in fact, witnesses to the affair. In the case of a true potlatch this means that they recognize the donor's legal right to his myth and name, with whatever prerogatives may be embodied therein. There are other types of ceremonies at which the recipients, for example, become witnesses to a marriage, to the right to perform a dance, or to the fact that the donor has used a certain amount of goods to make both "firm" and "soft" the place of his name; that is, his seat in the hall. To the Bella Coola it is absolutely unthinkable for a man to invite guests without compensating them for their attendance. Let me emphasize this by a recent example. Last winter some Kwakiutl Indians visited Bella Coola to perform a mourning ceremony that they legalized by gifts to the Bella Coola spectators. The latter decided to provide some entertainment for the strangers. Accordingly, they invited them to be present at a band concert, at which the performers were Bella Coola men who used the musical instruments of the white man. At the conclusion of the entertainment it seemed obvious to the hosts that they should recompense their guests by giving them a sum of money. Without this the band concert would have been considered a valueless affair.

It may be said that this legalizing function is the most important aspect of the potlatch among the Bella Coola.

The donor does not expect goods so distributed to be returned. In fact he unhesitatingly gives to white guests, to cripples, to children, or to old people whom he knows will never recompense him. He regards the goods as being wisely spent in validating whatever the ceremony may be. Furthermore, he has been able to display his chief-like nature. Some recipients carefully remember the value of the goods received and return at least an equivalent on some future occasion. By so doing they have demonstrated that they too have the minds of chiefs, but if they fail to do so, it is entirely their own affair.

The man holding the potlatch is careful not to give so lavishly that he has not sufficient left for a third distribution. In the first place, he must repay what may be termed "investment-gifts" received by himself when a guest on some previous occasion. Woe to the donor should he not have sufficient goods to do so! Nothing would be said openly to shame him, but all would realize that he had failed lamentably to uphold his position as chief, and his status in the eyes of the community would fall beyond recall. Further, he himself, realizing his own failure, would lose all self-respect and confidence. But it is almost unthinkable for a man to hold a potlatch unless he has sufficient wealth. Usually he is able to repay not only the principal, all that is obligatory, but interest as well. Such interest may be termed an "investment-gift." The donor's attitude is that of saying: "See! These are the glories of my ancestors of whom *I* am the descendant. I am a part of their history. To show my importance I give you from my wealth a mere trifle, a matter of no consequence to me who am established in the path of my ancestors."

Each guest receives his present with mixed feelings. On the one hand he has received goods that he is only morally bound to repay. But if he wishes to show that his name is likewise one of dignity, embodied in a myth of equal distinction, it is incumbent upon him to return a present of equal or greater value at a later date. Contrary to the practice among some coastal tribes there is no fixed rate of interest with the Bella Coola. Indeed it is seldom that the donor knows how much goods he will have available for "investment-gifts" until after the obligatory payments have been made. Then he decides quickly among whom to bestow the residue. As there is no system of writing or calculation, mistakes are by no means rare; the donor may even forget to repay some debt and so put himself to shame in the eyes both of the lender and the community at large. The position of the recipient of an "investment-gift" is closely akin to that of a guest at a dinner-party among ourselves. Though not legally bound to reciprocate his host's hospitality, a guest who habitually fails to do so in time loses his social position. Likewise, among the Bella Coola, the standing of a person who fails to repay is lowered, irrespective of the name that he bears.

Sometimes an "investment-gift" is bestowed with malicious intent. If the donor of a potlatch wishes to shame a guest he may do so by giving him a very valuable present, hoping that the recipient will be unable to repay with one of equal value. Should this be the case, the donor will have succeeded in establishing his name on a higher plane than that of his guest. But the latter may be equally wealthy, and if so he will return a gift of even greater value as soon as possible – sometimes immediately, if he has received warning of the plot. The original donor may again reciprocate, until a vendetta arises that may impoverish both parties. Another method of shaming a guest is to throw goods on the fire in order to demonstrate the wealth of their owner. It is sometimes said that this shows the heat-giving power of his name, though that may be a mere rationalization on the part of the Indians. At any rate the guest so shamed must quench the flames; that is, he must wipe out his antagonist's gifts by throwing ones of equal value on the fire. In such competition goods of considerable worth are sometimes destroyed. This aspect of the potlatch is neither as common nor as important in Bella Coola as it is among the Kwakiutl, so admirably described by Professor Boas.

Following, or sometimes preceding, the third and final distribution of presents the total value of the gifts is announced. The guests returning to their homes carry with them this remembrance of the donor's wealth. By it is judged his influence. The man's own feeling of mental superiority, though it cannot be measured in terms of blankets, is equally important as it enables him to assume, without fear, a position of influence in his community.

To conclude. The principles of the potlatch can be summed up in five brief headings.

First: A distribution of goods is essential to validate every transaction or ceremony, the recipients becoming legal witnesses.

Second: In addition to such presents as are necessary to validate a ceremony, further gifts are always made. These are of two kinds:

(A) Payments for services rendered.
(B) Investments.

Third: Investments must be returned or the recipient loses his social position. With this aim in view a chief sometimes shames a rival by giving him large presents.

Fourth: By giving ceremonies, legally validated by presents, a man engenders a feeling of mental superiority over those who have been unable to do likewise.

Fifth: A man's status and influence in Bella Coola is judged almost entirely by the goods he has distributed. As the Indians say, "It is the function of a chief to be generous."

Observations on the Medical Lore of the Bella Coola Indians, British Columbia

T.F. McIlwraith, Associate Professor of Anthropology, University of Toronto

Editors' note: This manuscript was found among the McIlwraith papers. It is published here for the first time.

The Academy of Medicine has recently acquired a medicine man's kit from the Gitskan Indians of Northern British Columbia that, by illustrating the practices of a relatively primitive community, throws light on the development and history of the science of medicine. Paraphernalia of this type are disappearing so rapidly that those responsible for the purchase are to be commended for their scientific forethought; they have also been extremely fortunate in enlisting the aid of Mr. C.M. Barbeau of the National Museum of Canada who has been carrying on ethnological investigations in western Canada for a number of years. Although the medical practices of every tribe differ to such an extent that a detailed account of the use of the outfit now owned by the Academy must await the publication of Mr. Barbeau's researches, there are sufficient general resemblances among all the coastal tribes of British Columbia that the following description of the beliefs of the Bella Coola will serve to explain the background of west coast Indian lore. The Bella Coola are a small tribe of the central littoral, among whom I worked for a number of months on behalf of the National Museum of Canada.

A white man coming in contact with primitive peoples is struck by the difference between their outlook on life and his own. In some cases, this has appeared so great that there has been attributed to the lower races a type of mental process dissimilar to that of Europeans. But the explanation of the difference in attitude rests not upon physiology or psychology but upon culture, itself the result both of environment and of slow historical development throughout the centuries. The twentieth-century European looks at life through scientific eyes, due to experience in a world of which the keynote is mechanical development; it is not too much to say that he is conditioned to a highly complex commercial and machine-made environment. Primitive man, on the other hand, exists in a world without writing, where the struggle for food and for other essentials of life must be carried out with the aid of crude tools of stone. Further, and perhaps still more important, to the native the supernatural is ever present and ever influencing the activities of the individual. This is so vital and so difficult for scientific minds to grasp that it is worthy of two illustrations. I remember one occasion when an old Indian and I started out from his house planning to be absent for two or three hours; we had gone some fifty yards when my companion stopped, remarked that he had not put enough wood on the fire to keep it alight, and turned back to remedy the oversight. On rejoining me he said with a smile:

"You see my *hichmanoas* was on the job."

By *hichmanoas* he meant a supernatural element, located in the back of the neck, which comes to the individual at birth and remains in his body throughout the whole of his life, the seat of his mental activities. What a white man would have regarded merely as a sudden thought was to the Indian the direct result of the activity of a supernatural part of his body, something bestowed on him by the supreme deity himself.

Another Indian was once talking about animals and spoke of their ability to transform themselves, mentioning an incident that had occurred a few years before, when a grizzly bear changed into a stump. He described the circumstance. As he and some others were paddling up a long fiord, they saw a grizzly bear on the shore ahead of them, the white sheen of its fur shining in the sunlight. Eagerly they paddled in behind a point out of sight and cautiously moved their craft forward; but, when they edged around the tip of the promontory within rifle shot, there was no bear but only a white, water-washed stump having somewhat the shape of the animal. Wild excitement followed: a bear had been there, they had all seen it, now there was a stump; therefore, the animal had turned into a stump! My Indian friend added that a white man had been in the canoe at the time and had been a witness of the transformation. At the first opportunity I sought out the main in question and asked him about the incident; he remembered it perfectly and confessed that he had certainly thought the stump to be a bear when first seen. But whereas his reaction was to admit an ocular delusion, that of the Indians was to consider that the bear had changed its form, a matter of no great difficulty in view of the nearness of supernatural powers and of the manifold ways in which they can come into contact with mankind.

It is no exaggeration to say that the Bella Coola Indian regards all things as swayed by the supernatural: success and failure, births and death, health or disease – all are due to the intervention of powers belonging to a different plane than that of human activity, a plane not necessarily above or below but definitely not the one on which ordinary mortals exist. One may ask whether this vivid belief in the nearness of supernatural powers does not produce a feeling of fear in the natives, but the answer is in the negative. It is true that they are faced at all times with diverse forces, but they know how to deal with them in prayer, by sacrifice, by magic, and by what might be regarded as embryonic science. A middle-aged Indian whom I knew intimately had been a patient at a white man's hospital when he had learned of the danger of germs.

"Surely," he said to me, "the white man must live in a perpetual state of fear knowing that whenever he enters a crowded street-car he may be sucking into himself countless invisible particles capable of giving him virulent diseases."

Just as we realize that germs are present, and know, more or less, how to circumvent them, so does the Indian know how to deal with the ever-present and very real creations of his own imagination.

Since disease, like everything else, is due to the supernatural, it follows that treatment must include either an appeal to supernatural powers or the use of remedies that have potency in themselves. Some of the latter are well known to all, others must be regarded as patented since they are owned by certain families; but in either case there are no ceremonial regulations with regard to their application. A few instances will suffice to illustrate the type. To ensure long life, a newborn infant is frequently rubbed with the body of a beaver or a wolverine in order that the child may have the strength of these hardy animals (remembering that to the Indian, a beaver is not a mere element in a fur coat or something occasionally to be seen in a zoo, but a creature endowed with powers of swimming and of obtaining food of a kind that human beings may well envy). Similarly, to give a child ability as a singer, he is rubbed with a bird of which the song is much admired; a squirrel is used to give climbing agility, a wasps' nest to make the baby a fighter, and so forth. Other remedies of the same type are applied at different periods throughout life. During pregnancy, the application of a fetal porcupine ensures easy delivery, a characteristic attributed to these animals. Some remedies are distinctly medicinal, such as the use of poultices for sprains, but equally efficacious in the beliefs of the people is the eating of pounded bear's heart for a stiff neck, while for whooping cough the favourite remedy is boiled cottonwood buds mixed with animal fat. The basis of all such cures is sympathetic magic, a belief that has played its part in the lives of all mankind.

Surgical practices are limited to cutting for boils and the removal of foreign substances, the practitioner being anyone who happens to possess ability along such lines. Likewise, the setting of fractured limbs calls for no skill of a professional nature. Other methods of treatment include immersion in hot springs and the use of steam baths, in principle akin to the Turkish bath. In some of the many hundreds of remedies belonging to the categories just enumerated there is a certain amount of medicinal value, and effective cures are the ones most likely to be handed on from generation to generation, although there is no realization of the scientific principles involved. Other ailments caused more directly by the invention of malignant powers require more drastic treatment with supernatural appeal. In all cases, however, a potent factor is the power of the mind; a man believes that the treatment will be effective and the probability is that he will be benefited thereby.

In more serious illness, it is natural for the Indian to call upon the individual who has supernatural healing power – the medicine-man, or, as I prefer to call him, the shaman. Bella Coola shamans are socially important for it is they who have received direct visitations from supernatural beings and are therefore in a class somewhat superior to their fellow men, irrespective of whether or not the visitation has given them the power to cure. Legends handed down from generation to generation attest to the power of shamans in the golden past. A favourite tale is that of Waowallis, who was the owner of a marvellous stick with one end of which he could deal death, and with the other restore to life. Other mighty men of old could roll back the tide, could pass through the mountains, or could support themselves from the end of a stick thrust against the flat under surface of a roof beam. Such traditions, believed in without question, serve to impress upon the hearers the prowess that may be granted by supernatural beings.

Modern shamans, in this degenerate age, lack the abilities of their forbears, but even they possess certain unusual powers that are a source of envy to their less fortunate tribesman – powers obtained from supernatural beings in dreams or in visions. Sometimes the parents of a lad notice that he is thoughtful and silent, unwilling to mix in the amusement of the village, and they wonder whether or not his behaviour is due to the tentative desire of a supernatural being to commune with him. This is particularly likely if some of the boy's dead relatives were shamans, and the hopeful parents urge their son to continue to live apart, to concentrate his thoughts on lofty matters, and to woo the supernatural in every possible way, hoping that in the course of years, he may have the good fortune to receive a real vision.

Most shamans, however, receive their power when they themselves are ill. If an individual is lying at death's door, he, and everyone else, knows that he can be saved only if Tlitcaplixwanna takes pity on him. She is an enormous supernatural woman, kindly though awe-inspiring, who sometimes comes to a dying man, restores him to health, and gives him both a name and a song. On recovery, the individual is accepted as a shaman with all the social prestige attached, and if there is mention in the song of a basin, he will be able to cure the sick.

Many Bella Coola undoubtedly believe that they have had visitations, and the explanation is not difficult to find; if a patient believes that his only hope of recovery is through hearing a voice and a song, it is not difficult for him to imagine such an experience in his weakened condition and to affirm it when restored to health. The following is a typical example of such a visitation.

One autumn, some thirty years ago, an individual was fishing when he contracted a malady that caused his flesh to waste away so that by December he was little more than a skeleton. Then, one morning, he heard whistling, which he was sure must be the voice of Tlitcaplixwanna. He wisely said nothing about it, nor was it heard by anyone else. The same sound was repeated on the next two mornings, and on the fourth the woman appeared.

"I am Anolximdimut,"[1] she said. "Everyone calls on me to visit the sick, and henceforth they will likewise seek you and your basin."

Something entered his stomach, causing it to heave violently, and he felt that the sickness had left him. He sent for the singers[2] and repeated to them the words that Tlitcaplixwanna had chanted; these formed the text of the shaman's song that he used on future occasions.

While giving them to the singers, he endeavoured to dance but was too feeble to do more than weakly shake his hands.

Another shaman gave a detailed account of his acquisition of power which, however, did not include ability to cure the sick. This man slept one night in the forest and saw, next morning, a trail of dried blood leading to his blankets. Examining himself, he found no wound and so concluded that the blood could not have come from his own body. A week later, he was working at the fire in his house when his nose began to bleed; the people tried the usual remedies, but they were without effect and the hemorrhage continued for several days, until he became weaker and weaker, at last sinking into unconsciousness. His friends had assembled, thinking he was on the point of death, when he recovered slightly, and his eyes roved around. It was realized that a supernatural being must have come to him in his hour of need and that he would become a shaman. A few days later, he had a relapse and was again in dire straits, when he heard inside his head a buzzing sound like that made by a bee; it was the tune and also the words of his shaman's song, which Tlitcaplixwanna was bringing to him. He could see her faintly and heard her utter the name that was to be his as a shaman, Nitsimdimut. He recovered completely and is regarded as a shaman since he was cured when at the point of death by Tlitcaplixwanna and received a name and song from her, though unable himself to effect cures.

It is believed that serious sickness is due to the presence in the body of some foreign substance that a shaman can often draw forth by means of the power located within his own body. When a person is ill one of his relatives requests the aid of a powerful shaman who answers grandiloquently that he will help the mortal. Then he dons his distinctive collars of cedar-bark and other professional articles of costume, and goes to the patient's house followed by a group of interested onlookers, including the musicians. He throws himself on or beside the sufferer and begins to feel for the sickness by pounding him, squeezing him, and kneading the flesh while he growls and grunts with half-closed lips, ejecting a flow of fine saliva over the patient. Friends and relatives crowd around, amid a pandemonium of wailing women, barking dogs, and howling children. In some cases, he is able to squeeze and suck the malady to the surface and produce it as a twig or a pebble, or to extract it although it is not displayed in visible form. In either case, it is carried solemnly to the door and blown away. In more serious illness, the shaman's power is itself thrust into the sufferer who, thus endowed, begins to grunt and gurgle in the same way and casts out the evil; the power is then returned to the owner and the cure is complete.

But frequently the sickness is too deep-rooted to yield to such simple methods, and the shaman needs the assistance of all and sundry. The musicians are in attendance and they may sing the shaman's own song while he dances with shaking rattle, an action that tends to concentrate his power. His basin is filled, placed near the patient, and he throws water as he kneads and pummels in the manner already described. Meanwhile, another shaman or someone accustomed to lead the musicians arranges the bystanders into two rows, facing one another between the door and the central fire. Each is provided with a beating stick about two feet long, and a sounding-board is placed before each row. He who has been commissioned to lead the orchestra of stick beaters stands near the door, and the musicians take their time from his movements. First he raises his arms higher, the noise increases, and he sways from side to side as if carried away by the music; as he does so the men towards whom he leans intensify their beating while those on the other side decrease theirs. Back and forth he sways followed by the beating; nearing the climax he treads mincingly, whereat the noise rises to thunder-pitch, then he jumps twice, and as he strikes the ground the drums beat and all the sticks come down with a final ear-splitting crash. Throughout the whole, the women drone, a constant eeeeeeeeeee. This elaborate beating of time is repeated four times, on each occasion concluding with the double jump, which calls forth the double thunder of drums and sticks. Thus encouraged, the shaman, who has been continuing his efforts to draw forth the sickness, frequently achieves his purpose.

It is not easy to sum up briefly the psychology of the shaman. The word "charlatan" comes to one's mind at once, but that is not an accurate description because, although the shaman uses deceit to increase the effect of his work, he is not a simple deceiver. His own recovery from disease appears to him as proof positive of his supernatural endowment and convinces him that it is his duty to increase the impressiveness of all he does. If, therefore, he knows that he can suck forth sickness, surely he is justified in exhibiting it, hence the subterfuge of the pebble or the twig.

Furthermore, the repetition of the same practice serves still more to convince him that he is acting with divine sanction. Mere quacks exist among the West Coast shamans, as, may one say, among all bodies of medical practitioners, but the majority of the individuals are activated by the sincere conviction that they have supreme authority for what they are doing – a viewpoint that can be understood only in the light of the nearness and constant influence of non-human powers upon the lives of mortals.

Notes

Introduction

1 For a more detailed account of McIlwraith's career and contributions, see Barker (1987; 1992).
2 Sapir to McIlwraith, 19 August 1921. Canadian Ethnology Service, Canadian Museum of Civilization.
3 Jenness to McIlwraith, 3 March 1927. Canadian Ethnology Service, Canadian Museum of Civilization.
4 These and other Nuxalk spellings follow usages in *The Bella Coola Indians* (hereafter BCI). See "Note on Text and Annotations" at the end of Introduction.
5 There was no single name for all of the speakers of the Bella Coola language. "Bella Coola" itself is a mispronunciation of a Kwakwala or Heiltsuk word that outsiders applied to the people of this area (Kennedy and Bouchard 1990, 338).
6 In 1911 the Pacific and Hudson Bay Railway received a charter to build a railway across the western provinces with a Pacific terminus near Bella Coola. Speculators rushed to the area, buying up land in anticipation of a port that boosters insisted would rival Vancouver's. Events reached a climax in early 1914, when surveyors arrived to lay out the line of the tracks. The project was effectively killed soon after, due to the completion of the Grand Trunk Pacific Railway route to the north in April and then the outbreak of war in Europe in August 1914 (Kopas 1970, 263-6). Some residents refused to give up the dream. Until its demise in 1917, the weekly *Bella Coola Courier* published a map of British Columbia in every issue showing the proposed rail line to Bella Coola.
7 For a complete list of early publications on the Nuxalk, see Kennedy and Bouchard (1990).
8 Two members of the Berlin troop, Alex Davis and Bill Jones, were still living in Bella Coola in the early 1920s (Tepper 1991, 179). Oddly, McIlwraith mentions neither in his letters or book, although Davis had once worked as Boas's informant.
9 McIlwraith's account (at an academic conference in England) of his experiences as a Nuxalk cannibal dancer attracted the attention of *Punch* magazine, whose correspondent commented: "We don't see anything extraordinary in Professor G.F. McIlwraith's [sic] description of the supernatural influence which impels him, as a member of a secret society of Indians in British Columbia, to rush about biting people. Professors are often like that" (*Punch*, 19 September 1928, 309).
10 In his excellent discussion of shifting styles of fieldwork, Sanjek (1990a) notes that Boas developed his approach to fieldwork gradually; his mature work is best understood as the twin product of a survey approach to fieldwork and a heavy reliance upon Aboriginal collaborators, especially George Hunt, who greatly augmented his collection of texts. The publication of Boas's field journals and letters in 1969 greatly contributed to the reassessment of his fieldwork and the huge body of published and unpublished materials that resulted from it (Rohner 1969).
11 In his introductory remarks on a chapter containing origin myths, McIlwraith comments that he felt that Boas's earlier publication of Nuxalk myths made any efforts on his part redundant. "The Bella Coola, however, are so intensely proud of the deeds of their first forefathers that several insisted on recounting them before they were willing to do other work; in consequence, a fair number of myths was collected through necessity" (*BCI* I, 292).
12 I do not mean to suggest that Europeans were never taken by Native peoples to be deities. A few years ago I was surprised to discover that some old people among the Maisin of Papua New Guinea, with whom I have worked since 1981, speculated that, when we first arrived, my wife and I might be returned ancestors. As Marshall Sahlins (1995) argues in his debate with

Gananath Obeyesekere over the interpretation of Cook's apotheosis, the reasons and implications of such acts are usually quite different from what the Europeans concerned imagine.

The First Season, March to July 1922

1 His family, in Hamilton, included his father and mother, Thomas Forsyth (1858-1932), and Mary Stevens McIlwraith (1858-1923). His older sister, Dorothy Stevens (1891-1976), was in New York City. His oldest sister, Marjorie Spafford (1888-1977), was most likely living in Burlington in 1922.

2 A comfortable passenger vessel of the Union Steamships, Ltd., lines. It was built in Scotland in 1904-5 and scrapped in 1936.

3 Alfred Cort Haddon (1858-1940), Reader in Anthropology at Cambridge, Curator of the Museum of Archaeology and Ethnology, and fellow of Christ's College. He was McIlwraith's closest Cambridge mentor.

4 Haddon and his daughter were keen collectors of string figures ("cat's cradles"). Appendix B of *The Bella Coola Indians* describes Nuxalk string figures, including several connected to the raven (*BCI* II, 543-69). See also K. Haddon (1930).

5 Joshua Moody. He had been suggested to McIlwraith by Harlan I. Smith because of his previous service to the latter. According to Smith (1924), Moody was about fifty-four years old in 1922. McIlwraith describes a conversation with Joshua in his *Toronto Sunday World* article, reproduced in this volume. He also describes Joshua's personality in the *Bella Coola Indians*, with the addition: "Not particularly practical, subject to fits of anger or moroseness, but with a meditative temperament which delights in seeking biblical parallels and synonyms for Bella Coola practices, his is the kind of mind which, in other walks of life, would have produced the professor of philosophy" (*BCI* II, 525). A photograph of Moody appears as Plate 2 in *BCI* I. See also H.I. Smith's photographs of Moody's commodious house (no. 49059), located near the town hall, and the group portrait of McIlwraith, Joshua and Eliza Moody, and Willie Mack and son in costume (no. 56872) (Tepper 1991, 33, 187).

6 McIlwraith's early rendering of *łım*, the ceremonial potlatch of the Bella Coola. See *Bella Coola Indians*, especially I, 182ff.

7 McIlwraith is here thinking of the work of William Halse Rivers (1864-1922), fellow of St. Johns College, Cambridge; retired lecturer; and, with Haddon and Sir William Ridgeway, the source of Cambridge's importance in anthropology. In a series of highly influential publications, Rivers (1910; 1914) placed the "genealogical method," which he had largely invented, at the centre of anthropological research in kinship-based societies. He argued that "pedigrees" provided field researchers with an invaluable framework within which to investigate a wide range of social conditions, including post-marital residence, totems, descent group membership, and migration histories as well as biographical information on individuals. Historian George W. Stocking (1983, 88) notes: "In his more confidently positivistic moments, Rivers tended to see the genealogical ... method as the solution to almost every ethnographic problem."

8 Edward Sapir (1884-1939), a German-American who trained under Franz Boas at Columbia University. He was appointed first chief of the Anthropology Division of the Geological Survey's Victoria Memorial Museum in 1910. He moved to Chicago in 1925.

9 Edward Sapir, *Language: An Introduction to the Study of Speech*. New York: Harcourt, 1921.

10 See 180n7.

11 The annual meeting of the British Association for the Advancement of Science, which had met in Edinburgh in September 1921. McIlwraith's paper, "Egyptian Influence on African Death-Rites," was presented on 13 September. It was never published, but an abstract can be found in the published proceedings (McIlwraith 1922), 442-3.

12 Rivers had been in Melanesia in 1908 and 1914.

13 The Chinook jargon is a simple trade language, made up of words drawn from various sources, that evolved into a widely used medium of communication before English became virtually universal.

14 Charles Lord is listed in directories as a canneryman or fisherman.

15 The reference is to a famous First World War legend that probably derived from a short story written by Arthur Machen for the *London Evening News*. This story soon took on a

life of its own. Outnumbered by German forces in their first battle at Mons in Belgium in August 1914, the British were forced into retreat, protected, it was said, by the divine intervention of St. George and a host of angels and ghostly warriors from English history.

16 See *BCI* I, 158-62.

17 This is not a Bella Coola word; most likely it is "tyee," which is Chinook jargon for "chief."

18 McIlwraith's initial spelling of *xιxmänoäs*, the supernatural spirit that dwells in the human body (*BCI* I, 94-7).

19 McIlwraith provides a more complex description of Nuxalk ideas concerning "the spirit" and "the living" in *BCI* (I, 98-100).

20 See *BCI* II, 107-11. In his fieldnotes, McIlwraith remarks that Joshua was one of the seven living men possessing the right to "eat" human flesh (McIlwraith 1922-4).

21 McIlwraith's alternate spelling of *ɬιm*, or potlatch.

22 Mr. and Mrs. Adolph Christensen, who ran a general store and boarding house at the townsite.

23 Iver Fougner (1870?-1947) arrived with the first Norwegian colonists and worked as the settlement's schoolteacher and editor of an early newsletter, *Nybyggeren* (*Pioneer*). Later, he served for many years as the Indian agent.

24 Reverend Samuel Spencer Peat and Hilda Peat. A Yorkshireman, Peat (1874-1943) had commenced his Methodist ministry in Alberta. He served in Bella Coola from 1921 to 1925, before taking up posts at Kitamaat, Skidegate, and Pender Island. In his later years, he worked with the Chinese and East Indian missions of the United Church in Victoria (Turner 1943).

25 The senior editor, John Barker, met the missionary's son, Spencer Peat, during a short visit to Bella Coola in 1990. This was the latter's own first visit to Bella Coola since leaving the place as an infant. According to Mr. Peat, the bear incident became a favourite family story in latter years.

26 Bert Robson, born Bertram George (1889-1964), son of a Hudson's Bay Company trader and a fishpacker skipper.

27 That is, the Protestant martyrs, Nicholas Ridley (Bishop of London) and Hugh Lattimer (Bishop of Worcester), executed by Queen Mary Tudor in 1555.

28 The force of this anecdote depends in part upon a realization that Northwest Coast Aboriginal languages contain no "r" sound and, like Chinese immigrants, they could only approximate it with an "l." The "d" was similarly lacking, but an Aboriginal "t" was a less discordant substitute.

29 Jean Newton McIlwraith (1859-1938), his paternal aunt. A successful author, she worked at this time as a publisher's editor in New York.

30 His older sister Dorothy (1891-1976), who had followed her aunt, Jean Newton McIlwraith, into editorial work in New York.

31 William McInnes (1858-1925), director of the Victoria Memorial Museum, Ottawa; John Marshall was responsible for its accounts.

32 See McIlwraith's letter to his father, 5 December 1923, for a description of the use of such whistles.

33 The Kwakwa̱ka̱'wakw (Kwakiutl) are a large group of Kwakwala-speaking peoples living in Vancouver Island and the opposite mainland; the Kitkatlas are a Coast Tsimshian group centred at the village of that name.

34 These are the winter dances of the *kusiut* secret society, dealt with at length in *BCI* II, chap. 1.

35 The dances of the *sιsaok* society, made up usually of high-ranking Bella Coola, having special names. See *BCI* I, 180-2.

36 The reference here is to Franz Boas's monograph, *The Mythology of the Bella Coola Indians* (1898).

37 "Potlatch."

38 Harlan I. Smith (1872-1940) was a museum archaeologist; C. Marius Barbeau (1883-1969) and Diamond Jenness (1886-1969) were museum ethnologists.

39 The first mechanical pencil, introduced in 1915 by Tokuji Hayakawa, who later memorialized his first great invention by naming his burgeoning electronics business the Sharp Corporation.

40 The Eastern Townships in Quebec. Mary McIlwraith was in New York to visit Dorothy.

41 Also spelled "eulachon," "olachen," and "oolichan," the small "candlefish" of the coast, from which Aboriginal people extracted a highly valued edible oil (Kuhlein et al. 1982).

42 Dr. W. Reinhard, provincial medical officer, who was succeeded by Dr. J.C. Carruthers. The white community constructed and managed a small hospital from 1910 to 1928, when the United Church took over its management. Many of the early doctors were well advanced "in their descent to degradation," and few lasted long. "One of them was the local bootlegger, dispensing the liquor in eight-ounce bottles with a label of instructions for suitable dosage. Another ended his life in Hagensborg with an overdose of sleeping pills, after being involved in a shooting affray" (Large 1968, 90).

43 Many of McIlwraith's photographs are retained among the family papers. Some were used in *The Bella Coola Indians,* and some are in albums at Cambridge University's Museum of Archaeology and Anthropology.

44 Harlan I. Smith, an archaeologist at the museum who worked in Bella Coola through the early 1920s.

45 Captain Myers is pictured in Tepper (1991, 188).

46 As we shall see, McIlwraith quickly developed a very close friendship with Captain Schooner.

47 McIlwraith took the Temiskaming and Northern Ontario Railway from Cochrane to North Bay.

48 That is, his sister Dorothy.

49 There were two canneries in the Bella Coola area, the Bella Coola Cannery (owned by British Columbia Packers) and the Tallheo Cannery (owned by Northern British Columbia Packers).

50 Ethlyn Trapp, who was nursing in the Interior. A few years later she returned to McGill, received her MD, and opened a practice in Vancouver.

51 J. Playfair McMurrich (1859-1939), professor of anatomy at the University of Toronto. McMurrich was anxious to hire an anthropologist for the university. He had decided upon McIlwraith after reading Haddon's recommendation and meeting with him, but he was awaiting funding for the position. See Cambridge University Library, Haddon Collection, env. 7, McMurrich to Haddon, 1 March 1922.

52 Charles Trick Currelly (1876-1957), director of the Royal Ontario Museum of Archaeology.

53 See *BCI* I, 5-16, for a list of Nuxalk village sites. Kennedy and Bouchard (1990) provide a detailed map.

54 See *BCI* I, 450, for a brief note on this practice.

55 As we will discover, this is Jim Pollard, with whom McIlwraith later gets on well. He describes him as a Kimsquit villager, descended from Smaoan, one of the earth's first settlers, and "a valuable and reliable informant. Jim is a man of great ability, who has given more potlatches than any other Indian of either Bella Coola or Kimsquit, and who, accordingly, has been able to validate very fully his ancestral myths and the names embodied therein" (*BCI* I, 340). Elsewhere McIlwraith adds: "Essentially practical he has devoted his energies to keeping abreast of changing conditions. He is the best singer and composer in Bella Coola, the best canoeman for miles; he has learnt to handle a motor-boat engine, to aid prospectors for minerals [sic], and has succeeded in amassing and saving a considerable amount of money. Jim excelled all other informants in clearness and logical presentation of his explanation, though he showed a slight tendency, intelligible enough, to gloss over aspects which he knew would be considered unpleasant. If Jim had been a white man, he would undoubtedly have made his mark in the world of business" (*BCI* II, 525). His photograph is seen in Plate 4, *BCI* I.

56 On 12 May 1917 Mary Nelson and her daughter Jessie Saunders were shot dead while working in their garden about two miles from Kimsquit. Iver Fougner, the Indian agent, heard rumours that this was a revenge killing but provided no further details in his initial report of the murders (DIA, vol. 1655, Fougner to Secretary, 17 May 1917; *Bella Coola Courier*, 19 May 1917). In an undated fieldnote, McIlwraith writes: "The ancestral story of Jack King George at Kimsquit is superior to that of Jim Pollard, but the latter has given more lims [sic] than Jack, accordingly he regards himself as superior and this has been a source of constant friction and ill feeling; the sister and mother of Jack King George were murdered a number of years ago and Jim has been suspected of the murder on account of the hard

feeling between the two families" ("Original Part One," n. 1878, p. 683, box 1, ACC. B79-0054, University of Toronto Archives). He revised his opinion in *The Bella Coola Indians*, suggesting that the King George family won the long-term enmity of the Pollards by never compensating them for a name acquired through marriage. Identifying Pollard by his Nuxalk name, McIlwraith suggested that one of Jim's relations committed the murders (*BCI* I, 395-6). He indirectly reaffirms this point later in the monograph, where he reports that a Bella Coola elder put a secret medicine on the neck of each of the corpses and that this resulted, at least in the eyes of the Kimsquit, in the death of the murderer, a Rivers Inlet man (*BCI* I, 719).

There were likely other complications in this case, notably Pollard's role as the chief witness against two Kimsquit men who were jailed for the murder of three men and a woman in a drunken shooting rampage on Dean Channel near the Kimsquit cannery in 1913 (*Bella Coola Courier*, 13 September 1913, 20 September 1913, 15 November 1913, 29 November 1913).

57 Probably A.S. Cruikshank (d. 1924), an honoured Hamilton teacher, is the grandfather to whom McIlwraith is referring.

58 Captain Charles Patrick Hardy was first an Atlantic steamer officer and then became president of Payne and Hardy, insurance brokers in Hamilton. They were family friends, and for several years the elder McIlwraith had a business association with the firm.

59 Florence Delson Sapir suffered from an abscess of the lung as well as schizophrenia. She died in 1924.

60 McIlwraith may be referring here to the smallpox epidemic, which devastated the northern coast tribes in 1862, leaving over 500 Nuxalk dead (Boyd 1990, 144). Boyd was unable to find reliable figures for the Nuxalk population prior to that date, but they must have been affected by the waves of epidemic diseases that swept the coast from 1775 onwards.

61 See Boas (1898).

62 The trouble here was that the Nuxalk insisted that stories were owned by particular ancestral families whose members possessed the sole right to tell them. In theory, McIlwraith should not have heard the same story more than once. In actuality, the elders were quite aware of disputes over the most important names and associated prerogatives. But having these brought into the open by McIlwraith would not only have cost him their trust it would also have forced conflicts into the open (with unpredictable outcomes).

63 In December 1921 Rivers received an invitation to the Labour Party candidacy for the University of London constituency and accepted it in the spring of 1922. Upon his death in June, H.G. Wells succeeded to the nomination – and finished at the bottom of the poll in the 1922 general election.

64 The Nuxalk followed a similar procedure to enhance a dog's ability to hunt beaver: "Wrap the puppy in the freshly removed skin of a beaver and throw it into the river to the accompaniment of hand-clapping from as many as happen to be present. After submersion for a few moments, remove the bundle and throw it in again. Repeat this twice more. This makes the dog grow up unafraid of water and, accordingly, useful in hunting beaver" (*BCI* I, 712).

65 This did not prevent McIlwraith and Harlan I. Smith from learning many details about Nuxalk medical belief and practice. See *BCI* I, 539-94, chap. 11; Smith (1925; 1929).

66 W.H.R. Rivers. See 180n7.

67 "Activities in the canneries would have interfered seriously with my work during the summer of 1922 if two men had not been confined to the village, Captain Schooner owing to an injured wrist, and Jim Pollard by the illness of his wife. These two men were willing to work half a day apiece without jealousy. Each was intensely proud of the traditions of his people and, realizing that their culture was passing away, was glad to assist in making it permanent in writing. An intimacy sprang up between Captain Schooner ... and myself culminating in an adoption, a circumstance which established and improved my position in the community. In this way I was enabled to collect a large amount of material before July when it was necessary for me to leave for the east" (*BCI* I, x). In *The Bella Coola Indians*, McIlwraith wrote that Schooner, "perhaps, came nearest to the original, uncontaminated Bella Coola type. Heavy in build, coarse in humour and expression, he had a heart of gold and was a fine example of a native gentleman. He was glad to assist most patiently in recording ancient lore, being intensely proud of the traditions of his ancestors. A friendship developed from

this which is one of the writer's happiest memories. Often in the evenings life in general was discussed, the war, the rush of progress in big cities, the quest for wealth, the spread of white civilization, and the problems raised by the contact of peoples. Schooner lacked the mental acumen of Joshua Moody and Jim Pollard, but he revealed himself as a tribal patriarch, proud of his family's history and eager to assist his grandchildren and great-grandchildren, but feeling himself lost and helpless in the struggle before them. With sadness, but without bitterness, he used to speak of the approaching end of Bella Coola culture, and his words brought home the tragedy which the spread of civilization brings to so many, and the responsibility resting upon the white people as a whole" (*BCI* II, 525-6). See also McIlwraith's tribute to Captain Schooner in the *Toronto Sunday World* article reprinted in this volume.

Harlan I. Smith (1924, 123) estimated Schooner to be about seventy-four in 1922. A photograph of Schooner appears in *BCI* I, Plate 3.

68 Harlan I. Smith concentrated on the material culture of the Nuxalk. He began to prepare a book but never completed it. His Nuxalk fieldnotes remain at the Canadian Museum of Civilization.

69 Sir Bertram Coghill Alan Windle (1858-1929), since 1919 professor of cosmology and anthropology at St. Michaels College, University of Toronto, and in 1922 special lecturer in ethnology at the university. Sir Bertram's wide-ranging erudition and abundant endowments did not qualify him as an anthropologist.

70 Wilson Dallam Wallis (1886-1970) had studied anthropology under Robert R. Marett while a Rhodes Scholar at Oxford in 1907. He moved from Reed to the University of Minnesota in 1923 and remained there until his retirement in 1954.

71 Here and elsewhere, McIlwraith was unfair in his assessment of Reed College, then and now an outstanding liberal arts institution.

72 Presumably Bert Robson.

73 The note was not published in *Folklore*.

74 In *The Bella Coola Indians* (I, 292), McIlwraith explains that he had not intended to give much attention to ancestral myths because of Boas's previous work on the subject. "The Bella Coola, however, are so intensely proud of the deeds of their first forefathers that several insisted on recounting them before they were willing to do other work." Many of the origin histories were contributed by Jim Pollard.

75 Presumably McIlwraith means that no ceremonies had been performed.

76 McIlwraith gives a detailed account of the funeral and memorial potlatch of Jessie, the wife of Samuel King, in *BCI* I, 474-95.

77 That is, Mr. Peat, the missionary.

78 See also *BCI* I, 477. The Bella Coola Indian Concert Band started in 1917 under the tutelage of Tullef Saugstad, the son of the Norwegian colony's pastor. Captain Schooner's grandson, Andy Schooner, acted as bandmaster from its inception to its demise, some fifty years later (Kopas n.d., 70).

79 The hall was located at the Indian reserve on the north side of the Bella Coola River. For several years it had been "used in place of the several large family homes of old and intermediate styles for ceremonial dances" (Tepper 1991, 32, see photograph no. 49062, p. 35).

80 See *BCI* I, 464-6, for a more detailed description of how mourning songs were composed. The songs on this occasion are described in *BCI* I: 485-6.

81 Reuben Schooner. He is pictured in *BCI* II, Plate 16, and is credited as the composer of several songs (*BCI* II, chap. 2).

82 Well aware that the government forbade potlatching, Captain Schooner had decided to hold the memorial potlatch for his daughter immediately so that the Indian agent would have no chance to suppress it. Some $864 was distributed after the whites had been cleared out (*BCI* I, 491-4).

83 In 1885 the federal government, at the urging of local government agents and missionaries (who saw the custom as detrimental to the promulgation of "civilization" among the Indians), amended the Indian Act to outlaw the potlatch. Enforcement was ineffectual until the Indian agent at Alert Bay undertook a concerted campaign against potlatching in the early 1920s. In April 1922 this resulted in the surrendering of ceremonial paraphernalia to the government and the incarceration of twenty-two individuals in the provincial prison (Cole and

Chaikin 1990, 125; see also LaViolette 1961). The deputy superintendent of the Department of Indian Affairs, Duncan Campbell Scott, was at this time an implacable opponent of Aboriginal traditions and an ardent proponent of Indian assimilation (Titley 1986). All the same, the anti-potlatching provisions of the Indian Act seem not to have been too vigorously enforced in Bella Coola. Iver Fougner, the Indian agent, had written to his superiors the previous November defending the winter dances and had received permission to use his "discretion" as to whether or not to interfere. He chose not to (Cole and Chaikin 1990, 125).

84 One must suppose that McIlwraith is writing about Christianity in general. There is no indication from his letters that the local missionary, Mr. Peat, held any particular attitude towards potlatching and other Nuxalk ceremonies or that he tried to suppress them.

85 He died suddenly on 4 June 1922 from an intestinal obstruction.

86 Oddly, McIlwraith does not identify the people involved nor link them with the funeral described in the previous letter. The "Indian friend" was actually Captain Schooner and the deceased relative his daughter Mrs. Jessie King. The alleged "poisoner," or sorcerer, was Willie Mack. Harlan I. Smith (1925, 120-1) relates the incident in his "Sympathetic Magic and Witchcraft among the Bellacoola." Jessie King's death had an unhappy aftermath, which McIlwraith later drew upon to illustrate the point that, "if it is believed that a man will die, he is almost certain to do so. In June 1922, a woman died in Bella Coola and her father claimed that she had been murdered by a certain man either with material poison or by magical means. He took no direct steps to revenge but stated emphatically that the man whom he suspected would die within a year. The threatened man knew this, and more than once said that he would probably fall a victim. He became ill in May 1923, and, though treated by a white doctor, grew steadily worse until he died in the latter part of June, three weeks after the year had elapsed. All the Bella Coola believe that this was due to the power of thought ... The doctor who attended this man stated that his patient had shown symptoms of melancholy and resignation during his last sickness; it seems clear that the expectation of death must have lessened his chance of recovery." He describes Schooner as "a powerful chief whose thoughts were accordingly potent" (*BCI* I, 697-8). Many Nuxalk believed that Mack's ghost took its revenge, killing Schooner a few days after his own death (737).

87 It actually retained the Norwegian spelling "Hagensborg."

88 McIlwraith is referring to the townsite here. There was a Methodist church on the Indian reserve.

89 Revivalists still stir the Aboriginal and White populations of the valley, although the Hagenborg church itself became part of the United Church of Canada in 1949.

90 Shore Pine (*P. contorta* Dougl. ex Loudon var. *contorta*) is probably meant.

91 The guide was Charlie West, also known as "Pretty," or "Handsome," Charlie, a Ulkatcho-Carrier who served as Smith's chief informant (Tepper 1991, 203). Wilfred Christensen recalled watching McIlwraith's progress up to the cave through Smith's binoculars (Wilfred Christensen interview, Bella Coola, 23 August 1991).

92 Details of McIlwraith's discovery of this practice appear in *BCI* I, 404-5.

93 McIlwraith came to a somewhat different conclusion when he wrote his monograph. He concluded that internment had always been the most common form of burial while tree burial was a relatively rare but fully accepted alternative (*BCI* I, 450).

94 *Nusmät·a,* the huge house of the supreme deity, *Äɬquntäm,* which is located in the flat land above the sky.

95 Sisauk is McIlwraith's alternate spelling of the *sɪsaok* ceremony.

96 Senior members of the *kusiut* impressed upon McIlwraith "that the most important duty of each member is to aid in impressing and deceiving the uninitiated (*BCI* II, 10), a goal that, in extreme instances, could necessitate murder. "Deception," in fact, struck the anthropologist as a major theme in Nuxalk culture – one that ran through most spiritual endeavours but that was most clearly evident in the secret societies and shamanism. However, McIlwraith (*BCI* II, 13) notes repeatedly that Nuxalk, though highly credulous of the supernatural, frequently saw through human-made performances but still chose to accept their reality, "entirely failing to use their common sense." Subsequent research on "secret" rituals, particularly in Melanesian societies, suggests that there is considerably more general knowledge

of these rituals than may at first meet the eye. The "deceived" act as performers within a larger religious drama – both deception and being deceived being aspects of stagecraft. In any case, by the 1920s, as McIlwraith found through personal experience the following year, the *kusiut* ceremonies held few secrets from the audience.

97 As we shall see, McIlwraith witnessed parts of the elaborate "Cannibal Dance" during the winter ceremonials of 1923-4.

98 In *The Golden Bough*, James Frazer (1922) speculated that most magical practices rested upon a belief that things operate upon each other over a distance through a sympathetic connection, either because they resemble each other or because they have some sort of symbolic connection.

99 Sapir was in the field near Calgary, working among the Sarcee, an Athapaskan group.

100 Provincial Archives of British Columbia, C.F. Newcombe Papers, McIlwraith to Newcombe, 28 August 1922.

101 Sir Grafton Elliot Smith (1871-1937), anatomist and anthropologist at University College, London.

102 Rivers's major work, published in two volumes in 1914 by Cambridge University Press.

103 Berthold Laufer (1874-1934), then a senior curator of anthropology at the Field Museum of Natural History in Chicago. Laufer was an outstanding scholar of Chinese and Tibetan cultures. Needless to say, not all would agree with McIlwraith (and Rivers's) dismissive assessment of collection practices at the Field.

104 Robert R. Marett (1866-1943) was reader in social anthropology at Oxford. His students also included Marius Barbeau and Diamond Jenness.

105 See 184n83.

106 Wilfred Christensen recalls that both Whites and Aboriginals made a variety of simple home brews by mixing yeast and sugar with berries, potatoes, peaches, canned tomatoes, or cherries (Interview, 25 July 1994). Whites also made dandelion wine, although this was not popular with the Nuxalk. As McIlwraith's letters make very clear, both the Aboriginal and White communities suffered from considerable alcohol abuse.

107 Presumably Captain Schooner.

108 See *BCI* I, 404-5, for details and evidence. Kennedy and Bouchard (1990, 328) question McIlwraith's conclusions, but, working among the Tlingit in Alaska, de Laguna (1990, 217-18) was told of high-ranking women in non-fraternal polyandrous unions.

109 There is a slight error here as Smith's presence was noted in a 17 June letter.

110 Boas (1898).

111 Also known as Alkatcho Carriers. The "Dene Syllabary" was a script devised in the 1880s by Father Adrien Gabriel Morice, OMI (1859-1938), and quickly adopted by the Carrier.

112 These, presumably, are Cambridge Museum numbers 1924.753-761, listed as donated by T.F. McIlwraith per A.C. Haddon. They include a stone adze head, fragments of an old coffin, three cedar-bark baskets, and, most notably, a *sɪsaok* mask.

113 C.F. Newcombe, M.D. (1851-1924), a British physician and naturalist who settled in Oregon, then Victoria. He became a major museum collector of Northwest Coast Aboriginal material and a resident expert on British Columbia Aboriginal peoples. In 1922 he was travelling with Pliny Earle Goddard of the American Museum of Natural History.

114 Haddon had been at the Alaska-Yukon-Pacific Exposition in Seattle in 1904.

115 Frank Armitage Potts (1872-1945), lecturer in zoology and demonstrator in comparative anatomy at Cambridge, had voyaged with Newcombe along the coast in the summer of 1911.

116 Further information on Roys is provided below in a note to McIlwraith's letter of 22 September 1923.

117 Probably the Thorson Creek site (Hill and Hill 1974, 168-72).

118 A heel ball is cobbler's wax; Reckitt's blue was a brand of fabric blueing that came in cube form.

The Second Season, September 1923 to March 1924

1 The hoist winch on the deck aft of the cargo hold used to lift and lower freight.

2 Ralph Loveland Roys (1879-1965), who would become a major figure in Maya studies, known principally for his transcriptions and translations of Mayan texts. From 1911 to 1940 Roys

lived in Vancouver, working at his family's lumber business and visiting Mexico during the "slack season" to pursue his scholarly passion (Thompson 1967).

3 "The Ritual of the Chiefs of Yucatan" (Roys 1923).

4 The surviving letters are all addressed to McIlwraith's father.

5 Smith attended Schooner's funeral in the Bella Coola dance hall on 25 July. Following the ceremony, he took several photographs of a dancer wearing a button blanket and a Heiltsuk mask belonging to Reuben Schooner. These represented his father's story (Tepper 1991, 130-1).

6 See 185n86 concerning these deaths. According to his son, Clayton, Willie Mack was about forty-six when he died from a burst appendix (Mack 1993, 20). He is featured dressed in a number of costumes and masks in a series of photographs taken by Harlan Smith in June and July 1922 (Tepper 1990, 115-24). McIlwraith apparently was not aware that Willie Mack was the son of John Clayton, a prominent trader in Bella Coola (see 187n11), and Q'uit, a Nuxalk woman who was his first wife.

7 This project is not mentioned in the annual reports of the Department of Parks for the period, which would seem to indicate that it received little serious consideration in Ottawa.

8 In August 1924 the Necleetsconnay again tore through the White town again, causing serious damage, and the decision was made to move the settlement across the river to its present site on land once owned by John Clayton, a former Hudson's Bay Company factor and local businessman. The Brynildsens, to whom McIlwraith is probably referring, rebuilt their store a block from the Christensen establishment. The Nuxalk moved from the north side of the Bella Coola River to their present location east of the White community following a serious flood in November 1938 (Kopas 1974, 266-7, 272-3).

9 Iris Peers Scott, affectionately called "Ips" by the Christensen children (Wilfred Christensen interview, Bella Coola, 25 July 1994).

10 As we shall see, this was J.C. Carruthers. Before McIlwraith arrived, the Bella Coola Hospital Board decided to fire the doctor and shut down the hospital (Bella Coola Hospital Minute Book, 1 August 1923, Add. MSS 1474, Reel A-0704, Provincial Archives of British Columbia). McIlwraith's letters indicate the good sense of this but give no indication that it was done.

11 Elizabeth Clayton, the widow of John Clayton, a trader who had bought out the interests of the Hudson's Bay Company in both Bella Bella and Bella Coola in the early 1880s and went on to establish several businesses in the two communities. Vinny was her son and Dorothy her daughter. In 1923 the Claytons lived on the south side of the Bella Coola River in the old Hudson's Bay Company house some distance from the townsite.

12 The previous spring, his mother was diagnosed with cancer. She died in August.

13 Sapir was at Camp Red Cloud, Pennsylvania, studying two Yukon Athapaskan languages, work made possible by the presence of two Alaskan Aboriginals in the camp.

14 This was the death of Willie Mack.

15 McIlwraith is obviously referring here to his problems with Nuxalk phonetics. See also his letter to Sapir, 15 January 1924, below.

16 More commonly known as "Coho" salmon.

17 Located at the head of Cousins Inlet near Bella Bella, Ocean Falls was a vibrant company town whose economic life centred on a massive state-of-the-art pulp and paper mill. The mill closed in 1980.

18 Mary McIlwraith Brian suggests that this might refer to Twelve Mile Creek, a favourite family picnic place a short distance northwest of Hamilton.

19 By this time most such easily accessible Aboriginal cemeteries had been stripped clean of artefacts (and often skeletons) by collectors. In his *Captured Heritage: The Scramble for Northwest Coast Artifacts,* Douglas Cole (1985) provides a useful discussion of the ethics of grave theft during an earlier period.

20 Susie Christensen, who married Murray Rhodes of Ocean Falls.

21 Ethel S. Fegan of Girton College, Cambridge. She assisted in the university museum, especially in the library.

22 An opening at the University of Cape Town, where A.R. Radcliffe-Brown, formerly of Cambridge, was establishing an anthropology department and a school of African studies.

23 Given the recent arrests in Alert Bay (see 184n83), McIlwraith had reason to fear that the winter dances might be called off. It seems highly unlikely, however, that he himself would run much danger of being arrested for participating in them.
24 Presumably an adaptation of Longfellow's famous poem.
25 Louis Colville Gray Clarke (1881-1960), curator of the Cambridge Museum of Archaeology and Ethnology from 1922 to 1927.
26 McIlwraith indicated in his letter to Haddon on 29 August 1922 that he had already been given three names. These, however, would not have been validated in a potlatch or related ceremony.
27 During the summer of 1923 Clarke had participated with archaeologists from the Museum of the American Indian in a major excavation at early Pueblo village sites near Zuni.
28 The dog appears with its human companions in Plate 11 in *BCI,* I. McIlwraith explains that its owner, almost certainly "Steamboat" Annie and her husband Tallio Charlie, were childless and so bestowed some ancestral names upon their dog, validating this action with presents. Consequently, when the dog died "it [would have been] mourned as a chief," and its owners had in fact already begun amassing return presents to be used at the dog's funeral (*BCI* I, 175). McIlwraith indicates that the dog had accumulated at least five names originating in four ancestral stories related to him by Steamboat Annie (*BCI* I, 130, 310, 322, 356).
29 A mattress.
30 Clayton Mack recalled in 1991 that his mother, Mary, told McIlwraith stories "all day," with his sister, Eliza, providing a translation (Clayton Mack interview, Bella Coola, 21 August 1991).
31 Unfortunately, we are missing McIlwraith's previous letter to his father and sister, but he is almost certainly referring here to his part in the rescue of young Wilfred Christensen under horrific conditions. He briefly describes the incident in a later letter to Haddon (16 March 1924) (see 192n98).
32 See also McIlwraith's letter to his father dated 6 October 1923. In 1903 the Bella Coola Pulp and Paper Company acquired the site, which had a good anchorage and a nearby source of cheap hydroelectric power. Within a year of the new pulp mill going into operation, the (now) Ocean Falls Limited went into receivership and was taken over by Pacific Mills Limited, which successfully expanded the operation (Anonymous 2000).
33 Andy Christensen, the eldest of the Christensen children. As we shall see, McIlwraith acted as the best man at his wedding.
34 O.E. Prud'homme, artist for the Anthropology Division of the museum.
35 Boas was in Bella Bella in November and December 1923. George Hunt (1854-1933), an English-Tlingit man who grew up in Fort Rupert, served as an assistant to several anthropologists, especially Boas.
36 *The World's Work* was a popular monthly magazine.
37 The Hamilton Tigers football team, known as the Tiger-Cats since 1950.
38 As we shall see, McIlwraith had assumed the position of a "marshal." Traditionally, each village had four or five marshals who had the special duty of preserving the "dignity and awe of the society" (*BCI* II, 15-16). Among other duties and privileges, the marshals ate first at *kusiut* performances and gave the first address to the audience. They punished infringements of the *kusiut* and possessed the right to strike and even kill offenders (*BCI* II, 16-17).
39 "It was always a sign of poverty if a person were obliged to eat berries without olachen grease" (*BCI* I, 3; see also *BCI* II, Appendix A). Nuxalk continue to enjoy similar dishes, as is indicated by the berry soup recipe in *Kanusyam a Snknic – "Real Good Food": A Nuxalk Recipe Book* (Program 1985, 100).
40 McIlwraith reflects on this experience in his *Toronto Sunday World* article, which is included in this book: "Closing his eyes and hoping that he would not be ill on the spot he swallowed a mouthful. It tasted as it smelt, horrible. But details of this kind must be experienced by an anthropologist as part of the day's work. Though he never grew to like this Indian delicacy, after a few meals the investigator was able to eat it without experiencing the stomach-ache which followed his first taste."
41 This is almost certainly McIlwraith's early rendering of the name *Xwotsɛ̓kmis,* translated in *BCI* II as "The Destroyer" (16) and "The One Whose Work Has Failed" (629). This was

the professional name of a *kusiut* marshal, originally created "on account of an elaborate *kusiut* ritual that failed" and passed through time as an ancestral prerogative.

42 "*Kukusiut* are always ready to assist one of their fellows, so that three or four friends are always willing to accompany the dancer ... Particularly in those dances fraught with danger to the performer, it is customary for any number of his friends, either men or women, to dance to 'help' him" (*BCI* II, 46-7).

43 McIlwraith can surely be forgiven for this incautious claim. Many Whites had witnessed Nuxalk ceremonials over the years and some took part in them, although perhaps not to the extent that McIlwraith did (see Mack 1994). A possible exception is a rather mysterious individual, Samuel Shields, or "White Sam," who plays a large romantic role in Kopas's (1974, 139-63, 187-97) popular history of Bella Coola. According to Kopas, Shields was raised by the Hudson's Bay Company factor, George Clayton, after being stranded in Bella Coola at age fourteen. He became close with the Nuxalk, learned their language, and was eventually adopted, taking the name Quinoa and then marrying a Nuxalk woman. Kopas's White Sam becomes a leading chief, giving many potlatches, rising up through the ranks of the secret societies, gaining fame as a warrior, and negotiating relations between the Nuxalk and the Whites. Although McIlwraith relates several of the same war stories as does Kopas, he makes no mention of either a White Sam or Quinoa. However, he does list "Qwinao" as an ancestral name of a Kimsquit family, which does fit Kopas's account (*BCI* II, 608). Smith took a photograph of "White Sam" (Tepper 1991, 206), and Clayton Mack (1994) remembered him as a White man who lived with Aboriginal people and spoke only Nuxalk.

44 "The uninitiated, and perhaps some of the *kukusiut* as well, believe that Cannibals are carried away to the land above where they are exposed to great dangers, and to prevent this an effort is always made to bind the dancer" (*BCI* II, 72). This drama, which McIlwraith describes at greater length in the *BCI* II (73-4), also occurs early in the ceremonies surrounding the Scratcher Dance.

45 Eagle down typically marked occasions as being ceremonial. McIlwraith does not report on any further symbolic significance. See *BCI* I, 109, 223.

46 "As his songs are sung, [the cannibal] dances in the usual *kusiut* style, but more violently than most, and growling at intervals. The women drone and his four guardians stand close by, spitting into his ears to soothe him" (*BCI* II, 83). In his letter to Fanny Rose Haddon on 9 December, McIlwraith identifies this as a cannibal dance, although he makes it clear that the Nuxalk did not consider him to be an initiate.

47 See *BCI* II, Plate 2, for a photograph of *kusiut* whistles. As the voices of the supernatural sponsors of the dances, they have an importance second only to the masks (*BCI* II, 28).

48 A private boys' high school in Hamilton that McIlwraith had attended.

49 This was *Änoᵒlikwotsaix,* who appeared at every *kusiut* performance. She is said to have deposited all of the ancestral prerogatives in various repositories in Nuxalk territory. "*Änoᵒlikwotsaix* travels only during the ceremonial season when she is present at every *kusiut* dance in the form of a woman with a long, thin face and pointed chin ... who 'explains' the significance of the figures to the uninitiated in a peculiar high-pitched voice. She is well able to do so since as guardian of repositories she knows the prerogative of each member of the society" (*BCI* II, 9). See also Plate 13.

50 McIlwraith refers to such figures as Laughers, or Clowns, in *The Bella Coola Indians.* Few men can make the hoarse sound for long, "and they are always asked to appear as comedians. They are entitled to make witticisms, often of an obscene nature, at the expense of any of the spectators." The Clowns would be called out at various times "to keep the audience amused while waiting for the more important beings" (*BCI* II, 179).

51 A copy of "Good King Wenselaus," typed on McIlwraith's machine, can be found among his original fieldnotes: McIlwraith papers, no. 3004, box 12, B79-0054, University of Toronto Archives.

52 The exact line is, "To make me forget the thing I am and the man I used to be," from Service's "The Low-Down White," published in *Spell of the Yukon and Other Verses* (1907).

53 Spiritual Thunder and his human representative are considered the senior *kusiut* in both the upper land and on earth. Thunder calls upon all supernatural beings to witness his dances; the earthly dancer may do the same. The thunder dance was performed as part of several

kusiut ceremonies. It has continued into the present as one of the favourite and most important Nuxalk performances. See *BCI* II, 205-11 and Plate 9.

54 After Thunder finishes each circuit of the central fire, "Rainwater appears and drenches the audience, as rain accompanies a thunder-storm. The dramatic skill displayed is always impressive" (*BCI* II, 207). In a 1991 performance witnessed by John Barker, the part of the rain was played by Laughers, who sprinkled members of the audience with water from soda cans.

55 In the early ceremony, *Tƚoqots* (the Defamer) appeared with Thunder's herald, calling upon supernatural beings not to come even a̧s the herald summoned them. Wearing a "Huge mask" and said to be jealous of Thunder, *Tƚoqots* "does his utmost to belittle Thunder," adding "a touch of comic realism" to the ceremony (*BCI* II, 182-3, 206-7).

56 The Nuxalk had their own version of the Cannibal Dance, described at some length in *BCI* II, 71-117. In *BCI* McIlwraith gives somewhat contradictory information about the performance described in this letter. He states that the Fort Rupert dance was performed in Bella Coola for the first time in 1923-4 by *Ƚxwuntnam,* a Kwakiutl man who "had long been resident in Bella Coola" (*BCI* II, 309); but elsewhere he credits the son of "an old Kimsquit Indian" who had long lived in Smith Inlet and had inherited the dance from his mother (*BCI* II, 117). The song used for this dance was composed and/or translated by Kimsquit Alec and later recorded for McIlwraith by Jim Pollard. Its text is given in *BCI* II, 309.

57 That is, the cause of the dancer's possession. The Nuxalk had only a vague knowledge of this figure, which resembled their own *haohao*, a large supernatural bird (*BCI* II, 117).

58 Although the Nuxalk Cannibal Dance resembles the more famous *hamatsa* of the Kwakwa̱ka̱'wakw (Kwakiutl), it is based on a different understanding of supernatural empowerment. McIlwraith notes that the Nuxalk were intensely interested in the spectacle of the Kwakiutl dance, especially the representation of the cannibal spirit as a huge snapping bird: "one had only to listen to their remarks when wondering what it might be, to be convinced that the Cannibal spirit is a strange concept to them … The Bella Coola greatly admired the dance, and were by no means ashamed to confess their inferiority as dancers to the Kwakiutl" (*BCI* II, 117).

59 The elaborate marriage exchanges are described in *BCI* I, chap. 7. The most important of these, the "repurchasing" of wives, entailed the transfer of wealth and ancestral prerogatives between families and generations. In 1923 this was "one of the few customs preserved tenaciously amid the ruins of their ancient culture" (*BCI* I, 414).

60 McIlwraith probably received the name *X̣ekαlus,* which referred to an infamous corpse-eating cannibal. "This name had been dormant for a number of years until conferred on the writer, who failed to uphold the prerogative" (*BCI* II, 110).

61 McIlwraith felt awkward about being placed in a situation where he might have to praise Nuxalk traditions before the representatives of official assimilation. See his letter to Harlan Smith, 7 January 1924, below.

62 In his letter to Haddon, 16 March 1924, McIlwraith identifies this as a *sιsaok* costume. See *BCI* I, 206-7 for a description.

63 For more details, see *BCI* I, 376, 393-5. Annette B. Weiner's *Inalienable Possessions* (1992) provides a useful, if controversial, general discussion of how "inalienable" objects are transacted in small-scale societies.

64 This was Jim Pollard.

65 Rendered as *äs·iko·tƚ* in the *BCI* (II, 580) glossary, it translates as "second part of a song" and as "second oldest sibling."

66 The Bella Coola marriage register, including the page recording Andy and Dorothy's wedding, is preserved in the United Church Archives at the Vancouver School of Theology.

67 *Qoƚliaotεmx̂,* a figure in the Cannibal complex of dances. See *BCI* II, 113-14.

68 Possibly H.D. Tanton, listed in *Wrigley's B.C. Directory* as a silver/black fox farmer.

69 That is, soapberries *(Shepherdia canadensis).*

70 Rendered as *älxotƚa* in the *BCI.*

71 McIlwraith includes two additional lines in Nuxalk, presumably listing his other names, but the handwriting is too faint to make out accurately. *Wina* was McIlwraith's own favourite name, and the name by which he was later remembered by the Nuxalk as well as by close friends in the White community. The term refers primarily to a raiding party and, by

extension, a warrior, but it "is also applied to a context in any game of skill, especially one in which teams or individuals from different villages take part" (*BCI* I, 620). In the 1970s Dorothy Kennedy was told that McIlwraith got the name after roaming through the Indian village singing the song that occurs in a well known story, "Raven and the Berries" (Kennedy, personal communication). Two versions of the story appear as "Raven and His Sisters" in *The Bella Coola Indians* (II, 408-10). See also "At Home with the Bella Coola Indians" in this volume, where McIlwraith renders his name as "Weena."

72 See *BCI* II, 239, for a brief description of the dance. McIlwraith also records a story, "The Orphan Hunter" (second version), which involves supernatural cedar-bark beaters (*BCI* I, 639-40).

73 See *BCI* II, 192, for a brief description. The salmon was probably part of the Supernatural Bark-Beater Dance, but it could also have been part of the dance of *Winwina* (*BCI* II, 187-96).

74 The Mosquito often accompanied the dance of Thunder. During the performance, Thunder's herald explains to the audience that Thunder would like to taste human flesh but is both too big and too hot; so he sends Mosquito as his messenger. While the figure might appear to be rather comic, McIlwraith was convinced that it demonstrated the fear *kusiut* dancers could inspire in the uninitiated – those who stood in danger of being jabbed (*BCI* II, 207-8).

75 The "*haohao* is an enormous bird with bony wings and long, flexible beak. As it flies, the wings rattle violently, and its note, an oft repeated 'Hao, hao, hao,' can be heard for miles ... The *haohao* is feared for its practice of inserting its long beak into the rectum of anyone sleeping carelessly in the forest and drawing forth his entrails" (*BCI* I, 64). The dance and giant masks are briefly described in *BCI* II, 186.

76 The reference is to the Hamilton Tigers football club.

77 By Alfred Noyes (1880-1958).

78 A.M. Cunningham and Son, prominent Hamilton photographers.

79 Sapir (1916). Other offprints could have been any of a number of Sapir's pieces on the Nuu-Chah-Nulth ("Nootka") and Northwest Coast.

80 The British Association for the Advancement of Science met in Toronto, 6 to 13 August 1924. McIlwraith's paper, "Certain Aspects of the Potlatch in Bella Coola," was read on 12 August. It is reprinted in this book.

81 William Ridgeway (1853-1926), a classical specialist who was a fellow of Gonville and Cauis College, Cambridge; Disney Professor of Archaeology; and Brereton Reader in Classics.

82 There is some confusion here. Clarke had written Sapir on 11 November and Sapir had replied to him on 23 November expressing absolutely no objection to McIlwraith collecting for Cambridge (Sapir Papers, Canadian Ethnology Service, Canadian Museum of Civilization).

83 See *BCI* I, 167, for a fuller explanation of this "adoption," probably by Steamboat Annie. The woman gave presents to validate her adoption, thus "saving herself from the disgrace of having one of her songs used as if it were a matter of no consequence, free to anyone."

84 When beaten with an equal amount of water, soapberries yield a light froth popularly known as "Indian ice cream." Prized by many First Nations peoples, others find the sour-bitter foam an acquired taste (Turner 1975, 133-6).

85 "The Siwashes [Indians] of the interior are called 'Stick Indians' because they live among the timber and call all trees sticks" (*Bella Coola Courier*, 31 May 1913, p. 1, Public Archives of British Columbia).

86 Unfortunately, McIlwraith's previous letter, which must have provided details of this incident, is now missing.

87 McIlwraith is probably referring here to a tendency, beginning in the 1860s, for men to seek wives outside their own ancestral families. Prior to this marriages tended to be endogamous. McIlwraith (*BCI* I, 121, 378) did not believe that this change had been triggered by White intrusion. He notes in Chapter 7, however, that by the 1920s marriage had become less important as a means of transferring ancestral prerogatives. To an increasing extent, young people arranged their own marriages based on mutual attraction and resisted lengthy engagements with their associated exchanges. A large number of marriages now ended in divorce.

88 Compare with McIlwraith's early speculations on Nuxalk ideas in his letter to Rivers, 3

March 1922. His mature conclusions on Nuxalk conceptions of the human "spirit" and "life" can be found in *BCI* I, 94-100.

89 According to Sapir's annual report, fifty-eight records and 118 pages of transcriptions/translations (Canada, Parliament, *Sessional Papers*, 1925, vol. 2, no. 15, p. 39).

90 "It was soon found that few people were qualified to sing into the machine. Some became confused and forgot the words; some began to laugh; and some lacked the poise to attempt to sing. One elderly Kimsquit man, Jim Pollard, was found to be the best and most reliable singer, and he was used almost exclusively for phonographic work." (*BCI* II, 267). Many of the texts are reproduced in *BCI* II, chap. 2. By the 1970s the quality of most of the records McIlwraith had recorded had deteriorated to the point where the sounds could no longer be made out (Kolstee 1982).

91 Catalogued by the National Museum of Man under nos. VII D 441-464. His 1922 collection is no. VII D 284-322.

92 "The Bella Coola agree that the most important of their supernatural beings is *Äɬquntäm*, the supreme deity, the maker of man and animals ... The word *Äɬquntäm* is said to derive from xquntam, 'foreman,' or 'chief.' He is chief of the supernatural beings" (*BCI* I, 32).

93 In a letter to McIlwraith dated 18 March 1924, Sapir replied, "if you assure me it is something which would justify a glowing feeling in the region of the heart (or is it liver in Bella Coola belief?), I am prepared to be exceedingly flattered and pleased" (T.F. McIlwraith records, B72-0030, box 2, University of Toronto Archives).

94 This presumably refers to the institution of a chair at the University of Sydney, which A.R. Radcliffe-Brown occupied from 1925 to 1931.

95 A New York journal, published weekly.

96 McIlwraith's father had moved to Burlington. John Street was his business address.

97 See 184n83.

98 See McIlwraith's letter to his father, 11 November 1923. Seventy years later Wilfred Christensen remembered the incident vividly, although he had forgotten about McIlwraith's part in his rescue. On 5 November Wilfred and two friends came across a partly cut alder while hiking on the south side of the Bella Coola valley. One of his friends hacked at the tree with a hatchet. It suddenly fell, knocking Wilfred on the head and pinning his right leg. Wilfred regained consciousness with his badly twisted leg in excruciating pain. One of the boys ran to the store for help. A fisherman returned, splinted the leg, and helped carry Wilfred on a stretcher back to the town. The doctor arrived, reeking of vanilla and rum, and declared that Wilfred's ankle was merely sprained. After the rough night trip to Ocean Falls, Wilfred spent two weeks in hospital (his right leg was broken in two places). He returned on crutches to Bella Coola on 24 December (Wilfred Christensen interview, Bella Coola, 25 July 1994).

99 The partially constructed basket is Cambridge Museum of Archaeology and Anthropology no. 1924.689 and is listed as Nootka. The tump line is no. 1924.690, catalogued as "Esquimalt Sanitch." Both were procured while McIlwraith was visiting Charles Newcombe.

Observations on the Medical Lore of the Bella Coola Indians

1 One of the names by which the woman is known; this would henceforth be his designation as shaman (note in original).

2 Formerly there were singer-musicians in every Bella Coola village who played a leading part in all rituals (note in original).

References

Anonymous. 2000. "A Brief History of Ocean Falls." Victoria: British Columbia Public Archives. Available at <http://www.bcarchives.gov.bc.ca/exhibits/timemach/galler02/frames/oceanhis.htm> (accessed October 2002).

Barker, John. 1987a. "'At Home with the Bella Coola Indians' by T.F. McIlwraith." *BC Studies* 75: 43-60.

–. 1987b. "T.F. McIlwraith and Anthropology at the University of Toronto, 1925-1963." *Canadian Review of Sociology and Anthropology* 24, 2: 252-68.

–. 1992. "T.F. McIlwraith among the Nuxalk (Bella Coola Indians)." In *The Bella Coola Indians,* ed. T.F. McIlwraith. ix-xxxvii. Toronto: University of Toronto Press.

–. 2000. "Toward a History of Canadian Departments of Anthropology (Comment)." *Anthropologica* 42: 95-7.

Boas, Franz. 1898. *The Mythology of the Bella Coola Indians.* Memoirs of the American Museum of Natural History, vol. 2. Anthropology, vol. 1, part 2. *The Jesup North Pacific Expedition,* vol. 1, part 2.

Boyd, Robert T. 1990. "Demographic History, 1774-1874." In *Handbook of North American Indians.* Vol. 7: *Northwest Coast,* ed. W. Suttles, 135-48. Washington, DC: Smithsonian Institution.

Burke, Colleen. 1993. "The Politics of Representation: A 'Rational' History of the Ethnological Collections of the National Museum of Canada 1910-1925." MA thesis, Carleton University.

Codere, Helen. 1966. Introduction to *Kwakiutl Ethnography,* ed. F. Boas. xi-xxxii. Chicago: University of Chicago Press.

Cole, Douglas. 1973. "The Origins of Canadian Anthropology, 1850-1910." *Journal of Canadian Studies* 8, 1: 33-45.

–. 1982. "Franz Boas and the Bella Coola in Berlin." *Northwest Anthropological Research Notes* 16, 2: 115-24.

–. 1985. *Captured Heritage: The Scramble for Northwest Coast Artifacts.* Seattle: University of Washington Press. Reprint, Vancouver: UBC Press, 1995.

Cole, Douglas, and Ira Chaikin. 1990. *An Iron Hand upon the People: The Law against the Potlatch on the Northwest Coast.* Vancouver: Douglas and McIntyre.

Darnell, Regna. 1998. "Toward a History of Canadian Departments of Anthropology: Retrospect, Prospect and Common Cause." *Anthropologica* 40, 2: 153-68.

de Laguna, Frederica. 1990. "Tlingit." In *Handbook of North American Indians.* Vol. 7: *Northwest Coast,* ed. W. Suttles, 203-28. Washington, DC: Smithsonian Institution.

Frazer, J.G. 1922. *The Golden Bough.* London: Macmillan.

Gruber, Jacob W. 1970. "Ethnographic Salvage and the Shaping of Anthropology." *American Anthropologist* 72: 1289-99.

Haddon, Kathleen. 1930. *Artists in String: String Figures; Their Regional Distribution and Social Significance.* London: Methuen.

Hill, Beth, and Ray Hill. 1974. *Indian Petroglyphs of the Pacific Northwest.* Saanichton, BC: Hancock House.

Jackson, Jean E. 1990. "'I Am a Fieldnote': Fieldnotes as a Symbol of Professional Identity." In *Fieldnotes: The Makings of Anthropology,* ed. R. Sanjek, 3-33. Ithaca: Cornell University Press.

Kennedy, Dorothy, and Randy Bouchard. 1990. "Bella Coola." In *Handbook of North American Indians.* Vol. 7: *Northwest Coast,* ed. W. Suttles, 329-39. Washington, DC: Smithsonian Institution.

Kirk, Ruth. 1986. *Wisdom of the Elders: Native Traditions on the Northwest Coast.* Vancouver: Douglas and McIntyre.

Kolstee, Anton F. 1982. *Bella Coola Indian Music: A Study of the Interaction between Northwest Coast Indian Structures and Their Functional Context.* Ottawa: National Museum of Canada.

Kopas, Cliff. 1974. *Bella Coola.* Vancouver: Tenas Tiktik Publishing.

–. n.d. "The Bible in Bella Coola." In *United Church Archives.* Vancouver: Vancouver School of Theology.

Kuhlein, Harriet V., Alvin C. Chan, J. Neville Thompson, and Shuryo Nakai. 1982. "Oolichan Grease: A Nutritious Fat Used by Native People of Coastal British Columbia." *Journal of Ethnobiology* 2, 2: 154-61.

Large, R. Geddes. 1968. *Drums and Scalpel: From Native Healers to Physicians on the North Pacific Coast.* Vancouver: Mitchell Press.

LaViolette, F.E. 1961. *The Struggle for Survival: Indian Cultures and the Protestant Ethic in British Columbia.* Toronto: University of Toronto Press.

Loram, C.T., and T.F. McIlwraith, eds. 1943. T*he North American Indians Today.* Toronto: University of Toronto Press.

Mack, Clayton. 1993. *Grizzlies and White Guys: The Stories of Clayton Mack.* Madeira, BC: Harbour Publishing.

–. 1994. *Bella Coola Man: More Stories of Clayton Mack.* Madeira Park, BC: Harbour Publishing.

Malinowski, Bronislaw. 1922. *Argonauts of the Western Pacific.* New York: Dutton.

McIlwraith, T.F. 1922. "Egyptian Influence on African Death-Rites." British Association for the Advancement of Science. *Report of the Eighty-Ninth Meeting,* 442-3. London: John Murray.

–. 1922-4. "Bella Coola Fieldnotes." In Manuscript Collection No. 60. University of Toronto, Rare Book Collection.

–. 1925. "Certain Beliefs of the Bella Coola Indians Concerning Animals." Ontario Provincial Museum, Archaeological Report for 1924-5, 17-27.

–. 1948. *The Bella Coola Indians.* 2 vols. Toronto: University of Toronto Press.

–. 1964. "Facts and Their Recognition among the Bella Coola." In *Fact and Theory in Social Science,* ed. G.T. Bowles. Syracuse: Syracuse University Press.

Mead, Margaret. 1977. *Letters from the Field, 1925-1975.* New York: Harper and Row.

Nater, H.F. 1984. *The Bella Coola Language.* Ottawa: National Museum of Man.

–. 1990. *A Concise Nuxalk English Dictionary.* Hull: Canadian Museum of Civilization.

Program, Nuxalk Food and Nutrition. 1985. *Kanusyam a Snknic – "Real Good Food": A Nuxalk Recipe Book.* Bella Coola: Nuxalk Food and Nutrition Program.

Rivers, W.H.R. 1910. "The Genealogical Method of Anthropogical Inquiry." *Sociological Review* 3: 1-12.

–. 1914. *Kinship and Social Organization.* London: Constable.

Rohner, Ronald P. 1969. *The Ethnography of Franz Boas.* Chicago: University of Chicago Press.

Roys, Ralph L. 1923. "The Ritual of the Chiefs of the Yucatan." *American Anthropologist* 25, 4: 472-84.

Sahlins, Marshall. 1995. *How Natives Think: About Captain Cook, for Example.* Chicago: University of Chicago Press.

Sanjek, Roger. 1990a. "The Secret Life of Fieldnotes." In *Fieldnotes: The Makings of Anthropology,* ed. R. Sanjek, 187-270. Ithaca: Cornell University Press.

–. 1990b. "A Vocabulary for Fieldnotes." In *Fieldnotes: The Makings of Anthropology,* ed. R. Sanjek, 92-121. Ithaca: Cornell University Press.

Sapir, Edward. 1916. "The Social Organization of the West Coast Tribes." Proceedings and Transactions of the Royal Society of Canada for 1915, vol. 9, sec. 2: 355-74.

–. 1921. *Language: An Introduction to the Study of Speech.* New York: Harcourt.

Service, Robert. 1907. *Spell of the Yukon and Other Verses.* New York: Barse and Hopkins.

Smith, Harlan I. 1924. "A Bellacoola, Carrier, and Chilcotin Route Time Recorder." *American Anthropologist* 26: 293.

–. 1925. "Sympathetic Magic and Witchcraft among the Bella Coola." *American Anthropologist* 27: 116-21.

–. 1929. "Materia Medica of the Bella Coola and Neighbouring Tribes of British Columbia." National Museum of Canada, Annual Report for 1927, Bulletin 56: 47-68.

Stocking, George W. 1983. "The Ethnographer's Magic: Fieldwork in British Anthropology from Tylor to Malinowski." In *Observers Observed.* Vol. 1: *History of Anthropology,* ed. G.W. Stocking, 70-120. Madison: University of Wisconsin Press.

Stott, Margaret. 1975. *Bella Coola Ceremony and Art.* Ottawa: National Museum of Man.

Suttles, Wayne, and Aldona Joanaitis. 1990. "History of Research in Ethnology." In *Handbook of North American Indians Northwest Coast.* Vol. 7: *Northwest Coast*, ed. W. Suttles. 73-87. Washington, DC: Smithsonian Institution Press.

Tepper, Leslie H. 1991. *The Bella Coola Valley: Harlan I. Smith's Fieldwork Photographs, 1920-1924.* Hull: Canadian Museum of Civilization.

Thompson, J. Eric S. 1967. "Ralph Loveland Roys, 1879-1965." *American Antiquity* 32, 1: 95-9.

Titley, E. Brian. 1986. *A Narrow Vision: Duncan Campbell Scott and the Administration of Indian Affairs in Canada.* Vancouver: UBC Press.

Turner, John. 1943. "Rev. Samuel Spencer Peat." In *United Church Observer,* December 1943.

Turner, Nancy J. 1975. *Food Plants of British Columbia Indians.* Part 1: *Coastal Peoples.* Victoria: British Columbia Provincial Museum.

Walmsley, Christopher. 1987. *Changing the Future: A Social Development Plan for the Nuxalk Nation.* Bella Coola: Nuxalk National Council.

Weiner, Annette B. 1992. *Inalienable Possessions: The Paradox of Keeping-While-Giving.* Berkeley: University of California Press.

Sources and Permissions for Letters

Canadian Museum of Civilization (© Reproduced with the permission of the Canadian Museum of Civilization)

T.F. McIlwraith to Edward Sapir: 14 March 1922, 2 April 1922, 27 May 1922, 30 July 1922, 29 September 1923, 12 November 1923, 14 November 1923, 26 December 1923, 15 January 1924, 7 February 1924, 4 March 1924

T.F. McIlwraith to Harlan I. Smith: 1 May 1922, 7 January 1923, 27 October 1923

Haddon Collection, Cambridge University Library (reproduced with permission)

T.F. McIlwraith to E.S. Fegan: 13 October 1923

T.F. McIlwraith to A.C. Haddon: 14 March 1922, 16 March 1924, 7 June 1922, 29 August 1922

T.F. McIlwraith to F. Haddon: 9 December 1923

T.F. McIlwraith to W.H.R. Rivers: 21 March 1922

Cambridge Museum (reproduced with permission)

T.F. McIlwraith to L.C.G. Clarke: 19 October 1923, 16 January 1924

McIlwraith Family (reproduced with permission)

T.F. McIlwraith to Dorothy McIlwraith: 22 September 1923

T.F. McIlwraith to family: 7 March 1922, 26 March 1922, 28 April 1922, 4 May 1922, 12 May 1922, 17 June 1922, 24 June 1922, 30 June 1922, 15 July 1922, 28 July 1922

T.F. McIlwraith to father: 12 May 1922, 26 September 1923, 6 October 1923, 18 October 1923, 26 October 1923, 11 November 1923, 20 November 1923, 27 November 1923, 5 December 1923, 10 December 1923, 19 December 1923, 24 December 1923, 1 January 1924, 6 January 1924, 13 January 1924, 22 January 1924, 29 January 1924, 6 February 1924, 19 February 1924, 26 February 1924, 7 March 1924

Index

Note: Numbers in italics refer to the photographs.

Printed and bound in Canada by Friesens

Set in Stone by Brenda and Neil West, BN Typographics West

Copy editor: Joanne Richardson

Proofreader: Carina Blåfield

Cartographer: Eric Leinberger